AF877513

FIRST EDITION

PRACTICAL MANAGERIAL ACCOUNTING

CONCEPTS AND TOOLS SUPPORTING BUSINESS

By John Brooks Peacock and Chris Akroyd

cognella® | ACADEMIC PUBLISHING

Bassim Hamadeh, CEO and Publisher
Kristina Stolte, Senior Field Acquisitions Editor
Christian Berk, Associate Production Editor
Miguel Macias, Senior Graphic Designer
Natalie Lakosil, Licensing Manager
Joyce Lue, Interior Designer
Natalie Piccotti, Senior Marketing Manager
Kassie Graves, Director of Acquisitions and Sales
Jamie Giganti, Senior Managing Editor

Printed in the United States of America.

ISBN: 978-1-63189-347-6 (pbk) / 978-1-63189-348-3 (br)

cognella® | ACADEMIC PUBLISHING

CONTENTS

THE GATEWAY TO MANAGERIAL ACCOUNTING

1

Opening the gateway requires understanding units, behavior, and segments

THE QUESTIONS WE TRY TO ANSWER

- What impact would a new branch have on our firm?
- Why can't we get an appointment with any venture capital people?
- Why are we losing business to our competitors?
- Why does the online group always exceed its forecasts and why do the stores always fall short of their forecasts?
- Does anyone remember what we forecasted?
- Why aren't we making a decent profit on our most popular product?
- How can we expand by adding a new product?
- How many tax returns do we need to prepare before we make a profit?
- How can we show our donors the effects and benefits of donating to our museum?
- Can we make any profit on the special order just received?
- Can we continue to grow?
- Should we expand by opening four large stores or ten small stores?

INFORMATION USERS

These and many other questions drive our efforts to lead an organization forward or start a new endeavor. As we address these issues, readily available data from our accounting system can be used to generate information such as the following:

Revenues	$150,000	Assets	$250,000
Expenses	$130,500	Liabilities	$ 95,000
Profit	$ 2,500	Equity	$155,000

LEARNING OBJECTIVES

LO1: Identify the different objectives, uses, and users of both financial and managerial accounting information.

LO2: Explain the common sources of information used by both financial and managerial accounting professionals.

LO3: Identify and explain the differences between cost behavior classifications: fixed costs, variable costs, and mixed costs.

LO4: Calculate variable cost per unit, total variable cost, total fixed cost, and fixed cost per unit.

LO5: Explain the difference(s) between absorption costing and variable costing methods.

LO6: Prepare income statements using both the absorption costing method and the variable costing method.

LO7: Explain the importance of segment reports.

LO8: Describe the planning, evaluating, and decision-making aspects of managerial accounting.

LO9: Describe the ethical issues and professional practice environment for management accountants.

This information, as presented, does not help us find answers to these kinds of questions. This information is aggregated and lacks any supporting operational information. We cannot ascertain the effect of individual business activities, and we cannot determine where additional investment would have the most benefit for the firm.

External Users

Creditors, investors, regulators, taxing authorities, critical suppliers, and large customers (among others) find great value in using general-purpose financial statements, including income statements, balance sheets, statements of cash flow, and the myriad of other disclosures required by any of the financial accounting reporting standards, such as U.S. Generally Accepted Accounting Principles (US GAAP, or GAAP) and International Financial Reporting Standards (IFRS). Individuals and institutions outside the business use these general-purpose financial statements, along with related disclosures, to evaluate the overall performance of a business and make predictions about potential future cash flows or potential revenue growth as well as to make comparisons between different firms.

External users are limited to the information provided in the general-purpose financial statements and related disclosures. External users do not have direct access to the information captured and maintained by a firm. The information provided in general-purpose financial statements and associated disclosures is often highly aggregated, or consolidated, into the four standard financial statements. Aggregated or consolidated financial information does not provide critical information about 1) cost behaviors, 2) units produced and sold, and 3) operating segments and other sensitive strategic business areas. The financial statement disclosures provide some limited information regarding unit volumes and operating segments, but even the additional disclosures fail to provide enough information for significant detailed analysis.

To facilitate analysis from this aggregated information, external users have developed ratio analyses and extensive financial models to estimate future company performance, which they use to value companies and project future stock prices. These analyses and models are based on estimated values that can be complex.

Internal Users

But, none of the answers we seek as internal financial information users can be found in the general-purpose financial statements. Internal users require very different financial information. If the general-purpose financial statements and disclosures are useful for external users, who are internal users and what information do they need to make decisions?

Who are we?

Founders – Owners – Managers – Supervisors – Strategic Planners

Where do we work?

Finance – Accounting – Treasury – Operations – Production – Compliance – Planning – Human Resources – Marketing – Research – Development

What do we do?
Make operational decisions—every day

What do we use?
The three keys to opening the gateway to the information we need to make internal decisions and answer operational questions:

Unit (or activity) volume
Cost behaviors
Segmented information

Moving from externally oriented financial information to internally oriented financial information, we can begin by understanding the source of financial information. All financial information is captured and stored within the accounting information system, and that information is used to prepare both financial statements and disclosures for external users and is the base of financial analyses for internal users.

FINANCIAL ACCOUNTING AND MANAGERIAL ACCOUNTING COMMON GROUND

The same accounting information system is used for both financial accounting and managerial accounting purposes. Financial accounting purposes include the preparation of general-purpose financial statements and financial statement disclosures. Managerial accounting purposes include planning or forecasting future performance, evaluating current performance, and providing analysis for ongoing business decisions. No matter the use or user of financial information, the information source is the same. To show how information is organized we start with the accounting cycle.

The Accounting Cycle

Both the financial and the managerial accounting functions use the same accounting system, which revolves around the same accounting cycle. It starts when an organization records business transactions. These transactions are then analyzed and put in the general journal or a special journal and posted to specific accounts in the general ledger. At the end of the accounting period the account balances are listed in a trial balance.

For financial accounting purposes, the information in the trial balance (T/B) is adjusted and used to prepare general-purpose financial statements according to the financial reporting standards used by the firm, either GAAP or IFRS. After the statements have been prepared, the nominal, or temporary, accounts are closed.

For managerial accounting purposes, internal users take the same information from the general ledger and trial balance to make ongoing business decisions.

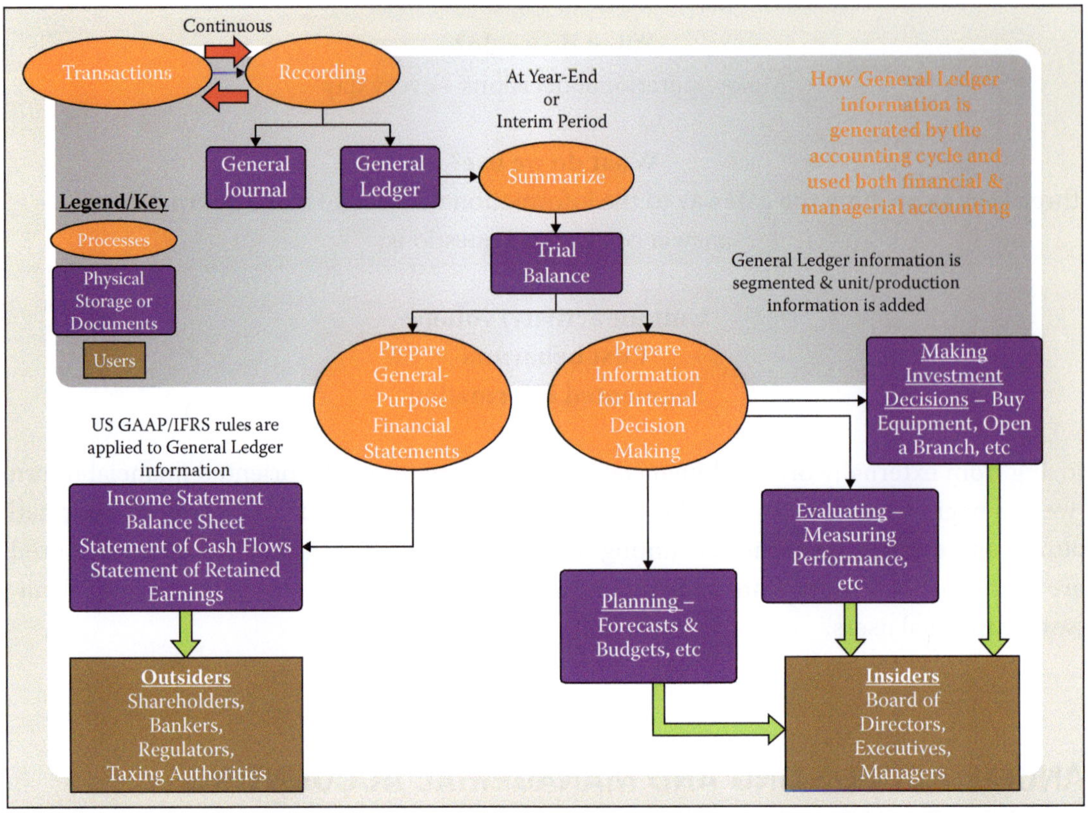

Fig. 1.1 The Accounting Cycle

Trial Balance

The same accounting system that captures the financial elements of the transactions that the business used to prepare the general-purpose financial statements is used by internal users. Sales, purchases, collections, billings, orders, contracts, and other financial activities are recorded in the accounting system with debits and credits and then summarized in each accounting period. This summation is what we call the trial balance. This is the common ground for both financial and managerial accounting as well as the point at which the needs of the two types of users go in different directions.

No matter how financial information might be used, revenue is recognized and treated the same way for both external reporting and internal decision making. The difference between internal and external user groups is how costs (also called expenses) are identified, reported, and analyzed.

To communicate to external users, financial accounting professionals use the trial balance to create the general-purpose financial statements: income statement, balance sheet, statement of changes in owner's equity, and statement of cash flow. These statements are audited and distributed to the (external) users of those statements. The expense/cost information presented in the general–purpose financial statements is divided into Cost of Goods Sold (COGS)—which includes the expenses related to the manufacturing of products—and Selling, General and Administrative (SG&A) Expenses, which includes all the non-manufacturing costs incurred during the period such as salaries for managers and salespeople, rent for office space, and advertising.

Home Plate, Inc.
Trial Balance
For the year ended December 31, 20XX

	Debit	Credit
Cash	$22,000	
Accounts receivable	$16,000	
Inventory	$27,500	
Prepaid expenses	$6,750	
Equipment	$175,000	
Accumulated depreciation—Equipment		$44,750
Furniture & Fixtures	$90,000	
Accumulated depreciation—Furniture & Fixtures		$42,500
Accounts payable		$26,000
Business loan		$69,000
Common stock		$25,000
Additional paid-in capital—Common Stock		$5,000
Retained earnings		$125,000
Revenue		$150,000
Purchases	$86,000	
Rent expense	$28,000	
Salary expense	$24,000	
Advertising expense	$4,500	
Insurance expense	$2,900	
Utilities expense	$4,600	
	$487,250	$487,250

Fig. 1.2 Home Plate, Inc. Trial Balance

ABSORPTION AND VARIABLE COSTING

One of the key differences between the information used in external reporting and the information used in internal decision making is how costs are defined and treated. In the general-purpose GAAP income statement, costs are divided into two categories: product costs and period costs. Product costs are those expenses directly related to manufacturing products in COGS, while period costs are the non-manufacturing SG&A expenses a business carries out during a given time period. This method of costing is referred to as full or absorption costing. External users are interested in understanding the costs incurred to generate the revenues recognized on the income statement and in understanding the nature and presentation of expenses as related to either product-focused manufacturing or selling and administrative non-manufacturing activities.

On the other hand, internal users of financial information are interested in how costs behave in relation to changes in unit production and sales volume, which requires costs to be identified and reported as either fixed or variable. This is referred to as the contribution margin or variable costing method, with information presented on a contribution margin or variable costing income statement. Owners and managers are responsible for both creating a firm's strategy to compete in the marketplace and executing that strategy. Strategy and execution responsibilities require information that allows decision makers to identify and understand the results of their decisions as well as assess the options available in a changing competitive environment. In order to make financial information useful for internal uses, additional information about cost behavior, units produced and sold, and segments needs to be collected and analyzed.

Both absorption and variable costing methods treat direct materials (DM), direct labor (DL), and the variable portion of manufacturing overhead (VOH) as costs associated with individual product units and capitalized as part of the manufacturing process. Fixed manufacturing overhead (FOH) is treated very differently between the absorption and variable costing methods. Under absorption costing, fixed manufacturing overhead is treated as a product cost, capitalized as part of the inventory costs, and put into the inventory account(s). Under variable costing, fixed manufacturing overhead is considered a period cost and not a product cost, so it is fully expensed in the period in which it is incurred. Even though variable sales expenses are variable costs, they are not product costs under variable costing, even though they are combined with manufacturing-related variable costs such as direct materials and direct labor, as they are not related to manufacturing activities.

To illustrate the difference between how fixed manufacturing overhead is treated between the absorption and variable costing methods, the following diagram isolates fixed manufacturing overhead and depicts the results of how absorption and variable costing treat fixed overhead (FOH).

In Figure 1.3, we isolate the fixed overhead as the only cost incurred to make our product because all other costs, direct material (DM) and direct labor (DL), are treated the same way under both absorption and variable costing. The absorption costing method capitalizes the fixed overhead into inventory as a product cost. The $28,000 is incurred to produce all 10,000 units during the period. While 10,000 units were produced, only 9,000 units were sold during the period. The fixed overhead per unit produced ($28,000/10,000 units) is $2.80/unit. When each unit is sold, then the $2.80 is released from the finished goods (FG) inventory and recognized as an expense on the income statement as cost of goods sold (COGS). If one unit is not sold during the period, the $2.80 remains in finished goods inventory and recognizing the cost as an expense on the income statement is deferred until the next period. The absorption method capitalizes (or absorbs) all of the manufacturing or product costs (direct material, direct labor, manufacturing overhead) into inventory accounts.

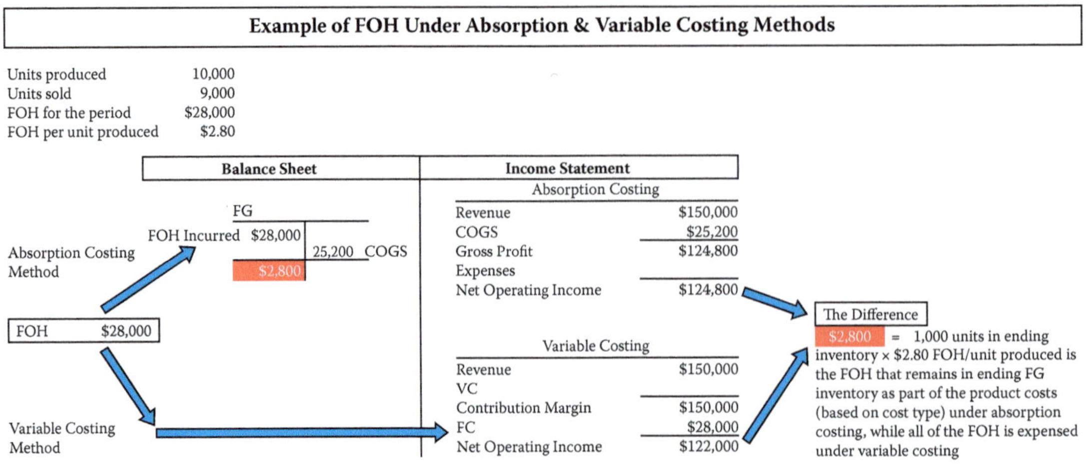

Fig. 1.3 Variable & Absorption Costing

The absorption method provides external users with an understanding of the costs that were incurred for the number of units sold during the period (based on the matching principle). The effect is to report the results of a period by matching revenue earned with the costs incurred, allowing external users to evaluate company performance or compare the company to its competitors or to companies in other industries.

The variable costing method classifies costs based on their behavior and how costs react to changes in unit volumes or activity. In Figure 1.3, the variable costing method treats the fixed overhead as a period cost (as opposed to a product cost), and, as such the fixed overhead is recognized as an expense on the variable costing (contribution margin) income statement in the same period in which the costs are incurred.

In the short term, and possibly the medium term, fixed manufacturing overhead costs cannot be easily changed. The argument might be made that fixed overhead represents costs that must be incurred irrespective of unit volume and should be recognized on the income statement as a cost during the period or analogous to a period cost because fixed overhead behaves like a cost related to time instead of being related to units produced (volume).

General-Purpose Income Statement (GAAP & IFRS)

The general-purpose income statement is based on classifying costs based on their type. Under GAAP and IFRS, product costs include all the costs related to manufacturing products: direct materials (DM), direct labor (DL), and manufacturing overhead (MFGOH). Period costs include those costs that relate to being in business during a period of time: advertising, rent, salaries, insurance, etc., and are often referred to as selling, general, and administrative (SG&A) costs, selling and administrative (S&A) costs, or simply operating expenses.

Figure 1.4 presents a general-purpose income statement that should be familiar from financial accounting. This income statement is based on GAAP, which requires the use of the absorption costing method. The absorption costing method is also required by IFRS.

The cost of goods sold section shows external users the amount of beginning and ending inventory and the purchases during the period, as well as the total cost for the products sold to customers. The expense section shows the users the expenses incurred for being in business during the year, which often are referred to as selling, general, and administrative expenses (SG&A). The net operating income (NOI) reflects how the business performed during the year, according to the financial reporting standards used (GAAP or IFRS) by the firm.

The presentation of information in this format allows external users to see the results of a firm's activities and operations in a given accounting period, but this information doesn't help internal users understand how to make any of the internal decisions like those listed earlier in the chapter. What would happen if Home Plate opened another office in a neighboring state? How would adding a new product affect profitability? What would be the financial impact if the current production facility was remodeled and expanded? These kinds of questions cannot be answered using these general-purpose financial statements and related disclosures because they are based on cost categories and not cost behavior.

Home Plate, Inc.
Balance Sheet
December 31, 20XX

Cash	$22,000	Accounts Payable	$26,000
Accounts Receivable	$16,000	Loan	$69,000
Inventory	$27,500		$95,000
Prepaid	$6,750	Common Stock	$25,000
Equipment, net	$130,250	Additional Paid-In Capital	$5,000
Furniture & Fixtures, net	$47,500	Retained Earnings	$125,000
	$250,000		$250,000

Home Plate, Inc.
Income Statement (Traditional Format–Absorption Costing)
For the year ended December 31, 20XX

Rev		$150,000	Bl	$25,000
COGS		($83,500)	Purch	$86,000
		$66,500	El	($27,500)
Expenses			COGS	$83,500
Rent	$28,000			
Salary	$24,000			
Advertising	$4,500			
Insurance	$2,900			
Utilities	$4,600	$64,000		
Net Operating Income		$2,500		

Fig. 1.4 Home Plate, Inc. Balance Sheet and Traditional Income Statement

Manufacturing Overhead (MFGOH)

Manufacturing overhead (MFGOH) costs are those costs incurred by a business to maintain their current productive capacity. In order for a firm to manufacture their product(s), they incur costs such as the following:

1. Rent for the manufacturing plant
2. Repairs and maintenance of equipment
3. Utilities for the manufacturing plant
4. Insurance for the plant and equipment
5. Many other expenses

Manufacturing overhead is critically important to a firm's strategic and financial success by maintaining its productive capacity and supporting its manufacturing processes. Manufacturing overhead costs are separate from the direct product costs, such as direct materials used to produce the products, and are separate from the direct labor costs incurred to make the products.

The manufacturing overhead costs are incurred for any and all manufacturing or production activities.

In an absorption-based general-purpose income statement, the fixed manufacturing overhead costs are capitalized into the work-in process and finished-goods inventory accounts (as part of the direct product costs). One of the problems created by absorption costing is a firm producing a different number of units than the number of units sold in an accounting period. If a firm produces more units than it sells, then some of the fixed manufacturing overhead costs remain in finished-goods inventory and are deferred until the goods are sold in a future accounting period. If a firm sells more units that it produces, then some of the fixed manufacturing overhead from previous periods is released out of finished goods inventory and moved into the income statement in cost of goods sold. Here is a summary of the effects caused by different unit production and unit sales:

Units Produced > Units Sold → Current Costs Deferred into Future Income Statements

Units Sold > Units Produced → Prior Costs Released into Current Income Statement

Contribution Margin (Variable Costing) Income Statement

Internal decision makers need information that helps them plan for the future, monitor and evaluate current operations, and make decisions that impact the productive capacity of their firms. These types of needs require information that is useful for not only evaluating current operations, but also for projecting future operating results. These needs are better met by using costs identified according to their behavior and their reaction to changes in the units produced and in the units sold. What happens to a cost when production increases? What happens to a cost when sales decrease?

Figure 1.5 presents a contribution margin income statement. The contribution margin income statement is structured based on the variable and fixed behavior of the costs a firm incurs.

Home Plate, Inc.
Contribution Margin Income Statement
For the year ended December 31, 20XX

	Total		Per Unit		Percentage
Revenue		$150,000		$10.00	100.00%
Variable costs:					
Variable product costs	$63,500		$4.23		10.00%
Variable selling and administrative costs	$4,600		$3.10		31.00%
Total variable costs		$68,100		$4.54	45.40%
Contribution margin		$81,900		$5.46	54.60%
Fixed costs:					
Fixed manufacturing costs	$28,000				
Fixed selling and administrative costs	$31,400				
Total fixed costs		$59,400			
Net operating income		$22,500			

Fig. 1.5 Home Plate, Inc. Contribution Margin Income Statement

The contribution margin income statement provides valuable information for internal decision makers. The contribution margin income statement can be shown with total amounts, amounts on a per-unit basis, or in percentages. The contribution margin per unit and the contribution margin percentages will be particularly useful throughout this textbook and in practice.

Variable Costs

Variable costs (VC) are those costs that change directly in relation to a change in the number of units sold. Variable costs are the same for each unit of product. In other words, they are consistent on a per unit basis. If more units are sold, the variable costs increase in total. Home Plate, Inc. manufactures baseballs that it sells to schools, baseball teams, and baseball leagues. If it costs Home Plate $10 for direct materials and labor to manufacture a box of baseballs it sells for $25, the more boxes sold increases the total amount spent. Here is an example:

	(Consistent per unit)	(Varies in total)
Boxes Sold	Cost per Box	Total Spent
1	$10	$10
10	$10	$100
50	$10	$500

The variable costs to make a box of baseballs remains the same no matter how many boxes are sold; only the total amount spent increases. This is the nature and result of variable costs: Variable costs are the same per unit and only change in total with changes in the volume of units produced.

Fixed Costs

Fixed costs are those costs that must be paid no matter the volume of units produced or sold. If the owner of Home Plate, Inc. decides to give all the employees a month of vacation, the rent for the Home Plate, Inc.'s facilities must still be paid because Home Plate, Inc. signed a long-term lease agreement to pay $2,000 each month for 10 years for their facilities, and they cannot change the lease. If Home Plate sells 10,000 boxes of baseballs or ten (10) boxes of baseballs in a month, the same $2,000 for rent must still be paid each month. If 10,000 boxes are sold in a month, then each box covers $0.20 of the rent. If ten (10) boxes are sold in a month, then each box must cover $200 of the rent. In either scenario, the $2,000 in rent must be paid. The following table presents an example of how fixed costs per unit sold changes.

(Fixed in total)		(Varies per unit)
Monthly Rent	Boxes Sold	Rent/Box Sold
$2,000	10	$200
$2,000	100	$20
$2,000	1,000	$2

For internal users, managerial accounting professionals take information from the trial balance and use the information based on predominantly three specific differences from financial reporting information to facilitate internal analysis and the needs of internal users:

1. The behavior of the amounts
2. The volume of activity
3. Segments, if applicable, to facilitate analysis

Applying a cost behavior approach to financial information (as opposed to cost categorization), allows the presentation of information, which shows how costs respond and react to the changes in the number of units sold, giving the information better predictive value.

The definition or identification of costs is one of the most significant differences between the general-purpose income statement (using full or absorption costing) and the contribution margin income statement (using variable costing). The general-purpose income statement reports costs/expenses based on the expense category (product or period), while the contribution margin income statement reports costs/expenses based on their behavior (variable or fixed). If the same accounting system is used to capture transaction information, why is the net operating income different between the two income statements? The reason is that costs/expenses are treated and reported differently: product/period cost categories for external financial reporting and variable/fixed cost behaviors for internal analysis. In the contribution margin income statement, the fixed manufacturing overhead costs are treated as period expenses and recognized as expenses on the income statement in the same period in which they were incurred. The number of units produced or sold will not affect the timing of when the fixed manufacturing overhead is reported on the income statement. Figure 1.5 illustrates the treatment of FOH as a period expense.

COMPANY VERSUS SEGMENT REPORTS

External Users Need Company Reports

External users need information on the company as a whole to make investment and credit decisions. The general-purpose financial statements provide a consistent format to report financial information on a company-wide basis, which can then be compared to other accounting periods or to other companies. Comparisons of companies in different industries are essential to making decisions like buying stock, holding stock, or selling stock, and whether to extend a loan to a company. Without general-purpose financial statements, these types of analyses become difficult.

External users, such as lenders and stockholders, require information about the performance of a company. A lender extends a loan to a company and must be able to evaluate the risk that it might default on the loan. Stockholders buy shares in the company and desire to estimate the future amounts and timing of cash flows, dividends, and potential growth that impact the current and future price of the company's shares. Owning stock in, or lending money to, a company like Walt Disney means owning a piece of, or lending money to, all of the operating activities the Walt Disney Company owns and manages. These types of relationships and arrangements require information on the company as a whole, making highly aggregated, consolidated financial statements useful to external users.

Beaver Pizza Segment Reports

This is the process of disaggregating or separating into operating/segmented units

	Consolidated Beaver Pizza		= East Campus		+ North Campus				North Campus		= Delivery		+ Dine-In	
Revenue	$1,000,000	100%	$400,000	100%	$600,000	100%	→	Revenue	$600,000	100%	$250,000	100%	$350,000	100%
VC	$220,000	22%	$100,000	25%	$120,000	20%	→	VC	$120,000	20%	$50,000	20%	$70,000	20%
CM	$780,000	78%	$300,000	75%	$480,000	80%	→	CM	$480,000	80%	$200,000	80%	$280,000	80%
FC-Traceable	$670,000	67%	$280,000	70%	$390,000	65%	Separating the traceable FC	FC-Traceable	$310,000	52%	$160,000	64%	$150,000	43%
SM	$110,000	11%	$20,000	5%	$90,000	15%		SM	$170,000	28%	$40,000	16%	$130,000	37%
FC-Common	$60,000	6%	xx		xx			FC-Common	$80,000	13%	xx		xx	
NOI	$50,000	5%						NOI	$90,000	15%				

Fig. 1.6 Segment Reporting

Internal Users Need Segment Reports

Internal users of accounting information need specific information on the aspects of an organization that allow them to understand how all the parts perform individually, as well as how those parts work together. Aggregated information loses the specific characteristics and attributes that an owner or manager needs when making decisions like expanding a product line, opening a new office or branch, replacing equipment, outsourcing a part or service, closing a division, or launching a new product or brand. These decisions require information on individual products, departments, locations, costs, and sales volume (among other things) that allow a decision maker to understand specific performance and identify the effect of any given option for change.

Figure 1.6 shows aggregated information for Beaver Pizza and its two operating segments, East Campus and North Campus, on the left half of the figure. On the right half of the figure, the North Campus segment is disaggregated into more detailed operating activities: delivery and dine-In. With sufficient disaggregation, financial information can be combined with operating information to illuminate metrics and ratios, which can be evaluated and compared.

Internal users are responsible for three general areas or activities of their firms: planning, evaluating, and decision making. These management responsibilities are valid at the individual operating unit (segment) level, as well as at the company level. These responsibilities should also correlate to a company's strategic plans and efforts. To execute planning, evaluating, and decision-making responsibilities effectively requires different types of accounting information.

PLANNING ACTIVITIES

Planning the future course of a business requires owners and managers to design and implement a strategic plan. These plans often use historical information to gain an understanding of how different activities behave, how they have changed, and the resources they require. Knowing how activities have been performed in the past, along with current information, is the starting point of a strategic plan.

A traditional forecast (also known as a "budget") has long been a resource owners and managers have used to implement strategic plans. The traditional forecast provides an opportunity to identify the impact of how changes in strategic direction or daily operations may financially affect both the individual activity and the firm as a whole. The challenges of the traditional forecast include difficulties trying to motivate employee participation in the forecasting process, time spent with seemingly little value generated in the process, and the potential for using results as a tool, which don't add value to the business. Beyond the traditional forecast, there are some alternative options that firms are now using, such as continuous or rolling forecasts. These have been designed to decrease the time required to create a forecast and to increase the value from the forecasting process.

When planning the future direction of an activity or segment, managers require information regarding the costs of specific segments, how those costs behave when the level of activity in the segment changes, and what effects might be anticipated on the net operating income of that segment. This is widely known as cost-volume-profit (CVP) analysis, which allows internal users to understand the profit effects a change in sales volume would have.

Planning requires a thorough and intimate knowledge of the costs in a firm or segment and understanding the behavior of those costs is a critical factor in effective planning. One of the most challenging aspects of planning is how a firm treats overhead, and it can play a critical role in the analysis and evaluation processes.

Some businesses also find value in developing standard costs: a function of standard quantities and standard prices for the inputs they purchase to make their products or deliver their services. Standard costs provide a framework to evaluate the use of resources within an activity and can provide insights into not only problems or issues, but also potential solutions to those problems.

EVALUATING ACTIVITIES

Internal users need tools that allow activities to be monitored and evaluated. Forecasts and standard costing contribute to an analysis of activities, which provides owners and managers with the ability to identify and observe differences. These differences, or variances, give feedback on the effectiveness of the managers operating the segments.

Monitoring and evaluating the performance of employees and operating units alike requires tools and methods that can show actual performance compared to expectations. The degree of performance over time or against competitors can be monitored using quality measures, key performance indicators, benchmarks, risk measures, and balanced scorecards.

One of the most important aspects of monitoring and evaluating individual employees, as well as organizations, requires the use of professional and ethical standards of conduct. A framework of standards communicated throughout an organization allows individuals to determine appropriate behavior, evaluate behavior, and appropriately discipline any ethical violations.

DECISION-MAKING ACTIVITIES

Owners and managers make decisions that affect the firm not only in the present, but also long into the future. Almost daily, internal decision makers face choices in how an operating unit or a firm executes its activities in creating and delivering value to its customers. Within a firm's operating capacity, managers must make decisions on a myriad of issues such as accepting a customer's special order, whether to make or outsource a part, whether a product line should be sold off or continued at a different location, or how to most effectively use a limited resource.

Decision makers also address issues surrounding how the firm's productive capacity might be either temporarily changed or permanently changed without a major new investment. Owners and managers may need to address the financial effects of temporarily increasing a firm's productive capacity by offering overtime to increase the availability of direct labor resources or evaluate whether they should continue to make a part or buy it from a contract manufacturer. Buying from a contract manufacturer, or service provider, is commonly known as outsourcing and can permanently change the productive capacity of a firm without a significant investment of capital.

Managers must also evaluate opportunities to permanently expand capacity, increase production, grow market share, access new markets, develop talent, respond to competitive challenges, and react to customer expectations. These decisions cannot be made solely with accounting information. Owners and managers also need market, operational, legal, regulatory and cultural information. This comprehensive analysis is crucial to provide decision makers with a wide view and in-depth understanding of the situation. Managerial accounting is not bounded by any type of reporting standard or limited by any regulatory body. Managerial accounting is not hindered or filtered by national boundaries. Instead, the goal is to provide appropriately detailed information in a timely manner to those within the organization who are responsible for making decisions with a financial impact. Our own professional capacity and the decision maker's needs are the driving forces that lead us to create value and achieve goals.

PROFESSIONAL STANDARDS AND ETHICS

Accounting professionals practicing in private industry face very different challenges and conflicts than those practicing in the public accounting environment. Although the principles, standards, and professional characteristics are similar throughout the accounting world, the dilemmas faced and the parties involved are generally based in an employee/employer relationship as opposed to a client/contractor relationship. To build a foundation of understanding, we present the IMA Statement of Ethical Professional Practice and the CIMA Ethics Checklist as reference for our work.

THE INSTITUTE OF MANAGEMENT ACCOUNTANTS (IMA)

IMA® is a worldwide association of accountants and financial professionals in business. The organization was founded in Buffalo, N.Y., in 1919 as the National Association of Cost Accountants (NACA) to promote knowledge and professionalism among cost accountants and foster a wider understanding of their role in management. In 1957, the name was changed to the National Association of Accountants (NAA), beginning an era in which they would later develop the hallmark credential, the CMA® . The IMA are the only organization to offer the CMA® (Certified Management Accountant), the is earned through a multi-part exam. In 1991, the organization's name was again changed to the Institute of Management Accountants (IMA), signifying a broader role as the association for accountants and financial professionals working inside organizations.

Source: Copyright © by Institute of Management Accountants, Inc.

Effective July 1, 2017

Members of IMA shall behave ethically. A commitment to ethical professional practice includes overarching principles that express our values and standards that guide member conduct.

PRINCIPLES

IMA's overarching ethical principles include: Honesty, Fairness, Objectivity, and Responsibility. Members shall act in accordance with these principles and shall encourage others within their organizations to adhere to them.

STANDARDS

IMA members have a responsibility to comply with and uphold the standards of Competence, Confidentiality, Integrity, and Credibility. Failure to comply may result in disciplinary action.

I. COMPETENCE

1. Maintain an appropriate level of professional leadership and expertise by enhancing knowledge and skills.
2. Perform professional duties in accordance with relevant laws, regulations, and technical standards.
3. Provide decision support information and recommendations that are accurate, clear, concise, and timely. Recognize and help manage risk.

II. CONFIDENTIALITY

1. Keep information confidential except when disclosure is authorized or legally required.
2. Inform all relevant parties regarding appropriate use of confidential information. Monitor to ensure compliance.
3. Refrain from using confidential information for unethical or illegal advantage.

III. INTEGRITY

1. Mitigate actual conflicts of interest. Regularly communicate with business associates to avoid apparent conflicts of interest. Advise all parties of any potential conflicts of interest.

2. Refrain from engaging in any conduct that would prejudice carrying out duties ethically.
3. Abstain from engaging in or supporting any activity that might discredit the profession.
4. Contribute to a positive ethical culture and place integrity of the profession above personal interests.

IV. CREDIBILITY

1. Communicate information fairly and objectively.
2. Provide all relevant information that could reasonably be expected to influence an intended user's understanding of the reports, analyses, or recommendations.
3. Report any delays or deficiencies in information, timeliness, processing, or internal controls in conformance with organization policy and/or applicable law.
4. Communicate professional limitations or other constraints that would preclude responsible judgment or successful performance of an activity.

Exhibit 1.1a IMA Statement page 1

RESOLVING ETHICAL ISSUES

In applying the Standards of Ethical Professional Practice, the member may encounter unethical issues or behavior. In these situations, the member should not ignore them, but rather should actively seek resolution of the issue. In determining which steps to follow, the member should consider all risks involved and whether protections exist against retaliation.

When faced with unethical issues, the member should follow the established policies of his or her organization, including use of an anonymous reporting system if available.

If the organization does not have established policies, the member should consider the following courses of action:

- The resolution process could include a discussion with the member's immediate supervisor. If the supervisor appears to be involved, the issue could be presented to the next level of management.
- IMA offers an anonymous helpline that the member may call to request how key elements of the *IMA Statement of Ethical Professional Practice* could be applied to the ethical issue.
- The member should consider consulting his or her own attorney to learn of any legal obligations, rights, and risks concerning the issue.

If resolution efforts are not successful, the member may wish to consider disassociating from the organization.

IMA Ethics Helpline Number for callers in the U.S. and Canada:
(800) 245-1383
In other countries, dial the AT&T USA Direct Access Number from www.att.com/esupport/traveler.jsp?tab=3, then the above number.

Exhibit 1.1b IMA Statement page 2

IMA Statement of Ethical Professional Practice

The IMA Standards are built around four principles and four standards:

Principles (Behaviors)	Standards (Abilities)
Honesty	Competence
Fairness	Confidentiality
Objectivity	Integrity
Responsibility	Credibility

The standards are the behaviors that accounting professionals must exhibit and the abilities they must possess. As an accounting professional enters the workforce and begins his or her chosen career path, these principles and standards can provide the individual professional with the tools he or she needs to effectively evaluate almost any ethical or professional dilemma and make appropriate decisions.

THE CHARTERED INSTITUTE OF MANAGEMENT ACCOUNTANTS (CIMA)

CIMA is the world's largest and leading professional body of management accountants. CIMA has a partnership with the American Institute of Certified Public Accountants (AICPA) to support and give a voice to the 150,000 Chartered Global Management Accountants (CGMAs) around the world. CIMA helps individuals and businesses to succeed by harnessing the full power of management accounting—not just accounting for the balance sheet, but accounting for business. CIMA provides continuing professional development services, funds academic research, develops thought leadership, monitors professional standards, maintains a code of ethics for members, and works with external tuition providers and assessment services to provide the best study and examination experience.

Source: Copyright © by CIMA.

CIMA Ethics Checklist

The CIMA Code of Ethics for Professional Accountants is built on five fundamental principles:

Integrity
Objectivity
Professional Competence and Due Care
Confidentiality
Professional Behavior

CIMA has also published a checklist for professionals to use to assist them in navigating professional or ethical dilemmas and situations.

Common Professional and Ethical Dilemmas

As professional management accountants, we have duties and responsibilities in many different relationships. We have duties to our employers, duties to our clients, duties to our immediate superiors, duties to our employees, duties to outside shareholders and owners, and duties to various professional and regulatory bodies, to name just a few. We can experience conflicts among the interactions of these duties no matter where or how we practice. For our purposes, we will address and explore issues we might face when working in private industry.

When we work as management accountants, we work in a business that is either privately or publicly owned. Our basic professional relationships center on 1) the employee/employer relationship between ourselves and our boss or our subordinates, 2) the agency relationship between ourselves and our firm's owners and stakeholders, and 3) our responsibility to the general public.

As an employee, we might have a standard set of responsibilities outlined in a job description for our current position and then another group of responsibilities that have been delegated to us

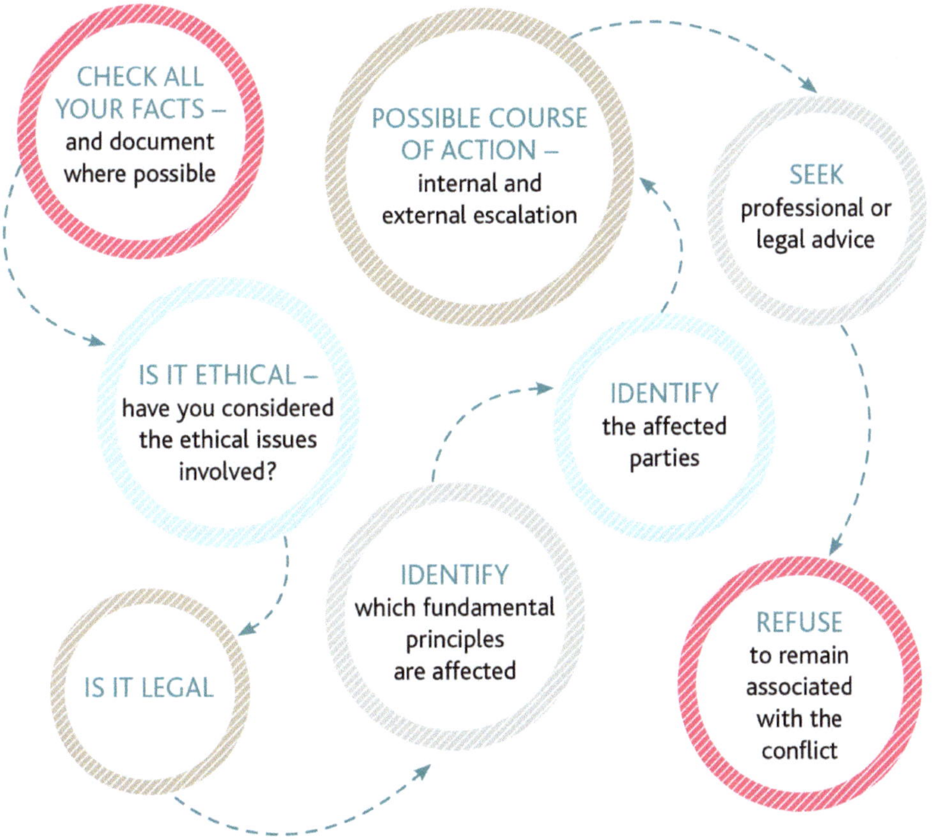

Exhibit 1.2 CIMA Ethics Checklist

by our boss. We must perform those responsibilities not only in accordance with our professional standards but also in accordance with our agency relationship.

An example where a conflict might arise between our employee/employer relationship and our agency relationship is in the area where decisions favor short-term profit objectives to the detriment of long-term growth goals. This could be caused by managers being compensated based on certain performance factors related to short-term financial results, current stock price performance, or both. These types of incentives are intended to align management's interests with the interests of shareholders/owners but the intent isn't always achieved, creating an apparent functional conflict of interest.

Fraud Detection and Reporting

As we discussed, one of our duties is created in our relationship to our shareholders/owners and another is created in our responsibility to the general public. As professional management accountants, we see information from inside the organization, we see many different internal aspects of the organization, and we have a significant degree of stewardship over financial information generated by an organization. Our stewardship is reflected both internally as we generate information that supports the creation, execution, and evaluation of strategic plans, and externally through the preparation and distribution of general-purpose financial statements as required by various generally accepted accounting principles throughout the world. To execute our stewardship, we create internal control structures and reporting structures to facilitate the integrity of information and fulfill our responsibilities to both shareholders/owners and the general public.

Sustainability

Sustainability has become an important aspect in the business world. An organization must be able to continue its operations, produce its goods or services, remain profitable, and maintain a level of social responsibility without depleting or permanently damaging the environment, scarce resources or commodities, or its employees. Every business, government, non-profit group, charity, or other type of organization must recognize the threats that can result from a resource or product input that can no longer be obtained, possibly resulting in a reduction, or even the cessation, of the firm's operations.

The Chartered Global Management Accountants (CGMA) published *Ten Key Elements to Sustainable Business Practices in SMEs*. The elements fall into three categories:

These elements provide a framework to evaluate a firm's sustainable operations and an approach to identifying potential sustainability issues.

THE TEN ELEMENTS

STRATEGY AND PLANNING

1. Take a broad view of sustainability.

Understand the key sustainability drivers, risks and opportunities for your organisation. As important as they are, remember to look beyond environmental issues. Finding innovative ways in which your company can be a good corporate citizen to the benefit of employees, customers and suppliers will yield benefits to your business.

2. Define in detail what sustainability means to your company.

With a clear definition to which everyone in the company can refer and clear success measures, any efforts to invest in sustainability or change business practices will focus on the right goals.

3. Engage all stakeholders.

Talk to customers, suppliers, investors and employees about sustainability, so that their voices can be heard in the debate, and the strategy you develop will be able to address all of their needs. Include them and get as much of their weight behind the strategy as possible.

EXECUTION AND ALIGNMENT

4. Remember that you are not alone.

National, international and industry-wide initiatives exist that help businesses become more sustainable. Engage with these organisations, tap into their knowledge and experience. This way, implementing a sustainability strategy will be quicker and easier.

5. Establish responsibility and communicate widely.

The delivery of any strategy is more successful if an organisation knows who is in charge of it. Have senior management drive the policy, appoint sustainability champions and communicate the importance of sustainability to every level of the company.

6. Take it step by step.

Becoming more sustainable is usually a process of evolution, not revolution. By making small changes now a company can affect significant change in the future.

7. Walk the talk.

Any company can talk about being more sustainable, but if it does not back up its words with meaningful actions its claims will quickly be seen through. Customers and investors are wise to greenwashing, so never make the mistake of seeing sustainability as a marketing exercise.

PERFORMANCE AND REPORTING

8. Tie sustainability to profit. Becoming more sustainable often means being more efficient. Resource efficiency, for instance, benefits the environment and reduces the cost of running a business. Make the link between consuming less water and electricity, or producing less waste, and improving profits clear within your business.

9. Measure, monitor and review.

Tracking progress towards the goals of a sustainability strategy is vital in justifying it to management, and in fully understanding the commercial benefit it brings. Develop clear metrics, review them regularly and whether progress is fast or slow, keep setting realistic, attainable targets.

10. Invest in the future.

Investing in sustainability does not always require huge capital expenditure. Many SMEs say the biggest investment is management time.

Exhibit 1.3 CGMA Ten Key Elements to Sustainable Business Practices in SMEs

Figure Credit

FORECASTING

2

LEARNING OBJECTIVES

LO1: Explain the purposes and uses of a traditional operating forecast.

LO2: Prepare a traditional operating forecast for a manufacturing firm.

LO3: Prepare a sales forecast.

LO4: Prepare a production forecast.

LO5: Prepare a direct material forecast.

LO6: Prepare a direct labor forecast.

LO7: Prepare a manufacturing overhead forecast.

LO8: Prepare a selling and administrative expense forecast.

LO9: Prepare a cash forecast.

LO10: Identify alternatives to the traditional operating forecasts and explain the reasons they are used.

THE QUESTIONS WE TRY TO ANSWER

- What would happen if unit sales increased by 25 percent?
- What would be the effect of a supplier dealing with a labor strike?
- What would happen if we sold more of our products on credit?
- What would be the effect of a competitor lowering prices?
- What might happen to our profitability if we opened three new branch offices?

FORECASTING OBJECTIVES AND PURPOSES

Forecasting is the process of quantifying the financial effects of a plan for a business, an operating unit, a charity, a non-profit organization, a school, or any other type of organization that includes some type of financial aspect. A forecast is a tangible product of the forecasting process and can vary from relatively simple to very complex. A forecast can be as simple as a few numbers written on a scrap of paper during a lunch meeting with a colleague or friend and can be as complex as complete computer programs used by large, multinational corporations. To forecast is to project or to predict. The definition of *forecast* from Merriam-Webster's Collegiate Dictionary is as follows:

> "To calculate or predict (some future event or condition) usually as a result of study and analysis of available pertinent data."

The objectives of forecasting can be diverse as every business situation is different. Organizations need to take this into account each time a forecast is created or updated. The needs of decision makers also change, not only because of internal changes, but also because the external environment changes.

A forecast can provide a powerful tool that can be used for both planning and evaluating activities. Two overarching objectives for any forecast are 1) to examine what potential results might be expected from a particular strategy and 2) to evaluate how actual performance relates to the expectations.

Starting a Business

A business starts when an idea for a product or service is conceived and someone decides to act upon that idea to deliver it to a market. The idea then needs to be communicated by those who created the idea to others. The idea may be communicated with words, pictures, illustrations, and other means, but the financial effect is expressed with numbers. To the financially literate, the numbers represent an intricate and detailed view of the idea's potential—the forecast.

Acquiring a Business

When a person or business acquires an operating business, the needs of the prospective buyer may be very different from those of the seller. While the seller has operated the business and generated results, the buyer might have ideas on how to operate the business differently. A forecast provides the buyer with the opportunity to examine the potential outcomes if his or her ideas are implemented. The potential outcomes give context to the buyer's expectations of the purchase price and the performance of the possible acquisition.

Growing a Business

An operating business generates results that become the historical record for the entity. The results came from a set of circumstances that are known and identifiable. The results can allow decision makers to consider possible changes by providing an understanding of how the business behaves. The historical results of the business are the starting point for managers to predict results for changes and decisions they could make to expand production, add products or enter new markets.

The process and tools of forecasting can be applied to for-profit businesses, not-for-profit and charitable organizations, educational institutions, governments, and family businesses. While the focus of this textbook is on for-profit businesses, the tools and techniques presented are also applicable to not-for-profit organizations. Growth is a natural objective and consequence of business activities in all types of firms (service, merchandising, and manufacturing). An overview of the different types of firm and examples of the reasons they would want to prepare a forecast are as follows:

Service firms provide services to their customers. Examples include Bank of America, law firms, and accounting firms like Moss Adams. Because they only provide services, they do not have any inventory accounts. Service firms would want to forecast to better understand the resources they need to deliver their services or the effects of developing and selling a new service.

Merchandising firms resell products purchased from suppliers. Examples include Amazon, Macy's, Ross, Safeway, and Home Depot. These types of firms only have one inventory account called "merchandise." These firms would want to forecast to better understand the resources they need to operate a store or open a new store.

Manufacturing firms create, produce, and sell products. Examples include Bob's Red Mill, Ford, and Precision Castparts. These firms have three inventory accounts: "raw materials inventory," "work-in-process inventory," and "finished goods inventory". Raw materials inventory includes all raw materials used in manufacturing a product. Work in process inventory includes all goods that are partway through the manufacturing process but not yet complete (raw materials plus some labor). Finished goods inventory includes completed goods that have not yet been sold (all costs associated with the product). While most manufacturers sell their finished goods inventory to merchandisers, some manufacturers sell their products directly to consumers. These firms would want to know how a change in material or labor cost or a new manufacturing technology would affect the firm.

One common process used to make a forecast in many firms is to calculate a standard cost for each of the firm's products or services. The idea of a standard cost is that for each product or service sold to a customer, the firm incurs the same cost to produce the product or deliver the service. In a manufacturing firm, the standard cost of a product is a function of the cost of direct material used to make a product, the cost of direct labor, and an allocation for overheads.

STANDARD QUANTITIES AND STANDARD PRICES

Developing a forecast that can adequately project future activity requires consistency in the relationships between both the quantity and price of the inputs (direct materials, direct labor, manufacturing overhead) used to produce finished products and services. Standard quantities of inputs are used to assist forecasting the amount of those inputs, which must be purchased to make the units we expect to sell. Standard costs are amounts we expect to pay (quantity × price) for the inputs we use in production. In effect, it is a forecast for one unit of production or delivery of a standard service.

Standard quantities of direct materials used to make a product or to deliver a service can be identified readily, but the challenge comes when we must also account for waste or rework that causes more direct material to be used than what is allocated to an individual product or service. For example, the surface area of a baseball is approximately 23.76 square inches, which is needed for each baseball produced. If 10,000 baseballs are produced, then 237,600 square inches of leather are required to meet production demand. While producing the baseballs, an employee might incorrectly feed the leather into the cutting machine, causing a complete sheet of leather to be cut in a way that cannot be used for baseballs. If all we have is the 237,600 square inches of leather, then we will not have enough to produce all 10,000 baseballs. Our goal is to not waste any input and to make each unit correctly each time, but people and processes are not perfect and the result is the inefficient use of resources. Therefore, if we need 23.76 square inches of leather for each baseball, we may set a standard quantity of 24.5 square inches based on experience and on the data we have collected in the past regarding the amount of material used in production.

The standard prices of our direct materials include not only the purchase price but also the miscellaneous costs of purchasing, transporting, and receiving the inputs. Often direct materials are purchased in large quantities that require transportation by truck or rail, and these transportation costs need to be added to the purchase price of the material. Larger quantities are

Number of baseballs	10,000.00	
Approximate surface area of one baseball	23.76	Square Inches
Total surface Area of 10,000 baseballs	237,600.00	Square Inches
Expected Waste		
Estimated amount of leather		
Used for each machine calibration	5,000	Square Inches
Number of baseballs produced between each calibration	3,000	
Number of calibrations for each 10,000 baseballs	3.33	
Estimated amount of leather needed for calibrations to product 10,000 baseballs	16,666.67	Square Inches
Total estimated amount of leather needed for each 10,000 baseballs produced	254,266.67	

Fig. 2.1 Scrap/Waste Example

also often insured while being transported, which adds another cost. The transportation costs and insurance costs are examples of the types of miscellaneous costs that can be incurred to acquire and receive direct materials. These costs must be included with the purchase price when calculating the standard cost.

Item	Cost/unit	Sq. in.	Total Cost
Leather, purchase price per square inch	$0.045	300,000	$13,500.00
Plus: Transportation Costs			$ 1,200.00
Plus: Insurance			$ 275.00
Total Cost for 300,000 square inches			$14,975.00
Cost per square inch (total cost/total sq. in. or $14,975/300,000)			$ 00.04992

TRADITIONAL OPERATING FORECAST

Much of the business world still uses traditional forecasting approaches. Because the traditional forecast is a long-standing and well-known activity, our time is well spent investigating how traditional forecasting functions, along with exploring its benefits and limitations. We will examine a manufacturing firm to illustrate a traditional operating forecast (also known as a planning forecast, original forecast, or static forecast).

Traditional Forecasting Benefits

The benefits of forecasting center on planning for certain levels of activity or specific operations. The process of forecasting requires detailed knowledge and understanding of the firm's operations and processes, including operational tendencies, capacity characteristics, capacity limitations, capacity bottlenecks, operational strengths, and operational weaknesses among others.

Traditional Forecasting Limitations

One of the most significant limitations of the traditional forecast is the cost in preparation. The time and effort that employees expended to generate a traditional forecast can be substantial. Significant time, effort, and resources can be consumed in the process of creating a forecast.

Along with time and effort, the traditional forecast can often be left unused until the next annual forecast needs to be created. Traditional forecasts can become so large and complex they lose their usefulness in the ongoing operations of an organization—never being used as a productive tool, but only as an annual ritual.

Although traditional forecasting isn't perfect, studying the traditional forecast can help us gain significant insight and understanding into the process of forecasting. Because understanding the production process is so valuable, we'll work through a traditional forecast for a manufacturing firm.

Forecasts in Manufacturing

A manufacturer has a distinct set of needs to forecast when considering future production and operations. A manufacturer combines direct materials by using direct labor in its manufacturing facility, which ultimately generates finished products.

For example; a baseball manufacturer employs people who operate general and specialized machinery that combine leather, cork, and string/yarn into baseballs. The baseballs must then be sold and delivered to customers. The idea of making and selling baseballs seems straightforward, but it requires a lot of work to create a tangible and successful product. We must identify how much direct material is required, how many direct labor hours it will take, which machines are needed, and a manufacturing facility in which to operate—all of which is dependent on how many baseballs we believe we can sell to customers.

Operating Forecast Diagram

As we begin to work through an operating forecast, we can use Figure 2.2 to help guide us through the intricacies of the forecast. Figure 2.2 is a complete diagram of all the individual forecasts and accompanying schedules we'll use in this chapter.

An operating forecast begins with the sales forecast and then flows to the production forecast, the direct materials forecast, the direct labor forecast, the manufacturing overhead forecast, and the selling and administrative forecast, and then ends with the cash forecast. Some firms also prepare and maintain forecasted income statements and forecasted balance sheets, which are commonly referred to as pro-forma financial statements. In this textbook, we will limit our coverage to the operating forecasts.

One critical issue to recognize in the operating forecasts is that the forecasts themselves (sales, production, direct material, direct labor, manufacturing overhead, and selling, general, and administrative), except for the cash forecast, are accrual-based forecasts. While the accrual-based forecasts provide needed information used in the pro-forma financial statements, owners and managers need to know the cash impact, which is included in the cash forecast.

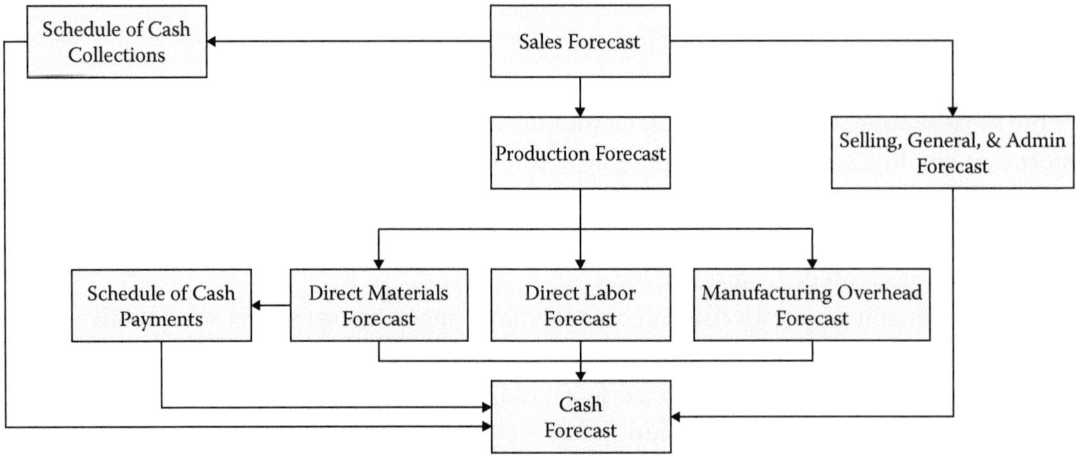

Fig. 2.2 Master Operating Forecast Diagram

Figure 2.3 provides an annotated diagram with the basis of accounting used in the forecasts.

Our objective in this chapter is to generate a cash forecast, which requires all of the forecasts to be adjusted to a cash-basis of accounting. We will first show how to prepare and use the accrual-based forecasts, then adjust them to provide cash-basis amounts.

Sales Forecast

Traditional forecasting always begins with the sales forecast, including the estimated or projected unit sales, as well as the sales price per unit. For a manufacturer, the estimated or projected unit sales volume drives the whole forecasting process. The estimated or projected unit sales volume governs production requirements, the production input needed, and the administrative support required to achieve the estimated or projected unit sales goals.

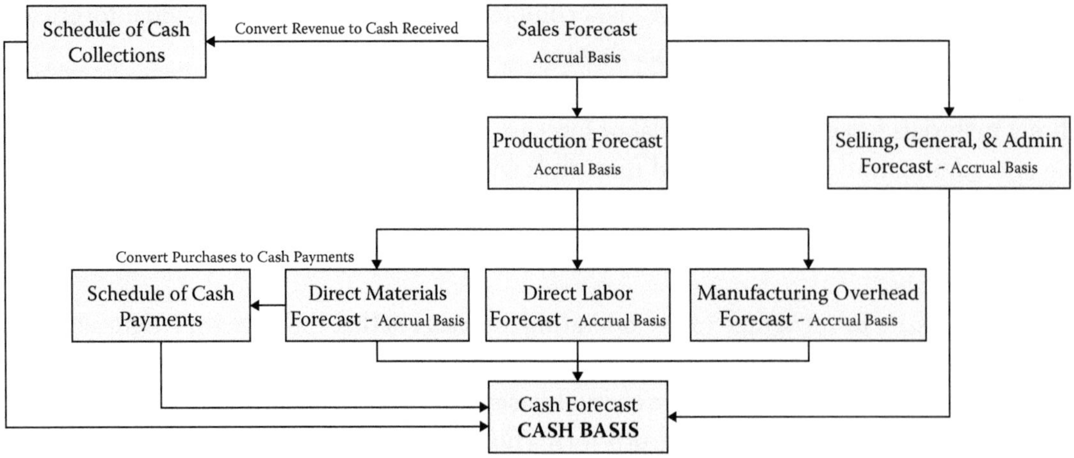

Fig. 2.3 Master Operating Forecast Diagram

Sales Forecast
Accrual-basis Sales Revenue

	Jan	Feb	Mar	1st Quarter total
Units Sold	25,000	35,000	30,000	90,000
Sales price/unit	$15	$15	$15	$15
Total Recognized Revenue	$375,000	$525,000	$450,000	$1,350,000

Estimated Collections of January Revenues

		Jan	Feb	Mar
Total Accrual-basis revenue		$375,000	$525,000	$450,000
Cash sales		$200,000		
Credit sales		$175,000		
		40%	40%	20%
Month of Sale	40%	$70,000		
Following month	40%		$70,000	
2nd month following	20%			$35,000

Fig. 2.4 Sales Forecast

From the volume of unit sales projected, we can apply 1) the sales price to determine total recognized revenue and 2) the estimated or projected collection expectation based on the firm's collection history and credit policies to forecast the timing of cash collections. Figure 2.4 provides an illustration of both the sales forecast and the conversion of accrual-based revenue in the month of January to the subsequent cash-basis collections of those revenues. In this case the firm expects to collect the January revenues in three different months: 40 percent in January, 40 percent in February, and the remaining 20 percent in May.

Figure 2.4 illustrates the collection pattern for a single month's revenue, isolating the collection pattern for the revenue generated only in January. When estimating revenue collections, each month will include cash collections from multiple months. Note that only the credit sales are subject to the cash collection pattern. Any cash sales will be collected at the point of sale. In some cases, revenue may not be segregated between cash and credit, which requires preparation to make and identify the assumptions they use in preparing the schedule.

Figure 2.5 illustrates the completed cash collection schedule for the months of January, February, and May. Included in January are collections from revenue generated in the previous November and December. The total amount of cash collected in each month will be used to prepare the cash forecast.

Production Forecast

The estimated or projected volume of unit sales drives how many units will need to be produced in a given period. We start the production forecast with the number of units projected to be sold during the month from the sales forecast. The number of units to be produced must cover all the units

Schedule of Cash Collections/Customer Receipts
Cash-basis Collections

		Jan	Feb	Mar	1st Quarter Total
Total Accrual-basis revenue		$375,000	$525,000	$450,000	
Cash sales		$200,000	$275,000	$240,000	$715,000
Credit sales		$175,000	$250,000	$210,000	
Month of Sale	40%	$70,000	$100,000	$84,000	$254,000
Following month	40%	$74,000	$70,000	$100,000	$244,000
2nd month following	20%	$30,000	$37,000	$35,000	$102,000
Expected Customer Collections		$374,000	$482,000	$459,000	$1,315,000

Collection expectations:		
Cash sales	100%	during month of sale
Credit sales	40%	during month of sale
	40%	during month following sale
	20%	during 2nd month following sale

Fig. 2.5 Cash Collection Schedule

expected to be sold, plus a number of units to remain in ending inventory at the end of the month so that on the first day of the next period, the firm has some products to sell to their customers.

The ending inventory requirement is created or determined by the firm as part of its standard policies and procedures for maintaining an ongoing operation. The amount of ending inventory can be expressed as a fixed number of units or as a percentage of the units to be sold the following month. One of the concerns management must address is the ability to fill customer orders without delay. In this traditional approach, management uses ending inventory as a tool to ensure customer orders can be filled promptly, while allowing for variations in the actual production schedule.

Figure 2.6 presents the production forecast. The expected number of units to be sold, forecasted in the sales forecast, is the starting point for each month's production forecast. For January, the firm must produce the 25,000 units they expect to sell in January, plus 8,750 units of ending inventory the firm wants to have on hand at the end of January, which can be sold in February, for a total of 33,750 units that must be produced. The 8,750 units of ending inventory in January equals 25 percent of the following month's (February) expected unit sales. The firm also has inventory on hand at the beginning of January that has already been produced and that can be subtracted from the total units needed to generate the total number of units that need to be produced during January.

The production forecast is denominated in number of finished or completed units. The beginning and ending inventory amounts relate to the finished goods Inventory.

Direct Materials Forecast

Once the number of units to be produced has been forecasted, we must plan for the amount of direct material needed to produce enough units to meet forecasted demand. The total units to be produced needs to be converted into the amount of direct material required for those units. When the required material for production has been identified, we then apply any operating procedures governing ending direct material inventory and beginning direct material inventory requirements. The materials inventory account is a separate inventory account and the firm will

Sales Forecast – Accrual-basis Sales Revenue	Jan	Feb	Mar	Qtr
Units Sold	25,000	35,000	30,000	90,000
Sales price/unit	$25	$25	$25	$25
Total Recognized Revenue	$625,000	$875,000	$750,000	$2,250,000

To translate units sold into units to be produced, we account for the units on hand at the start of the period & the units needed to be on hand at the end off the period.

The firm requires 25% of the following month's unit sales volume to be on hand at the end of the month.

Production Forecast		Jan	Feb	Mar	Qtr
Finished units to be sold		25,000	35,000	30,000	90,000
Ending Inventory	25%	8,750	7,500	6,875	6,875
Total units needed		33,750	42,500	36,875	96,875
Beginning Inventory		6,250	8,750	7,500	6,250
Units to be produced		27,500	33,750	29,375	90,625

Fig. 2.6 Sales and Production Forecast

have different amounts required as ending inventory requirements for direct materials than for finished goods inventory.

The forecast for direct materials is very similar to the calculation for cost of goods sold, but we are calculating the amount of purchases needed. It's important to recognize that the direct materials forecast is dealing with the direct materials inventory account.

DM	Forecast COGS	Purchases
DM for production	Beginning inventory	COGS
+ Targeted DM ending inventory	+ Purchases	+ EI
– DM beginning inventory	– Ending inventory	– BI
= DM to purchase	= COGS	= Purchase

The total units to be produced should be multiplied by the standard quantity of material that each unit requires in order to determine the amount of direct materials needed for the estimated production. After the amount of DM to be purchased has been identified, we then multiply the quantity of direct materials needed by the standard cost of the direct material.

Direct materials are an example of a variable cost. The cost for direct materials is consistent for each unit of product, and for every unit produced, the total cost of direct materials increases. The firm works to purchase its direct materials at consistent prices, usually entering into written contracts with suppliers or vendors to fix the price and guarantee sufficient quantities. These contracts fix the cost of the direct materials on a per-unit of material basis, or fix the cost for standard quantities of the direct materials.

Production Forecast – number of finished baseballs

		Jan	Feb	Mar	Qtr
Finished units to be sold		25,000	35,000	30,000	90,000
Ending inventory	25%	8,750	7,500	6,875	6,875
Total units needed		33,750	42,500	36,875	96,875
Beginning Inventory		6,250	8,750	7,500	6,250
Units to be produced		27,500	33,750	29,375	90,625

Producing units requires materials to be processed into products.
Units need to be converted into amounts of material to be ordered.

Direct Materials Forecast
Baseballs

		Jan	Feb	Mar	Qtr
Units to be produced		27,500	33,750	29,375	90,625
Materials used in each unit (square inches)		27	27	27	27
Total material for unit sales		742,500	911,250	793,125	2,446,875
Plus: Required Ending DM Inventory	35%	318,938	277,594	297,203	297,203
Total material needed – sq. in.		1,061,438	1,188,844	1,090,328	2,744,078
Less: Beginning DM Inventory		259,875	318,938	277,594	259,875
Total Quantity of DM to be Purchased		801,563	869,906	812,734	2,484,203
Square inches in a square foot		144	144	144	144
Total sq. ft. of material to be purchased		5,566.41	6,041.02	5,643.98	17,251.41
Price per square foot		$5.00	$5.00	$5.00	$5.00
Cost of material to be purchased		$27,832.03	$30,205.08	$28,219.92	$86,257.03

Estimated Payments of a Single Month's Purchases

		Jan	Feb	Mar	Qtr
Estimated purchases		$27,832.03			
		20%	60%	20%	
Amounts paid:					
In month of purchase	20%	$5,566.41			
In month following purchase	60%		$16,699.22		
In 2nd month following purchase	20%			$5,566.41	

Fig. 2.7 Direct Materials Forecast with Payments

Figure 2.7 illustrates the the direct materials forecast as well as the estimated payments for the direct materials purchases. The direct materials forecast begins with the number of units expected to be produced from the production forecast. The forecasted unit production must be converted to the amount of direct materials needed to produce the forecasted units. The amount of direct materials needed is then converted to the measurement or volume in which the material is purchased. In our example, each baseball requires 27 square inches of leather, and the firm has forecasted unit sales in January at 27,500 baseballs. The 27,500 baseballs to be produced will need 742,500 total square inches of leather.

Now that the expected unit production has been converted into direct materials amounts, we work through a similar process for the direct materials inventory. A desired amount of ending direct materials inventory is added to the amount of direct materials needed for forecasted unit sales, which gives us the total amount of direct materials needed. But, if we have any direct material inventory on hand at the beginning of the period, we subtract the beginning direct material inventory because we do not need to purchase what has already been acquired. In Figure 2.7, the ending direct materials inventory requirement is 35 percent of the following month's total material needed for unit sales. The 35 percent is an amount set by management, and each firm will have its own specific requirements, hence each business will have a different requirement. For our purposes, the 911,250 square inches of total material for unit sales in February is multiplied by 35 percent to calculate the 318,938 square inches of desired ending inventory for January.

January also has an amount of beginning direct materials inventory. The firm's desired ending inventory requirements can be applied to finding a month's beginning inventory levels. A month's beginning inventory is the prior month's ending inventory. To find the beginning inventory in January, we can calculate what the desired ending inventory should have been in December. December's desired ending inventory would have been 35 percent of January's total material needed for unit sales, so January's beginning inventory would be 35 percent of January's total material needed for unit sales.

This highlights an important aspect of inventory: One month's ending inventory is the next month's beginning inventory.

From the direct materials forecast, we must estimate when the payments will be made for the purchases. Similar to the cash collections estimate, the cash payments for direct materials purchases are often made over multiple months. The firm determines the timing of the expected cash payments based on current supplier contracts and on expected cash inflows. The result is to identify and estimate how much will be paid for direct materials purchases in each month.

Figure 2.7 illustrates the cash payments for the purchases in the month of January. The firm has determined an expected cash payment pattern. In this case, the firm expects to pay for a month's direct material purchases over three months:

20 percent paid in the month of purchase
60 percent paid in the month following purchase
20 percent paid in the second month following purchase

These percentages and their timing are decisions made by the firm's management. Every firm will have different pattern of payments. Each firm will have different percentages and different timeframes. Figure 2.8 illustrates a completed schedule for the estimated cash payments for direct

Schedule of Cash Payments for Purchases				
	Jan	Feb	Mar	Qtr
Estimated purchases	$27,832.03	$30,205.08	$28,219.92	$86,257.03
Amounts paid:				
In month of purchase	$5,566.41	$6,041.02	$5,643.98	$17,251.41
In month following purchase	$10,590.00	$16,699.22	$18,123.05	$45,412.27
In 2nd month following purchase	$2,515.00	$3,530.00	$5,566.41	$11,611.41
Total Amount Paid	$18,671.41	$26,270.23	$29,333.44	$74,275.08

Month of purchase	20%
Month following purchase	60%
Second month following purchase	20%

Fig. 2.8 Cash Payments Schedule

materials for the quarter. The schedule is color coordinated to assist the viewer in following the payments for a month's purchases. In this illustration, the January collections of $10,590 is from December purchases of $17,650, and the $2,515 of collections is from November purchases of $12,575. These amounts can be presented, in practice, as an amount of accounts payable that will be collected in the month.

Another aspect of Fig. 2.8 provides information on ending balances for accounts payable. At the end of any given month, the amount of any unpaid purchases can be used as the ending accounts payable balance.

Direct Labor Forecast

We forecast the amount and timing of direct labor needs based on the number of units to be produced from the production forecast. The firm establishes a standard amount of labor used to produce each unit of product based on the firm's production experience, as well as other measurements of direct labor input such as time-and-motion studies.

The standard cost for direct labor is a function of both the number of direct labor hours needed to produce a single unit of product (the standard quantity of direct labor) and the total amount an employer pays to employ its people (standard price of direct labor). The standard quantity of direct labor is based on the amount of time it takes an employee, or employees, to produce a single unit of product.

For small products or high volume, the time to produce a single unit maybe much less than an hour. An employee working in a pen or pencil factory may be able to produce hundreds or thousands of pens or pencils in an hour. The amount of time to produce a single pen or pencil might be found by dividing an hour by the number of pens or pencils produced to calculate the fraction of an hour needed to produce a single unit. Also, 60 minutes may be used to calculate the number of minutes needed to produce a single unit. For large products, the time to produce a single unit requires multiple hours.

The standard price to employ people must include not only the wage rate per hour (standard price) the employee receives, but also fringe benefits costs and ancillary employment costs. An employer is required to pay for costs such as unemployment insurance, worker's compensation insurance, and a portion of any employment/social welfare tax, in addition to the employee's base wage or salary. An employer may also elect to pay for some fringe benefits such as health insurance premiums or retirement plan contributions, which add to the cost of employing workers.

Employment	Cost	Percentage of Total
Wage per hour	$11.00	78.6%
Unemployment insurance premium	$0.50	3.6%
Worker's compensation insurance premium	$0.40	2.9%
Employer portion of social welfare tax	$0.80	5.7%
Fringe benefits	$0.80	5.7%
Retirement plan contribution	$0.50	3.5%
Total employment cost per hour	**$14.00**	**100.0%**

Production Forecast					
		Jan	Feb	Mar	Qtr
Finished units to be sold		25,000	35,000	30,000	90,000
Ending Inventory	25%	8,750	7,500	6,875	8,750
Total units needed		33,750	42,500	36,875	98,750
Beginning Inventory		6,250	8,750	7,500	7,500
Units to be produced		27,500	33,750	29,375	91,250

Producing units requires people to be processed into products
Units need to be converted into amounts of time employees spend making products.

Direct Labor Forecast				
	Jan	Feb	Mar	Qtr
Units to be produced	27,500	33,750	29,375	90,625
Materials used in each unit hours	0.2	0.2	0.2	0.2
Total material needed—hrs	5,500	6,750	5,875	18,125
Labor rate per hour	$14.00	$14.00	$14.00	$14.00
Cost of direct labor	$77,000.00	$94,500.00	$82,250.00	$253,750.00

Fig. 2.9 Production and Direct Labor Forecast

The total cost to employ people is significantly more than just the employee's hourly wage. In this example, the employee's wages are only 78.6 percent of the total cost to employ.

Figure 2.9 is an illustration of the direct labor forecast. The direct labor forecast begins by using the number of units to be produced from the production forecast. The number of units to be produced is then converted to the amount of direct labor time required to produce those units. In this example, employees must spend a total of .2 hours, or 12 minutes, to produce a single unit. Because in most businesses, direct labor wages are denominated in hours, the illustration in Fig. 2.9 converts the units to be produced into the number of direct labor hours to be congruent with the quotation of direct labor wages in hourly wages.

Direct labor is an example of a variable cost. For every additional unit produced, another .2 hours of direct labor time is needed to make that additional unit. As the total number of units increases, the total amount of direct labor cost increases as well.

Manufacturing Overhead Forecast

Direct material and direct labor are relatively straightforward costs to understand and calculate. Manufacturing overhead is much more challenging because the manufacturing overhead category includes many different costs as well as different cost behaviors: some costs are fixed, some costs are variable, and some costs are mixed (part fixed and part variable). Manufacturing overhead often includes indirect material, indirect labor, rent, utilities, property taxes, insurance premiums, repairs and maintenance, security, parts management, janitorial, and many other kinds of costs. The following list includes a sample of the various manufacturing overhead costs, along with the possible type of behavior each cost might exhibit:

Manufacturing Overhead	Cost Behavior
Indirect labor	Variable
Indirect material	Variable
Rent for factory	Fixed
Utilities in the factory	Mixed
Property taxes for the factory	Fixed
Insurance premiums for factory insurance	Fixed
Repairs and maintenance of factory equipment	Mixed
Security at the factory	Mixed
Parts inventory management	Mixed
Janitorial costs at the factory	Mixed
Depreciation of factory buildings and equipment	Fixed

To effectively forecast the amount of manufacturing overhead incurred and allocated at any given level of production volume, we must classify all of the firm's manufacturing overhead costs as either fixed or variable. At this point, we have classified all the manufacturing overhead costs as either fixed or variable. Later, in Chapter 3, we will address the issue of mixed costs and analyzing those mixed costs to separate them into their fixed and variable portions.

Here in Figure 2.10, we see one of the important reasons for mixed cost analysis, which is to allow more accurate forecasting of costs when unit volume changes.

Manufacturing overhead is comprised of various indirect manufacturing costs, as we discussed earlier. Because of the indirect nature of manufacturing overhead, the manufacturing overhead costs are allocated to individual units of product, batches of product, or product lines. Direct material can be found in, on, or around the finished product, and direct labor is the time employees spend making the products, represented by time cards and other documentation. Manufacturing overhead does not have a direct relationship to any individual unit of product. Manufacturing overhead is the costs incurred to maintain the productive capacity and productive environment in which employees can work to product the firm's products. Manufacturing overhead is essentially a portion of the cost of capacity. Because manufacturing overhead is indirect in nature and lacks a connection to individual units of product, the manufacturing overhead costs are allocated. Any allocation of costs is an arbitrarily determined process and uses a specific approach or method of allocation. We observe many allocation processes in the accounting records, such as depreciation, depletion, bond discount or premium amortization, and intangible amortization, to name a few. In this textbook and course, we will deal with manufacturing overhead allocation using different methods or approaches in future chapters.

To help understand the manufacturing overhead forecast at this point, we need to address how the manufacturing overhead is being allocated in Figure 2.10. In this example, the manufacturing overhead is being allocated using a single predetermined overhead rate (POR), which we will refer to as traditional costing. In Chapter 4, we will discuss both the single predetermined overhead rate along with activity-based costing methods of allocating manufacturing overhead. The single predetermined overhead rate is determined by selecting an allocation base and dividing the estimated manufacturing overhead by the estimated amount of allocation base. In our illustration in Figure 2.10, we use direct labor hours as the allocation base. For each hour of direct labor incurred, a predetermined amount of $5.50 of variable manufacturing overhead (VOH) will be allocated to the unit or batch.

Manufacturing Overhead Forecast				
	Jan	Feb	Mar	Qtr
O/H allocation base–DLH	5,500	6,750	5,875	18,125
VOH allocated per DLH (POR)	$5.50	$5.50	$5.50	$5.50
Total material needed–hrs	30,250	37,125	32,313	99,688
FOH	$12,500.00	$12,500.00	$12,500.00	$37,500.00
Total MFG O/H	$42,750.00	$49,625.00	$44,812.50	$137,187.50
Less: Deprciation	$4,500	$4,500	$4,500	$13,500
Cash-basis MFG O/H	$38,250	$45,125	$40,313	$123,688

Fig. 2.10 Manufacturing Overhead Forecast

Figure 2.10 illustrates the manufacturing overhead forecast. The number of units to be produced is used from the production forecast and multiplied by the $5.50 predetermined overhead rate to calculate the estimated amount of the variable portion of manufacturing overhead allocated to the units produced. To the estimated total allocated variable manufacturing overhead, the fixed manufacturing overhead is added. The total fixed manufacturing overhead includes all the fixed manufacturing overhead costs, including both cash and non-cash expenses, and are hence accrual-based expenses. This is an important point because the total fixed manufacturing overhead includes non-cash expenses, predominantly depreciation of factory equipment and buildings, for our purposes. In this chapter, the ending point for all the forecasts and schedules we produce is the cash forecast. The only amounts used in the cash forecast are those costs paid in cash. Therefore, the depreciation for the factory equipment and buildings must be subtracted from the total amount of accrual-bases manufacturing overhead expenses.

When preparing and using the manufacturing overhead forecast, it is crucial to recognize that it is both an accrual-based and cash-based forecast. The total accrual-basis expense must be adjusted for any non-cash expenses, mainly depreciation. Adjusting for depreciation converts the accrual-based expenses to the cash-basis payments for manufacturing overhead, which payments can then be used in creating the cash forecast while preserving the accrual-basis cost, which can be used in the pro-forma income statement.

Selling, General, and Administrative (SG&A) Forecast

Selling, general, and administrative (SG&A) costs are part of every organization and are critical costs in any successful organization. These costs include a wide array of amounts and behaviors. These costs are separate from the manufacturing or production functions while being directly related to the volume of units sold. The SG&A costs can include corporate office expenses, manager salaries, marketing, accounting, legal, research and development, logistics, advertising and marketing, human resources, treasury, and many others. The costs can behave like variable costs, fixed costs, or mixed costs. SG&A also includes non-cash expenses such as depreciation on corporate office buildings and equipment and amortization of various intangible corporate assets.

Sales Forecast—Accrual-basis Sales Revenue

	Jan	Feb	Mar	Qtr
Units Sold	25,000	35,000	30,000	90,000
Sales price/unit	$25	$25	$25	$25
Total Recognized Revenue	$625,000	$875,000	$750,000	$2,250,000

Selling, General, & Administrative Forecast

	Jan	Feb	Mar	Qtr
Unit Sales Forecast	25,000	35,000	30,000	90,000
Variable SG&A per unit	$0.75	$0.75	$0.75	$0.75
Total variable SG&A	$18,750.00	$26,250.00	$22,500.00	$67,500.00
Fixed SG&A:				
Executive Salaries	$10,000	$10,000	$10,000	$30,000
Insurance	$4,000	$4,000	$4,000	$12,000
Advertising	$6,500	$6,500	$6,500	$19,500
Property taxes	$1,300	$1,300	$1,300	$3,900
Depreciation	$4,250	$4,250	$4,250	$12,750
Total fixed SG&A	$26,050	$26,050	$26,050	$78,150
Total SG&A (variable & fixed)	$44,800	$52,300	$48,550	$145,650
Less: depreciation	$4,250	$4,250	$4,250	$12,750
Cash-basis SG&A	$40,550	$48,050	$44,300	$132,900

Fig. 2.11 Selling, General, and Administrative Forecast

Figure 2.11 illustrates the selling, general, and administrative expense forecast. When preparing the SG&A forecast, care must be taken to identify both the costs and cost behaviors. The forecasted unit sales are used as the starting point for the SG&A forecast. The unit sales are multiplied by the amount of variable SG&A costs to calculate the total estimated variable SG&A expenses. The estimated fixed SG&A expenses are then added to the total estimated variable SG&A expenses to find the estimated total accrual-based SG&A expenses. Note that the manager salaries, insurance, advertising property taxes, and depreciation listed in the illustration all relate to activities outside the manufacturing processes of the firm.

Similar to the manufacturing overhead forecast, the SG&A forecast identifies the total estimated accrual-based expenses and then adjusts the accrual-based expenses for any non-cash expenses (mainly depreciation, for our purposes) to identify the cash-based payments for SG&A.

Cash Forecast

The cash forecast is an important part of the operating forecast because it combines the cash receipts from sales with the cash payments for operations. A business must be able to access cash when payments are due to vendors, employees, taxing authorities, owners, and others. If a firm has irregular cash inflows from customers, then the firm must make financing arrangements that allow the firm to access a loan or line of credit to pay expenses.

The cash receipts from customers are added to the beginning cash balance to generate the total amount of cash available during the period.

From each of the forecasts and schedules we have prepared cash disbursements, which include payments for materials and inventory; direct labor; manufacturing overhead; and SG&A costs. Then dividends to stockholders and fixed asset purchases are also included as additional cash payments in the cash forecast as additional cash payments. Some firms maintain other forecasts for capital transactions (such as dividend and additional owner investment) and capital equipment purchases, but for our purposes we handle these kinds of payments in the cash forecast. All the cash payments are added to find the amount of total cash payments for each month.

The total amount of cash payments is subtracted from the total amount of cash available to calculate the period's cash balance (whether it's a positive amount (excess) or a deficit (deficiency)). At this point, the firm may have some form of standard operating procedures or business rules that address various issues such as any required ending cash balance for the firm. A business rule may state that a certain minimum balance must be maintained at the end of every accounting period, and if the cash balance falls below the minimum balance, then the firm will borrow money to meet the minimum cash balance requirement. While the firm may have standard rules or procedures for things like minimum balance requirements and lending activity, the bank or lender may also have their own borrowing and repayment terms that must be met according to the loan or line-of-credit agreement.

Banks and other lenders offer various types of loans and lines of credit to businesses, which often include various terms and conditions on how money is borrowed and repaid to the line of credit. Common terms for borrowing on a line of credit may include borrowing amounts in certain increments and at certain points in time. The bank may require borrowing increments of $1,000, $10,000, or some other amount. The bank may allow borrowing to occur only at the beginning of a month, while other agreements may allow borrowing at any time. Banks may restrict repayments to only at the end of a month or some other time frame. Banks may also stipulate when interest on the loan or line of credit is to be paid. The agreement may require interest to be paid at the end of each month on any outstanding balance or to be paid when any of the principal is repaid. One of the objectives a bank seeks is to maximize the amount of interest they earn on loans and lines of credit, and the borrowing and repayment terms are often structured to accomplish this objective.

Figure 2.12 illustrates a cash forecast. The beginning cash balance must be provided. The customer collections amount comes from the schedule of cash collection from customers. The amounts for direct materials comes from the schedule of cash payments for purchases and from direct labor, MFG, O/H, and SG&A amounts come from their respective forecasts. Amounts for dividends and asset purchases are also be included in the cash payments section of the cash forecast. The total cash payments is subtracted from the cash available to determine the amount of cash excess or (deficiency) for each month. The cash excess or (deficiency) is evaluated against the minimum cash balance requirement, and in this example the cash excess is $297,523.59, which is less than the minimum ending cash balance required by the firm. The firm must therefore borrow $53,000 in order to meet the minimum cash balance of $350,000. Even though the firm desires an ending cash balance of $350,000 at the end of any given month, the bank has a requirement that any withdrawals from the line of credit be made in increments of $1,000 and must be made at the beginning of the month in which the withdrawal is made. The firm must therefore borrow $53,000 to meet their $350,000 desired minimum balance and to comply with the banks withdrawal requirements.

Cash Forecaset				
	Jan	Feb	Mar	Qtr
Beginning Cash Balance	$125,000.00	$350,523.59	$585,435.86	$125,000.00
Customer Collections	$374,000.00	$482,000.00	$459,000.00	$1,315,000.00
Cash Available	$499,000.00	$832,523.59	$1,044,435.86	$1,440,000.00
Cash Payments:				
Direct Materials	$18,671.41	$26,270.23	$29,333.44	$74,275.08
Direct Labor	$104,005.00	$127,642.50	$111,096.25	$342,743.75
MFG O/H	$38,250.00	$45,125.00	$40,312.50	$123,687.50
SG&A	$40,550.00	$48,050.00	$44,300.00	$132,900.00
Asset Purchase				$0.00
Dividends				$0.00
Total Cash Payments	$201,476.41	$247,087.73	$225,042.19	$673,606.33
Cash Excess or (Deficiency)	$297,523.59	$585,435.86	$819,393.67	$766,393.67
Financing:				
Borrowings	$53,000.00			$53,000.00
Repayments			($53,000.00)	($53,000.00)
Interest Paid			($1,590.00)	($1,590.00)
Total Financing	$53,000.00	$0.00	($54,590.00)	($1,590.00)
Ending Cash Balance	$350,523.59	$585,435.86	$764,803.67	$764,803.67
Minimum Cash Balance	$350,000.00			
Annual Interest Rate	12%			
Withdrawal Requirements	$1,000.00	Increments		

Fig. 2.12 Cash Forecast

In this illustration, the bank has a repayment requirement at the end of any given month in which repayments are made, and that interest is paid when the principal is repaid. To calculate the interest paid on the borrowings, the $53,000 is borrowed at the beginning of January and then repaid at the end of May, meeting the banks borrowing and repayment requirements. The bank charges 12 percent annual interest on any funds borrowed on a line of credit. The amount of interest is calculated by multiplying $53,000 by 12 percent annual interest and then multiplied by 3/12 (3 months divided by 12 months) because the firm borrowed the money at the beginning of January and then repaid at the end of May. This is an application of the simple interest calculation method: principal × rate × time.

$$\text{Principal} \times \text{rate} \times \text{time} = \text{interest}$$
$$\$53{,}000 \times 12\% \times 3/12 = \$1{,}590$$

PRO-FORMA (FORECASTED) INCOME STATEMENTS, BALANCE SHEETS, AND STATEMENTS OF CASH FLOWS

After the operating forecasts have been completed, a common continuation of the process includes producing pro-forma income statements, balance sheets, and statements of cash flows based on GAAP or IFRS. These general-purpose financial statement forecasts are often generated or created by internal management accountants, but they serve an external reporting purpose and not necessarily an internal decision-making role. The pro-forma financial statements are often used to communicate expected performance to creditors or to provide financial analysts with earnings guidance if the firm is publicly traded. Although pro-forma financial statements are useful as a form of external reporting, we will not address the detailed preparation of pro-forma financial statements in this textbook and will leave the topic for more advanced accounting courses.

Various Forecasting Timeframes

In this chapter, we had presented an operating forecast for a three-month timeframe with a total for the calendar quarter. Forecasting will be based on various timeframes, depending on the needs of the firm and decision makers. The traditional operating forecast typically covers a 12-month period, usually assumed to be an operating cycle. Forecasts are commonly based on months, quarters, and years, but some firms may even use a weekly timeframe. No matter the timeframe, forecasting principles and techniques can be effectively applied to any timeframe.

BEYOND TRADITIONAL FORECASTS

Traditional forecasting can potentially become a tedious, arduous, and time-consuming task that generates significant stress without creating added value to the organization. The annual forecasting process can consume weeks and months of resources to produce a binder with many spreadsheets, charts, and graphs, and lengthy narratives that become fixtures on the shelves of owners and managers, gathering dust until the following year when the annual forecasting process starts again. This experience is an expensive resource drain on any organization.

Some organizations have implemented very different forecasting processes and models to decrease stress and reduce wasted time while increasing the tangible added value compared to traditional forecasting approaches. Jack Welch, former CEO of General Electric, summarized a forward-looking CEO's thoughts on traditional forecasting: "It sucks the energy, time, fun, and big dreams out of an organization. It hides opportunity and stunts growth. It brings out the most unproductive behaviors in an organization, from sandbagging to settling for mediocrity." We will explore one of the newer approaches to forecasting used by firms to simplify the forecasting process and to enhance the value of the process within the organization.

Rolling Forecasts

Rolling forecasts, or continuous forecasts, are used by firms as a way of constantly maintaining a forecast for the short term, between 12 and 18 months. A typical rolling forecast will include monthly forecasts for the prospective six (6) months and quarterly forecasts for the following four (4) quarters.

Functionally, responsible managers will forecast the next immediate six months and the following four quarters at the end of each quarter. On January 1, a company might have monthly forecasts for January through June of the current year, and a forecast for each quarter from July of the current year to June of the following year. At the end of the first quarter of the current year, managers will update the next six (6) monthly forecasts from April through September of the current year and then quarterly forecasts from October of the current year to September of the following year.

This approach maintains a constant six-month view with detailed monthly forecasts, along with an additional 12-month view of more aggregated quarterly forecasts. A manager works from the detailed information within a time frame that can reasonably be estimated while maintaining a less demanding quarterly forecast in a time window where the details of prices, quantities, and capacities, along with other general and specific economic conditions, are much less certain.

The following exhibit diagrams the continuous nature of a rolling forecast.

Figure 2.13 illustrates a rolling forecast. the forecasts are adjusted at the end of each quarter for each of the periods over the following two years. At the end of the first quarter, months four through six are updated, and quarter three is expanded into months seven through nine. This rolling approach maintains a detailed monthly forecast for the next six months, followed by quarterly forecasts for the next 12 months. All of the information in the forecast is subject to adjustment. The monthly and quarterly forecasts are adjusted for all known and suspected financial effects. In the example, both monthly and quarterly revenues are adjusted at the end of each quarter. Fixed costs are adjusted for planned investment as well as actual investment. Variable costs are adjusted for the effect of the increased investment and planned decrease in variable costs as the firm expands and sales volume increases.

Beyond Forecasting (Beyond Budgeting)

Some firms have deliberately discontinued (or have never had) any type of traditional or continuous forecasting/budgeting process and have still experienced high levels of success. One approach is to identify a key metric, such as net operating income, and require a standard 15 percent year-on-year increase. If last year the firm experienced a weekly net operating income of $35,000 then this year a goal would be $40,250, a 15 percent increase in net operating income over last year's net operating income. The simplicity of such an approach can bely a firm's commitment that nothing is allowed to deter the 15 percent year-over-year increase, no matter the circumstances. The financial goals are often supported with a number of non-financial goals such as on-time delivery or waste reduction. Also, firms with these simple goal-setting processes also usually have strong cultural and administrative controls. For this kind of approach to be successful, operating segments (divisions) need to be able to act as independent companies and have complete control over their operational activities.

Rolling/Continuous Forecasts

		Year 1								Year 2	
		Month 1	Month 2	Month 3	Month 4	Month 5	Month 6	Quarter 3	Quarter 4	Quarter 1	Quarter 2
Revenue		$35,000	$38,000	$46,000	$44,000	$55,000	$52,500	$156,000	$185,000	$140,000	$178,000
Variable Costs	35.0%	$12,250	$13,300	$16,100	$15,400	$19,250	$18,375	$54,600	$64,750	$49,000	$62,300
Contribution Margin		$22,750	$24,700	$29,900	$28,600	$35,750	$34,125	$101,400	$120,250	$91,000	$115,700
Fixed Costs		$27,500	$27,500	$27,500	$27,500	$27,500	$27,500	$27,500	$27,500	$27,500	$27,500
Net Operating income		-$4,750	-$2,800	$2,400	$1,100	$8,250	$6,625	$73,900	$92,750	$63,500	$88,200

		Month 4	Month 5	Month 6	Month 7	Month 8	Month 9	Quarter 4	Quarter 1	Quarter 2	Quarter 3
Revenue		$46,000	$52,500	$58,000	$51,000	$60,000	$58,500	$178,500	$178,500	$178,500	$178,500
Variable Costs	35.0%	$16,100	$18,375	$20,300	$17,850	$21,000	$20,475	$62,475	$62,475	$62,475	$62,475
Contribution Margin		$29,900	$34,125	$37,700	$33,150	$39,000	$38,025	$116,025	$116,025	$116,025	$116,025
Fixed Costs		$27,500	$27,500	$27,500	$27,500	$27,500	$27,500	$27,500	$35,000	$35,000	$35,000
Net Operating income		$2,400	$6,625	$10,200	$5,650	$11,500	$10,525	$88,525	$81,025	$81,025	$81,025

		Month 7	Month 8	Month 9	Month 10	Month 11	Month 12	Quarter 1	Quarter 2	Quarter 3	Quarter 4
Revenue		$52,500	$54,000	$60,500	$66,000	$62,500	$69,000	$185,000	$190,000	$187,500	$195,000
Variable Costs	28.0%	$14,700	$15,120	$16,940	$18,480	$17,500	$19,320	$51,800	$53,200	$52,500	$54,600
Contribution Margin		$37,800	$38,880	$43,560	$47,520	$45,000	$49,680	$133,200	$136,800	$135,000	$140,400
Fixed Costs		$35,000	$35,000	$35,000	$35,000	$35,000	$35,000	$35,000	$35,000	$35,000	$35,000
Net Operating income		$2,800	$3,880	$8,560	$12,520	$10,000	$14,680	$98,200	$101,800	$100,000	$105,400

Fig. 2.13 Rolling Forecasts

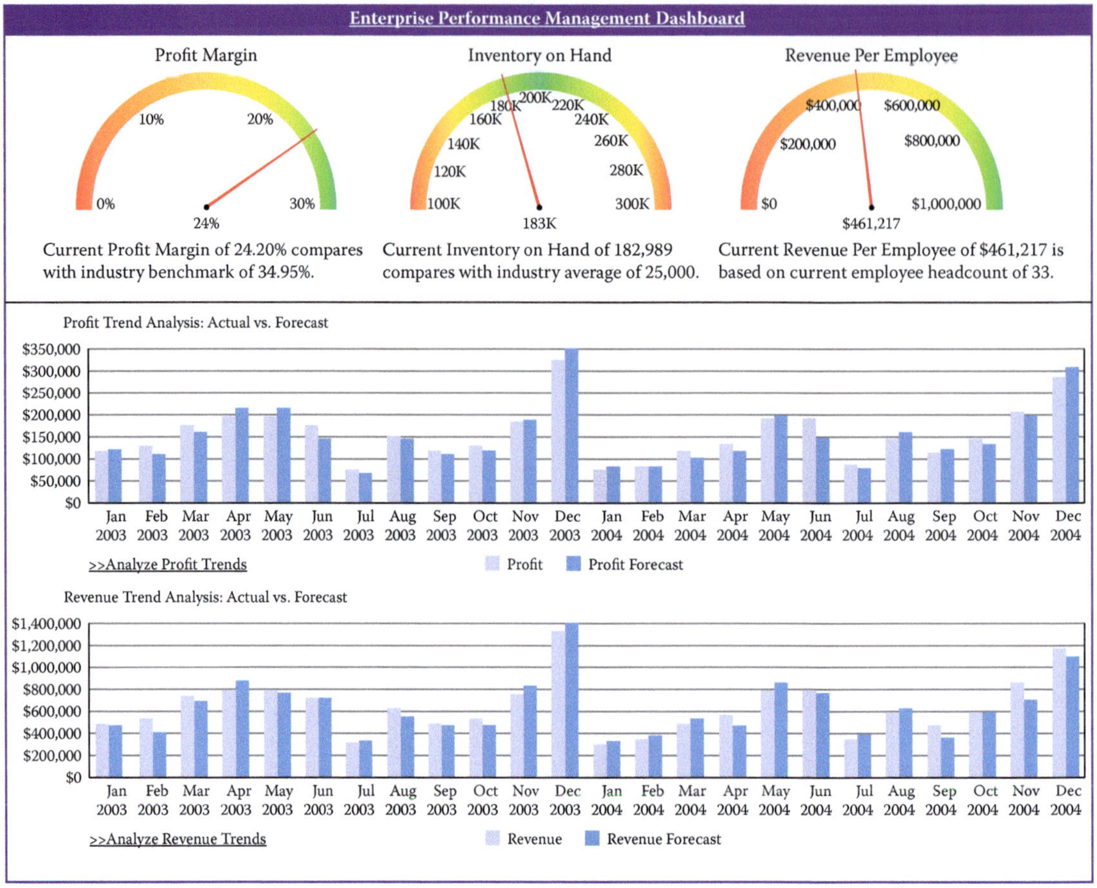

Fig. 2.14 Corporate Performance Management
Source: http://www.dashboards-metrics.com/corporate-performance-management/

Even though these firms have removed all the complexity and eliminated wasted excess time and resources, they still accomplish the essence of forecasting: to create and maintain a quantifiable goal based on the strategy of the firm that significantly impacts the performance of the firm.

3

COST-VOLUME-PROFIT (CVP) ANALYSIS

How changes in cost and volume affect profit

THE QUESTIONS WE TRY TO ANSWER

- How are our costs, sales volume, and profit related?
- What would happen to our profit if sales increased?
- What would happen to our profit if sales decreased?
- What is our breakeven point?
- How much do we need to sell to earn a specific amount of profit?
- What would happen to our profit if we purchased more efficient equipment?
- What is our cost structure, variable costs versus fixed costs?
- What would happen to our profit if a supplier increased their prices?

LEARNING OBJECTIVES

LO1: Explain the concept, assumptions, and components of CVP analysis.

LO2: Identify mixed costs and use the high-low method to separate fixed and variable costs.

LO3: Identify and explain the curves, points, and areas of the traditional CVP graph.

LO4: Explain the strengths and weaknesses of CVP analysis.

LO5: Explain the CVP staircase as a process tool.

LO6: Explain and calculate the breakeven point and target profit.

LO7: Explain and calculate the margin of safety and degree of operating leverage.

Objectives

Cost-volume-profit (CVP) analysis is used to forecast possible results of decision options (what-if analysis) so that owners and managers can see the effects that changes in cost structure and unit sales volume have on profit. The relationships among the costs of a product or service, the volume of unit sales, and the resulting operating profit or loss are critical areas a firm must understand to compete effectively in today's marketplace as well as plan future investments.

CVP analysis provides a view of a complete accounting period, usually a month or year, based on the predicted amounts for that period. This can be viewed as a type of marginal analysis because the analysis is based on the total expected unit sales volume of that period. CVP analysis is a short-term analysis tool because it assumes that the relationships between sales price, variable cost per unit, total fixed costs, and unit volume do not change during the period under analysis.

CVP analysis can also be used to understand the process of production or service delivery and the sustainability of profit margins, sales unit growth, and changes in cost structure. Thus, CVP analysis provides a tool for owners and managers to make day-to-day operational decisions.

Limitations

The main limitation of CVP analysis is that it is based on short-term marginal costs and revenue. The assumptions we make about the linearity of costs and revenue and the relevant range (of production or sales volume) limit the model's usefulness to narrow planning scenarios. Outside of the relevant range, the CVP model does not provide owners and managers useful guidance. Inside the relevant range the relationships may not be strictly linear. For example, an increase in sales volume could lead to lower material costs because larger orders of materials could get higher quantity discounts from suppliers.

One important aspect of the traditional CVP analysis model and graph is the use of total amounts: total revenue, total costs, and total sales volume. Because the traditional CVP graph only presents a view of one point in time it does not help owners and managers gain insight or understanding about how the results can be achieved and whether they are sustainable. These limitations will be considered further once we have an understanding of the traditional CVP model and graph. In order to gain an understanding of the effect that CVP analysis has on organizational processes, we end the chapter with a different graphical model, which we call the CVP Staircase.

The traditional CVP analysis model implies that unit volume is the single driver of cost. With unit volume displayed on the horizontal axis (x-axis), the volume is the single independent variable driving the end result of revenue and cost on the vertical axis (y-axis).

The traditional CVP analysis model also does not take into account inflation, price changes, operational efficiency changes, and the constant changes in the marketplace, and multiple products introduce complexity that the model cannot adequately address. Firms compete in dynamic environments and markets, while the traditional CVP model presents a relatively static view. For example, by holding sales price constant, the model takes the position of a price taker in the market, not able to influence the sales price. On the cost side, the model takes the position of having control over input prices. These types of inherent effects create weaknesses in the model, which owners and managers need to be aware of.

Benefits

Despite its limitations, the traditional CVP analysis model provides a good tool to explore and visualize a firm's current position and any short-term changes. The traditional CVP model is able to evaluate the position of a firm at a specific point in time with its current capacity. The model provides a tool to visualize the firm's immediate productive capacity and a context to understand the relationship between current productive capacities and decisions that need to be made regarding the firm's operations.

Later in this textbook we will use the traditional CVP model as a framework to evaluate operating and strategic decisions, which we view as essentially capacity issues. Traditionally, operating and strategic decisions have been grouped into two types of decisions: short-term decisions and long-term decisions. In this textbook, we take a much different approach to these types of operating and strategic decisions. We believe that the fundamental issue with operating and strategic decisions is that they are driven by capacity issues, not time issues. For example, long-term capital investment decisions and the need to make investments in plant and equipment are driven by increasing demand for the firm's products or services, not because of a five-year or ten-year timeline. While time might be a factor in the process of evaluating capacity decisions, time does not drive the need to make capacity decisions; demand alone drives those decisions.

Components and Assumptions

The components used in CVP analysis include total fixed costs, variable cost per unit, total variable costs, sales price per unit, total sales revenue, and unit volume. CVP analysis assumes that the relationships between costs, revenue, and volume are linear within a relevant range of activity.

FIXED COSTS

Most businesses have costs that must be paid no matter how many units they produce or sell. Rent for office and factory space is often negotiated in lease contracts that extend over multiple years. Land, buildings, and capital equipment are frequently acquired using some form of long-term financing or leasing. These types of contractual obligations cannot be changed without a significant impact on the resources of the business or without severe penalties. The obligations that cannot be changed in the short to intermediate term make them fixed for a known period of time. These costs do not change in total, no matter the volume of activity in which the firm engages. Whether a firm produces 10,000 units or 50,000 units in a month, the fixed costs are the same. As activity increases, then the fixed costs are spread over more units and the fixed costs per unit decrease.

Fixed costs are fixed in total and change on a per-unit basis as volume changes. No matter the unit volume of the firm, the fixed costs must be paid. Graphically, fixed costs can be represented by a horizontal line. Because fixed costs are fixed in total, as the number of units produced increases, the amount of fixed cost per unit decreases.

Figure 3.1 illustrates fixed costs with both a table calculation and a graphical presentation. In the right column of the table, the total fixed costs remain the same, $65,000, whether a single unit is produced or 100,000 units are produced, as shown in the left column. In the center column, the total amount of fixed costs is divided by the number of units produced. As the firm produces more units, the amount of fixed cost per unit decreases. We can also think about each unit of product paying for the fixed costs, and as the number of units increases, the amount each unit must cover decreases.

In the graph, the horizontal axis, the x-axis, represents the total number of units produced, while the vertical axis, the y-axis, represents the total dollar amount. As we view the graph, the fixed costs are represented as a horizontal line. As production increases from zero units at the origin of the graph, the amount of fixed costs remains the same. The graph does not depict the amount of fixed costs per unit.

Note that fixed costs should always be accounted for in total amounts. But, as you will see later in this textbook, we often allocate fixed costs to units on a per-unit basis. When we see fixed

Units	Per Unit Fixed Cost	Total Fixed Cost
1	$65,000.00	$65,000
100	$650.00	$65,000
1,000	$65.00	$65,000
10,000	$6.50	$65,000
100,000	$0.65	$65,000

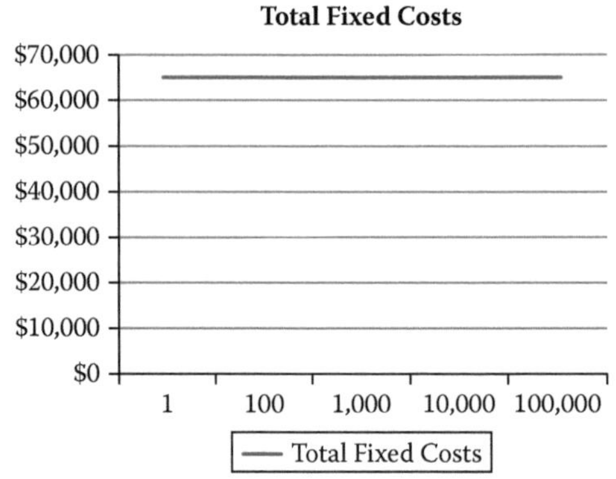

Fig. 3.1 Fixed Costs

costs presented on a per-unit basis, then the fixed costs per unit must be multiplied by the total number of units used in calculating the per-unit amount to find the total amount of fixed costs. Fixed costs should be accounted for in total because the per-unit amount of fixed costs cannot be known until the period is over and the exact number of units produced is known. For example, an amount of fixed costs per unit might be presented and used when forecasting, but that per-unit amount is an arbitrary allocation because the actual number of units is not known at the time the forecast is created; the actual number of units produced won't be known until after those units have been produced.

VARIABLE COSTS

When a business produces a product or service, each product or service requires specific costs. A baseball manufacturer must purchase a certain amount of direct materials such as leather, cork, and string/yarn to produce every baseball, and along with those costs there is a certain amount of direct labor time. The individual materials are combined and transformed into a finished product. The amounts of leather, cork, and string/yarn are consistent for each baseball produced and the costs for those materials are assumed to be relatively constant as well. Each time a baseball is made, the same amounts of and costs for direct material and direct labor are required. As more baseballs are produced, the total cost for direct materials and direct labor increases. Variable costs are directly proportional to sales volume.

Variable costs are consistent per unit and change in total as volume changes. Every unit produced adds its own variable cost, thus increasing the total variable costs for the period. Graphically, variable costs can be illustrated by an upward-sloping line. As the number of units produced increases, each unit adds the cost of the direct materials and direct labor incurred to produce that unit, thereby increasing the total amount of variable costs for the period.

Units	Total Variable Cost	Per Unit Cost
1	$2.50	$2.50
10	$25	$2.50
100	$250	$2.50
1000	$2,500	$2.50
10000	$25,000	$2.50

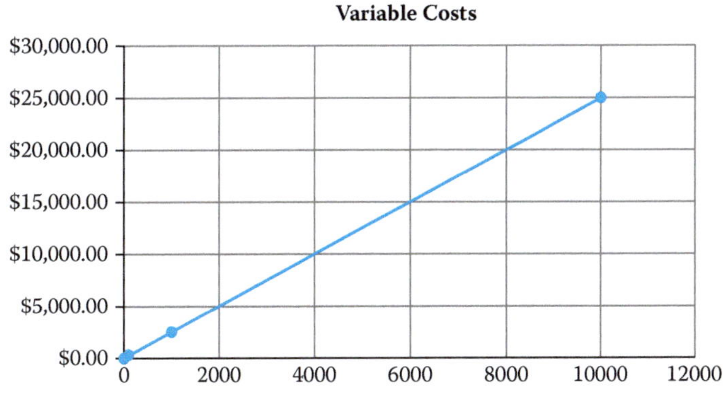

Fig. 3.2 Variable Costs

Figure 3.2 illustrates variable costs with both a table calculation and a graphical presentation. In the table, the variable cost per unit is shown in the right column and is a constant amount for each unit produced. As the number of units increase, as shown in the left column, the total amount of variable costs increases, as shown in the middle column. In the graph, the horizontal axis, the x-axis, represents the total number of units produced, while the vertical axis, the y-axis, represents the total dollar amount. Graphically, variable costs are shown as an upward-sloping line. The slope of the line increases at the rate of the amount of variable cost per unit: $2.50. Every unit produced adds another $2.50 to the total amount of variable costs incurred for the period. The graph does not explicitly depict the variable cost per unit.

When we combine the behaviors of fixed and variable costs side by side, we see the different ways the costs change based on those behaviors. Figure 3.3 presents a graph that includes both the fixed and variable costs together. The fixed costs of $65,000 are represented by the horizontal line. The upward-sloping line is the total of both the fixed and the variable costs. The slope of the line is the variable cost per unit, $2.50, but the line itself includes both fixed and variable costs. The upward sloping line represents the total costs because even when no units are produced, the fixed costs must still be paid. So, the point at which the fixed costs intersect the vertical axis is the point where the variable costs per unit are added to the fixed costs for the period.

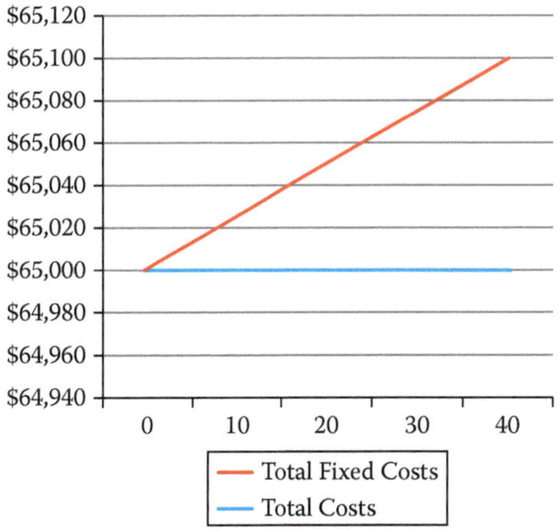

Fig. 3.3 Fixed and Variable Costs

SALES REVENUE

Sales revenue is also variable in nature in a CVP analysis. Each unit is sold at the same sales price per unit, and more units sold generates more total sales revenue. The terms "sales" and "revenue" can often be used interchangeably; both generally refer to the total amount received from the sale of the product or service. The total amount of sales or revenue is found by multiplying the total number of units sold by the sales price per unit.

For our purposes in this textbook, we will use the term "revenue," or "sales revenue," as the total amount received from customers from the sale of products or services. We will use the term "sales price," or "sales price per unit," to denote the amount each unit of product or services customers will pay.

UNIT VOLUME

Unit volume measurements apply to both product manufacturers and service providers. Naturally, many products are made as individual units, which may be bundled in boxes or cases for distribution. A small product, such as a baseball, may be packaged in a box of 72 or a case of 144 baseballs. Larger products, such as generators or airplanes, may be shipped as individual units. No matter how products are packaged or grouped, our work is focused on the individual product unit that can then be aggregated into various packaging options for a given sales price.

Services can also be measured in units, although defining the unit for a given service can be challenging. A unit of service must be discrete and identifiable. A bank may identify a customer opening a single account as a service unit. An accounting firm may identify a single tax return as a service unit. A sports team may identify a single home game as a service unit. Each service unit can be tracked with revenues and costs with which it is associated.

LINEARITY

The linearity assumption requires that sales price per unit, variable cost per unit, and total fixed costs not change within the relevant range of the CVP analysis. They are assumed to be static for the analysis. This assumption supports the CVP analysis and maintains the relative simplicity of the CVP tool.

One of the limitations of CVP analysis is embedded in the linearity assumption, because actual prices and costs are dynamic and can fluctuate, even in the short-term. A large customer might have enough bargaining power to negotiate a lower sales price than a smaller customer. A small vendor may be acquired by a larger competitor and attempt to exercise some degree of influence on the price of an important productive input, such as a scarce raw material or a limited production tool.

RELEVANT RANGE

The relevant range assumption places limits on CVP analysis to a relatively narrow range of activity and time wherein the sales price, variable cost per unit, and total fixed costs can reasonably maintain their linear relationships. Generally, the relevant range is bounded by current productive capacity and an implicit, relatively short-term horizon wherein capacity cannot change. Graphically, the top and right edges of the traditional CVP graph reflect the firm's current productive capacity, which we will refer to as the productive capacity boundary.

We will use this idea of the capacity boundary in later chapters to help us understand and visualize various types of decisions that managers must analyze regarding capacity issues. One issue addressed earlier, is that the driver of capacity decisions is demand for products and services, not time. Time is a factor and tool in the analysis of capacity decisions, but the driver that causes the need for those decisions is product or service demand.

CONTRIBUTION MARGIN—THE BASIS OF CVP

Contribution margin is one of the most important concepts in managerial accounting. Contribution margin is calculated by subtracting all variable costs from sales revenue. Conceptually, contribution margin is the residual revenue that first covers or contributes to fixed costs and then generates or contributes to operating profit after the fixed costs have been covered.

The contribution margin is a key tool used in breakeven analysis (discussed later in this chapter), segment analysis (discussed in Chapter 6), and incremental analysis (discussed in Chapters 7 and 8). Contribution margin can be expressed in total amounts, per-unit amounts, and percentages.

Contribution Margin: Per-Unit Amounts, Total Amounts, and Percentages

Contribution margin is the difference between sales revenue and variable costs and is the basis for presenting the contribution margin format of the income statement, as we discussed in Chapter 1. The contribution margin format of the income statement can be presented using any combination of three (3) formats: 1) total amounts, 2) per-unit amounts, and 3) percentages.

Note that when presenting contribution margin, fixed costs are always treated or accounted for in total amounts. Revenue, variable costs, and contribution margin are always present in all three formats. Figure 3.4 illustrates the presentation of the contribution margin in the contribution margin format of the income statement and in all three formats: per-unit amounts, total amounts, and percentages. The per-unit amounts include only the sales price per unit, the variable cost per unit, and the contribution margin per unit. The difference between the per-unit column and the total column is the unit volume; the per-unit amounts are multiplied by the unit volume, resulting in the amounts in the total column. In the total column, we also include the total amount of fixed costs.

The percentages can be found for revenue, variable cost, and contribution margin using either the per-unit amounts or the total amounts. Because we hold the revenue, variable cost, fixed cost, and unit volume relationships constant, the only difference between the per-unit amounts and the total amounts will be the number of units sold.

Contribution Margin Calculation

		Per Unit	%		1,000 Total	unit %
Sales Revenue		$250	100%		$250,000	100%
Variable Costs		$100	40%		$100,000	40%
Contribution Margin		$150	60%		$150,000	60%
Fixed Costs					$85,000	
Net Operating Income					$65,000	

		Per Unit	%		Total	%
Sales Revenue		$250	100%		$250,000	100%
Variable Costs:						
Variable manufacturing costs	$80			$80,000		
Variable SG&A costs	$20			$20,000		
Total variable costs		$100	40%		$100,000	40%
Contribution Margin		$150	60%		$150,000	60%
Fixed Costs:						
Fixed manufacturing costs				$35,000		
Fixed SG&A costs				$50,000		
Total fixed costs					$85,000	
Net Operating Income					$65,000	

Fig. 3.4 Contribution Margin

Figure 3.4 also presents the contribution margin format of the income statement in a condensed presentation as well as an expanded presentation. The expanded presentation gives the reader more insight into the relationships of the types of variable costs and fixed costs. This insight helps readers better understand the cost structure of the firm, and this detail makes the information much more sensitive. No matter the degree of detail presented, the contribution margin format of the income statement is used only for internal purposes because variable costing information identifies important aspects of a firm's cost structure, which is sensitive information and would be valuable to competitors.

For both the total amounts and the per-unit amounts, the percentages are the same for this analysis. Sales revenue is the denominator, or base amount, for calculating the percentages.

Using the total amounts, variable costs of $100,000 in total are divided by sales revenue of $250,000 to generate the variable cost percentage. The contribution margin of $150,000 is divided by sales revenue of $250,000 to calculate the 60 percent contribution margin ratio.

Using the per-unit information, the variable cost per unit of $10 is divided by the sales price per unit of $25 to generate the 40 percent variable cost ratio. The contribution margin per unit of $15 is divided by the sales price per unit of $25 to calculate the 60 percent contribution margin ratio.

Under either scenario (in total or per unit), the contribution margin ratio is the same. Within the relevant range, the sales price per unit and the variable cost per unit maintain a linear relationship that supports the CVP analysis and allows the managerial accountant to present a graphical representation of the relationship.

Identifying and understanding the relationships among the contribution margin components provides useful tools when only partial information is provided or available.

Mixed-Cost Analysis

Earlier we discussed the attributes and nature of variable and fixed costs. Some costs exhibit behaviors that are a mix of a fixed portion and a variable portion. These costs change when sales volume changes, but the change isn't directly proportional. Costs like repairs and maintenance, security, order entry, utilities, and many other costs behave as mixed costs, partly fixed and partly variable.

OBJECTIVE

To use contribution margin effectively in both planning and evaluating activities, all costs must be classified as either a fixed cost or a variable cost. Separating costs and classifying them as either a fixed cost or a variable cost can be a difficult process. The objective of mixed-cost analysis is to identify and separate the fixed cost and variable cost portions of a total mixed cost so that the mixed costs can be divided into their fixed and variable parts when evaluating changes in volume.

Mixed costs can be created by a contractual arrangement or by the nature of the cost itself. A contractual arrangement can stipulate a base amount plus an amount for each amount of usage, such a telephone service. The service provider might charge a flat $750 per month plus $00.02 per minute for phone calls. A credit-card processor might charge $25 per month plus 2.7 percent of the amount of each credit card transaction. In both cases, the flat monthly charge is a fixed cost that must be paid no matter the usage, while the per-minute and per-transaction fees are variable costs. The total bill each month is therefore a mixed cost containing a fixed and a variable portion. The contract is explicit in the amounts of both the fixed portion and the variable portion.

Some costs don't have a contract or payment arrangement, yet they fluctuate to some degree with the level of production or sales activity. These costs might include security costs or the repair and maintenance cost for a factory or production facility. The firm will have some minimum need for security or a minimum need to maintain its equipment no matter the volume or level of activity. Because the behavior of a cost changes with activity and without a direct correlation to volume, a number of methods can be used to analyze the costs and separate the fixed and variable portions of the total cost so the behavior of that cost can be used to plan for future needs as well to evaluate actual results.

The two methods we will use to demonstrate how mixed costs can be separated into their fixed and variable parts are the High-Low Method and the Least-Squares Regression Method.

HIGH-LOW METHOD

The High-Low method for analyzing mixed costs provides a reasonable and relatively simple approach that any business of any size can effectively use. In a manufacturing firm, the method uses the historical information from the trial balance, along with the number of units produced or sold, to analyze the cost.

Figure 3.5 provides a sample of the costs incurred during the calendar year. The financial information has been recorded in the accounting records and is typically found in the general ledger and included in the firm's trial balance. The account records the costs incurred for each month. The level of activity is not recorded in the general ledger and must be provided from records outside the accounting system.

High-Low Method of Mixed Cost Analysis

	Activity	Cost
January	25,000	$110,000
February	15,000	$65,000
March	22,000	$70,000
April	23,500	$79,000
May	21,500	$68,000
June	26,000	$125,000
July	35,000	$130,000
August	25,500	$112,000
September	26,000	$122,500
October	24,500	$83,000
November	22,000	$80,000
December	22,250	$84,000

High-Low Method Steps

1) Identify high & low levels of ACTIVITY & corresponding cost totals
2) Calculate the variable cost per unit at either the high or low activity level
3) Calculate the fixed cost portion using the variable cost per unit from step 2
4) Express the mixed-cost formula
5) Test the mixed-cost formula by using a volume level between the high & low

Step 1)	Identify high & low levels of ACTIVITY & corresponding cost totals		
	Low Volume Activity		
	February	15,000	$65,000
	High Volume Activity		
	July	35,000	$130,000

Step 2)	Calculate the variable cost per unit at either the high or low activity level				
	Rise	$65,000	=	$3.25	variable cost per unit
	Run	20,000			

Step 3)	Calculate the fixed cost portion using the variable cost per unit from step 2						
	$130,000	=	FC	+	$3.25	*	35,000
		=	FC	+	$113,750		
	$16,250	=	FC				

Step 4)	Express the mixed-cost formula						
	TC	=	$16,250	+	$3.25	*	volume

Step 5)	Test the mixed-cost formula by using a volume level between the high & low						
	TC	=	FC	+	VC/unit	*	Volume
	$89,375	=	$16,250	+	$3.25	*	22,500

Fig. 3.5 High-Low Method

The High-Low method uses the historical cost and activity data to analyze the behavior of the cost and separate the fixed and variable portions of the cost. The method uses the slope-intercept form of the following linear equation:

$$Y = a + bx$$

For our purposes, we can replace variables in the formula that better represent our needs in analyzing mixed costs, as follows:

Total Mixed Cost = Fixed Costs + Variable Cost/Unit (Unit Volume)

Or

TMC = FC + VC (Volume)

The High-Low method process has the following five (5) steps:

1. Identify the high and low levels of activity with their corresponding costs
2. Calculate the variable cost per unit at either the high or low level of activity
3. Calculate the fixed-cost portion at either the high or low level of activity, using the variable cost per unit found in step 2
4. Use the total cost formula, TC = FC + VC (Volume), to express the mixed-cost formula, using the variable cost per unit from step 2 and the total fixed costs from step 3
5. Test the formula using any activity level between the high and low levels identified in step 1

Using the information from Figure 3.4, we can analyze the mixed costs by following the five (5) steps:

1. Identify the high and low levels of activity with their corresponding costs

   High level of activity: July with 35,000 units and a total cost of $130,000
   Low level of activity: February with 15,000 units and a total cost of $65,000

2. Calculate the variable cost per unit at either the high or low level of activity

   Using the information from Figure 3.4, the variable cost per unit is the slope of the line drawn through the high and low activity points. The slope of any line is expressed as the rise over the run:

   $$\text{slope} = \frac{\text{Rise}}{\text{Run}} \quad \text{or} \quad \frac{\text{High Cost Point (Y2)} - \text{Low Cost Point (Y1)}}{\text{High Activity Level (X2)} - \text{Low Activity Level (X1)}}$$

   $$\text{slope} = \frac{\$130{,}000 - \$65{,}000}{35{,}000 \text{ units} - 15{,}000 \text{ units}} = \frac{\$65{,}000}{20{,}000 \text{ units}} = \$3.25/\text{unit}$$

3. Calculate the fixed-cost portion using either the high or low activity level and the variable cost per unit found in step 2

   We'll continue by using the high activity level to demonstrate how to find the fixed-cost portion by using the total cost formula:

   $130,000 = FC + $3.25 (35,000 units)
   $130,000 = FC + $113,750
   $16,250 = FC

4. Express the mixed-cost formula

   Total Mixed Cost = $16,250 + $3.25 (Unit Volume)

5. Use the mixed-cost formula to find TMC, using a volume level between the high and low activity levels identified in step 1

   TMC = $16,250 + $3.25 (24,000 units)
   TMC = $16,250 + $78,000
   TMC = $94,250

   The total mixed cost of $94,250 is expected at an activity level of 24,000, given the current behavior of the cost: $94,250 is between $65,000 and $130,000, and 24,000 units is between 15,000 units and 35,000 units. If the total mixed cost of $94,250 at 24,000 units is plotted on the graph, the point will be on the line and is congruent with our analysis.

High-Low Method Benefits

The High-Low method provides a relatively quick and simple method to analyze a mixed cost. The information is readily available from the general ledger and unit volume records. The math is straightforward and easy to be used and followed by a variety of employees across an organization.

High-Low Method Weaknesses

The High-Low method only uses two data points: the high and the low levels of activity. All other data about the levels of activity are excluded from the analysis, which creates a result missing the influence of constraints or anomalies generated by seasonal, operational, or financial forces.

LEAST-SQUARES REGRESSION METHOD

The Least-Squares (Simple) Regression method is a statistical analysis that fits a line through the data points that best represent the included information. Simple regression produces a line through the data points where the sum of the squared distances from the line to each data point is zero. The line fits such that the distance from the points above the line and the distance to the points below the line are equidistant from the line in total. Because simple regression includes all the information from all the data points, in this case all 12 costs and all 12 activity levels, the line is more accurate than the High-Low method, even though the line may not intersect any of the data points.

Using the monthly cost and activity information from the High-Low method example, we'll use simple regression analysis to separate the fixed and variable portions of the mixed-cost totals. Simple regression is applied to a mixed-cost scenario (see Figure 3.6 below).

TRADITIONAL CVP GRAPH

Overview and Description

The traditional CVP graph provides a visual representation of the relationships between a firm's costs, unit volume, and profit within a specific relevant range. The graph shows the end, or total, results from an accounting period, given the specific linear CVP relationship, illustrating a short-term marginal analysis. The horizontal axis (x axis) of the traditional CVP graph represents the total unit volume sold, while the vertical axis (y axis) represents total dollars.

The origin of the graph represents zero (0) unit sales and zero (0) sales dollars. Moving to the right from the origin, unit sales increase, which drives a corresponding increase in sales revenue and total costs. This demonstrates one of the weaknesses of the traditional CVP graph that can cause confusion: The revenue from the first unit sold is illustrated in the area of the graph denoted as fixed costs. The graph implies that the revenue from the first unit sold is paying for fixed costs when it is

Least-Squares Regression

	X Activitiy	Y Cost	X^2	Y^2	XY	X-Xmean	Y-Ymean	X-Xmean²	X-Xmen Y-Ymean	Regression analysis steps:
January	16,250	$122,000	264062500	$14,884,000,000	$1,982,500,000	(3,488)	16,100.00	12,162,656.25	(56,148,750.00)	1) Total the column of activity
February	15,000	$65,000	225000000	$4,225,000,000	$975,000,000	(4,738)	(40,900.00)	22,443,906.25	193,763,750.00	2) Total the column of cost
March	22,000	$74,000	484000000	$5,476,000,000	$1,628,000,000	3,263	(31,900.00)	5,118,906.25	(72,173,750.00)	3) Calculate the average activity
April	17,000	$85,000	289000000	$7,225,000,000	$1,445,000,000	(2,738)	(20,900.00)	7,493,906.25	57,213,750.00	4) Calculate the average cost
May	16,000	$86,900	256000000	$7,551,610,000	$1,390,400,000	(3,738)	(19,000.00)	13,968,906.25	71,012,500.00	5) Subtract the average actvity from the activity of each month
June	18,000	$125,000	324000000	$15,625,000,000	$2,250,000,000	(1,738)	19,100.00	3,018,906.25	(33,186,250.00)	6) Subtract the average cost from the cost from each month
July	35,000	$130,000	1225000000	$16,900,000,000	$4,550,000,000	15,263	24,100.00	232,943,906.25	367,826,250.00	7) Square the activity for each month
August	24,000	$112,000	576000000	$12,544,000,000	$2,688,000,000	4,263	6,100.00	18,168,906.25	26,001,250.00	8) Total the column created in #7
September	19,100	$122,500	364810000	$15,006,250,000	$2,339,750,000	(638)	16,600.00	406,406.25	(10,582,500.00)	9) Calculate the average of the column created in #7
October	15,500	$110,000	240250000	$12,100,000,000	$1,705,000,000	(4,238)	4,100.00	17,956,406.25	(17,373,750.00)	10) Multiple the activity by the cost for each month
November	19,600	$111,700	384160000	$12,476,890,000	$2,189,320,000	(138)	5,800.00	18,906.25	(797,500.00)	11) Total the column created in #10
December	19,400	$126,700	376360000	$16,052,890,000	$2,457,980,000	(338)	20,800.00	113,906.25	(7,020,000.00)	12) Calculate the average of the column created in #10
Sum	236,850	1,270,800	5,008,642,500	$140,066,640,000	$25,600,950,000	-	-	333,815,625	518,535,000	
Average (Mean)	19,738	105,900	417,386,875	$11,672,220,000	$2,133,412,500	-	-	27,817,969	43,211,250	
VC/unit	$5.11	XY Mean	$2,133,412,500		$1.55				$1.55	
		X^2 Mean	417,386,875							
FC	$5,014.63									

Total Cost = FC + (VC/unit volume)

$5,014.63 + $5.11

Fig. 3.6 Regression Analysis

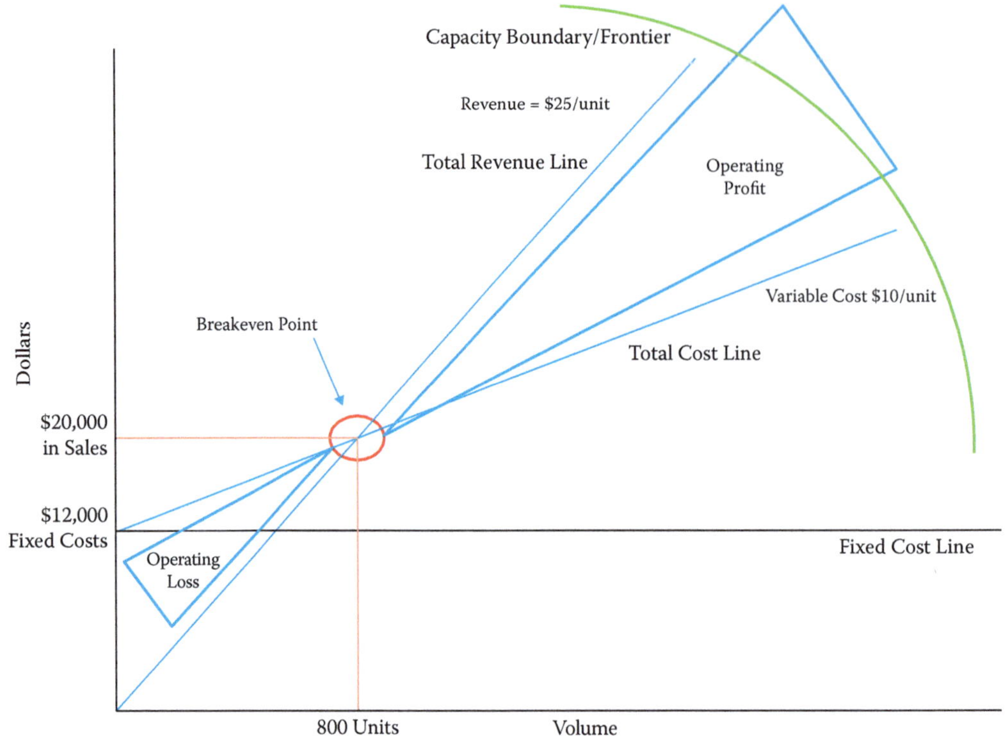

Fig. 3.7 Traditional CVP Graph

the variable costs that are paid first. Every time a unit is produced and sold, the variable costs of direct materials and direct labor must be paid before any fixed costs to ensure that production of additional units can continue.

The most important point on the CVP graph is the point where the total revenue line (unit sales x sales price per unit) intersects the total cost line (fixed costs + variable cost per unit (units sold)). This intersection is the breakeven point.

Fig. 3.7 shows the CVP graph, based on the information provided in the contribution margin section discussed earlier. The graph has a number of important and useful components:

Fixed costs—the horizontal line at $65,000

Total costs—start at the point where fixed costs intersect the vertical sales dollar axis at $65,000 and slopes upward at the rate of $10/unit (variable cost per unit)

Total revenue—starts at the origin and slopes upward at the rate of $25/unit (sales price per unit)

Operating loss—the area under the total cost line and above the total revenue line to the left of the breakeven point

Operating profit—the area above the total cost line and below the total revenue line to the right of the breakeven point

Productive capacity boundary—represented by the arc in the upper-right area of the graph

CVP Graph Boundaries

The boundaries, both vertical and horizontal, of the CVP graph imply a physical productive capacity limit or boundary. A firm can only produce a certain maximum number of units because the resources a firm can employ are naturally limited, or constrained. The physical productive capacity boundary is implied because a specific limit isn't necessarily identified on the graph, even though a firm would most likely know and understand its productive capacity limits. Treating the CVP boundaries as physical productive capacity boundaries can assist us in understanding the issues involved in the various types of productive capacity decisions that must be made within the firm and can provide some amount of context for those decisions. The arc in the upper right quadrant of the traditional CVP graph in Figure 3.7 represents the implied physical productive capacity boundary.

At this point, as we work with CVP issues, we are focused on the physical productive capacity of the firm: its ability to make products or deliver services. The physical productive capacity of a firm is only one type of capacity a firm must address. Other types of capacities might include financial capacities, intellectual property capacities, human capital capacities, regulatory capacities, etc. Capacity issues are critical issues, but for our purposes, our focus in this textbook is on the physical number of units of productive capacity a firm has available.

Common decisions that must be made by a firm include those that can be made within the firm's current capacity (short-term decisions such as accepting or rejecting special orders), those that may temporarily change the firm's capacity (intermediate-term decisions such as making/buying or outsourcing), and those that permanently change the firm's capacity (long-term decisions such as capital equipment investment and plant expansion) and require significant capital investment. We will address short-term, intermediate-term, and long-term decision issues later in the book, but the tools and approaches used to make those decisions are very different and can be explained, to a large degree, by how those decisions affect a firm's operating capacity.

CVP Graph Limitations

The traditional CVP graph is created using total units and total dollars across the relevant range of unit volume to show the effects of marginal changes in either the cost structure or the unit volume. Fig. 3.7 shows the CVP graph with a total relevant range from the origin to the arc in the upper right quadrant of the graph. One of the challenges of this graph is its reliance on total volume.

For example, when the first unit is sold, we move from the origin to the right by one unit of volume, and move up one unit of sales price ($25 in this example). The point on the total revenue line represents the first unit sold and the first $25 of revenue. That point lies within the area denoted as fixed costs, which doesn't necessarily represent the priority of payments from the revenue received from the first unit sold. The graph requires, and is dependent upon, the use of total unit volume, which can provide useful information regarding the effect of changing total unit volume and be used as a tool to evaluate the effect of possible changes in the linear CVP relationships, commonly referred to as what-if analysis. To use the CVP relationships and results as an operational or process tool, a different view of those relationships is required.

CVP STAIRCASE—CVP AS A PROCESS

To use the CVP relationships as an operational or process tool, we must change our view from a view of total units to a view of individual units. The contribution margin format of the income statement provides the basis and key to understanding the process-oriented nature of the CVP relationships.

The following information is the same as in our earlier discussion of the contribution margin:

The CM format is organized to show priority or order of payments that occur when producing a product or service. From sales revenue ($25/unit) the first cost paid is the variable cost ($10/unit), then the remaining amount, or contribution margin ($15/unit), can be used to begin paying the fixed costs. Once the fixed costs are paid, operating income is then generated.

Whether producing a product or a service, the variable cost must be paid before any of the fixed costs can be covered. For products, the direct material, direct labor, and manufacturing overhead must be paid so production can continue. For services, the direct labor and service overhead must be paid so services can continue. The fixed costs cannot be covered unless enough product or service has been sold to generate sufficient contribution margin to pay for them.

To demonstrate this process, Figure 3.8 shows the CVP relationships as a staircase. At the top of the staircase, a unit of product or service is sold for the sales price of $25; then, taking the first step to pay the variable costs of $10, the contribution margin of $15 remains. The $15 contribution margin takes the next step and begins filling the fixed-cost step. Once the fixed-cost step has been filled, the contribution margin can then take the step down to operating income, which increases at the rate of $15 per unit, or the rate of the contribution margin. Every period we must start over and rebuild the bottom step of the staircase as we need to cover the fixed costs before generating any net operating income.

The point where the fixed-cost step has been filled is the breakeven point. In the staircase, each unit sold must first pay its variable costs, and then the contribution margin generated by that unit goes to pay for (or cover) its portion of the fixed costs for the period. Once the fixed costs have been covered, the firm has reached its breakeven point and begins generating net operating income at the rate of the amount of contribution margin per unit. Each unit sold must take the same first step, which is to cover its variable costs before contributing to the fixed costs, and then eventually operating income.

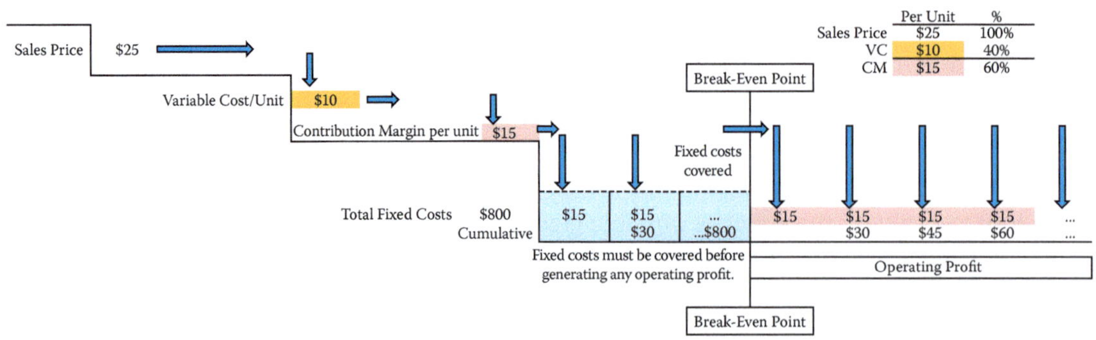

Fig. 3.8 CVP Staircase copyright by J. Brooks Peacock

BREAKEVEN ANALYSIS

Objectives

The linear relationships in the CVP analysis allow for a number of valuable planning tools. The first tool we'll use is the breakeven analysis. The breakeven point is the most important point on the CVP graph. Start-up firms are focused on the breakeven point so that they can manage their spending before becoming profitable. Ongoing businesses often seek to lower their breakeven points and evaluate how capital investment options might affect their breakeven points.

The breakeven point can be expressed as either a sales dollar amount or a sales unit number. In either expression, the fundamental approach is to determine how much activity needs to occur to create an adequate contribution margin to pay for the fixed costs. The breakeven point is where 1) total revenue covers both the fixed and variable costs and 2) the total contribution margin equals the fixed costs. From an equation perspective, the breakeven point is where the contribution margin minus the fixed costs equals zero:

$$\text{Breakeven point: Net Operating Income} = \text{Contribution Margin} - \text{Fixed costs} = \$0$$
$$\text{Breakeven point: Contribution Margin} = \text{Fixed costs}$$
$$\text{Breakeven point: Net operating income} = \$0$$

We will illustrate the breakeven point by showing the contribution margin format of the income statement used in Figure 3.3 as follows (some amounts rounded to the nearest dollar or percent):

	Total	Percent
Sales revenue	$108,333	100%
Variable costs	$43,333	40%
Contribution margin	$65,000	60%
Fixed costs	$65,000	
Net operating income	$0	
Breakeven point = $65,000 – $65,000 = $0		

To help simply and quicken the process to calculate breakeven points, we can use formulas based on the contribution margin concepts.

Breakeven Point in Sales Dollars

To find the breakeven point in sales dollars, we divide the fixed costs by the contribution margin ratio.

$$\text{Breakeven sales dollars} = \frac{\text{Fixed Costs}}{\text{Contribution Margin Ratio (CM\%)}} = \underline{\text{FC}}$$

$$\text{Breakeven sales dollars} = \frac{\$65{,}000}{60\%} = \$108{,}333.33 \sim \$108{,}333$$

In this example, the calculated breakeven point in sales dollars is in pennies and must be increased to reflect the next whole unit sold, or $108,333. Because units have a fixed sales price, calculating a breakeven point in sales dollars often generates an amount that does not correspond to the amount of revenue generated by selling whole units.

Breakeven Point in Unit Volume

To find the breakeven point in sales unit volume, we divide the fixed costs by the contribution margin per unit.

$$\text{Breakeven sales unit volume} = \frac{\text{Fixed Costs}}{\text{CM Per Unit}} = \frac{\text{FC}}{\$\text{CM/Unit}}$$

$$\text{Breakeven sales unit volume} = \frac{\$65{,}000}{\$150} = 433.3 \text{ units} \sim 434 \text{ units}$$

In this example, the calculated breakeven point in unit sales is in a fraction of a unit. Because products are sold in whole units, the calculated breakeven point must be increased to the next whole unit. Now, the rounded breakeven point in units, 434 units, can be multiplied by the sales price per unit, $250, to match the breakeven point in sales dollars of $108,333.

Note that Figure 3.9 provides an illustration of the breakeven point in both sales dollars and unit volume. In simple examples, the breakeven point in unit volume can be multiplied by the sales price per unit to find the breakeven point in sales dollars. Most examples in this textbook are a little more complex so as to reflect actual practice. For that reason, the breakeven point in unit volume cannot be multiplied by the sales price per unit to find the breakeven point in sales dollars. In practice, the linearity of the relationships is not constant and the intent of the examples in this chapter is to present scenarios that reflect some of the difficulties faced in practice.

Breakeven Point with a Sales Mix

A sales mix is the relationship between the quantity of sales of different products sold during an accounting period. One challenge we face when dealing multiple products is that the relationship of how many units of each product sold in a period is always fluctuating. To use CVP for finding the breakeven point we have to assume the relationship of the number of units of each product will remain constant.

In Figure 3.10, we assume that the firm will always sell five (5) baseballs for each bat sold. In practice, this assumption is risky because unit volume relationships are almost always changing, except in the case where one product is a required purchase with another product.

The breakeven analysis is slightly more complicated with a sales mix with multiple products, but we can think of the breakeven sales mix analysis like the single-product analysis in proportions. Each product has its own revenue, variable cost, and contribution margin. The total revenue and total variable costs for the individual products are aggregated for the firm's total revenue and total variable cost, from which the firm-wide contribution margin can be calculated. The firm's total

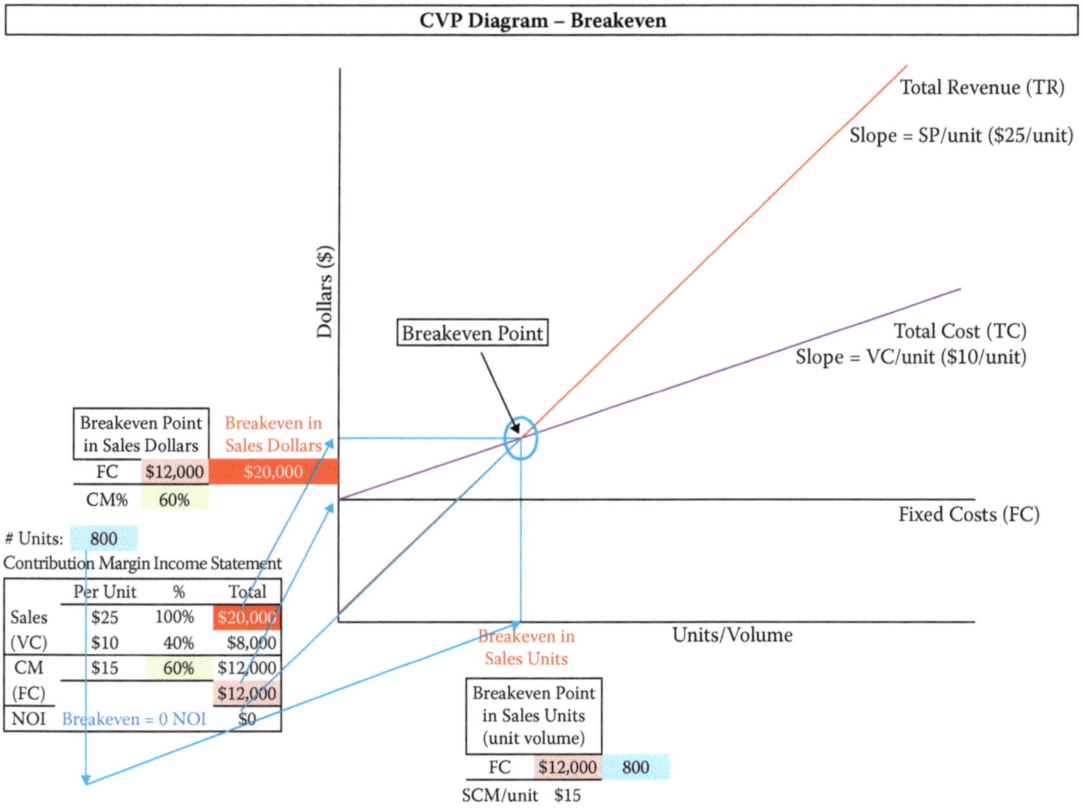

Fig. 3.9 Breakeven Point Example

contribution margin is generated at the rate of each product line and the total therefore reflects the proportion of each product line's unit sales as well as the proportion of each product line's contribution margin.

In Figure 3.10, five baseballs are sold for every bat sold, giving the firm a sales unit of six (6) individual products. Figure 3.10 shows how to find the contribution margin in both total dollar amounts and individual unit amounts. Both approaches generate the same contribution margin for either the average per individual units or per sales unit.

Figure 3.10 shows both the total contribution margin, as well as the contribution margin per sales mix unit, which is essentially a weighted average of the contribution margins. We use the total contribution margin amounts to calculate the breakeven point in sales dollars for the sales mix. Calculating the breakeven point in unit sales is more challenging because of sales mixed proportions. For our purposes, we present the breakeven point in sales dollars to demonstrate the issues related to sales mixes without introducing any additional issues related to the per-unit issues.

Breakeven Point with a Sales Mix

Per Unit	Baseballs	Bats	Total	
Units Sold	80,000	16,000	96,000	
Selling Price/unit	$6	$38		
Variable Cost/unit	$3.25	$18.90		
Contribution Margin/unit	$2.75	$19.10		
Total	**Baseballs**	**Bats**	**Total**	**Percent**
Total Revenue	$480,000	$608,000	$1,088,000	
Total Variable Cost	$260,000	$302,400	$562,400	
Total Contribution Margin	$220,000	$305,600	$525,600	48.31%
Total Fixed Cost			$465,000	
Net Operating Income			$60,600	
Per Sales Mix Unit	**Baseballs**	**Bats**	**Total**	
Units	5	1	6	
Revenue	$6	$38	$68	
Variable Cost/unit	$3.25	$18.90	$35.15	
Contribution Margin/unit	$2.75	$19.10	$32.85	48.31%
Fixed Costs			$465,000	

Breakeven point in sales dollars: $\frac{\$465{,}000}{48.31\%} = \$962{,}557.08$

Fig. 3.10 Sales Mix Breakeven

TARGETED PROFIT ANALYSIS

Overview

The objective of the targeted profit analysis is to identify the sales dollar value or the unit volume that must be achieved to generate a specific amount of net operating income. The owner or manager may desire to set specific goals for net operating income. The firm's breakeven point identifies the point at which profit begins to be generated, but additional work must be done to know how far past breakeven a firm must operate to achieve the targeted amount of profit desired.

In larger firms, targeted profit may be used as a tool when evaluating a project proposal or when evaluating a project's ongoing performance.

Targeted Profit Calculation

The targeted profit calculation is an expansion of the breakeven calculation for both sales dollars and unit volume.

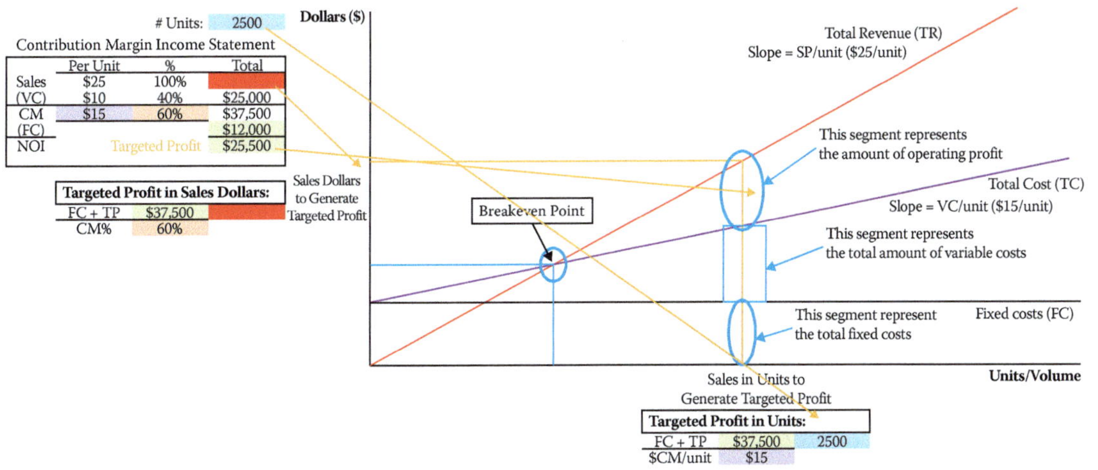

Fig. 3.11 Targeted Profit

$$\text{Targeted Profit Sale Dollars} = \frac{\text{Fixed Cost} + \text{Targeted Profit Amount}}{\text{CM Ratio}}$$

$$\text{Targeted Profit Unit Volume} = \frac{\text{Fixed Cost} + \text{Targeted Profit Amount}}{\text{\$CM per unit}}$$

Figure 3.11 illustrates the concept of targeted profit on the CVP graph.

OPERATING LEVERAGE

Overview

The idea of operating leverage is to explain the potential effect on net operating income when sales change. The magnitude of the change in net operating income when sales change refers to the degree of operating leverage, and the degree of operating leverage is dependent on the level of sales in relation to the firm's breakeven point. Operating leverage shows how a firm's fixed and variable costs might affect net operating income.

From a graphical viewpoint, the concept of operating leverage can be identified as the arc between the total revenue line and the total cost line at the breakeven point. The greater the difference between sales price and variable cost per unit, or the greater the contribution margin, the greater the operating leverage, represented by a wider arc between total costs and total revenue.

Operating Leverage Calculation

The degree of operating leverage (DOL) employed by a firm at any given volume is found using the following equation:

$$\text{Degree of Operating Leverage} = \frac{\text{Total Contribution Margin}}{\text{Net Operating Income}}$$

Figure 3.12 presents the calculation of the degree of operating leverage at four different levels of sales activity. At the breakeven point, the degree of operating leverage cannot be calculated because the firm has zero net operating income. As the sales increase, the degree of operating level declines because the rate of change slows as sales increase.

MARGIN OF SAFETY

Overview

The margin of safety (MOS) is a measurement of how much sales could fall before reaching the breakeven point. Understanding the relationship between current sales, or a targeted sales amount, and the breakeven point in sales provides a sense of the severity of a decrease in sales while still generating some degree of net operating income. Margin of safety provides a sense of the size of the cushion between targeted or actual sales and the breakeven point in sales dollars.

Calculating a firm's margin of safety is a two-step process. First, the margin of safety in dollars is calculated. Second, the margin of safety in dollars is divided by the targeted or actual sales dollars.

Margin of Safety in Dollars

The margin of safety in dollars is calculated as the difference between the actual/targeted amount of sales and the breakeven point in sales dollars.

$$\text{Margin of Safety in Dollars} = \text{Actual/Targeted Sales Dollars} - \text{Breakeven Sales Dollars}$$

The margin of safety in dollars represents the amount of sales that can be lost before hitting the breakeven point.

Degree of Operating Leverage

$$\text{DOL} = \frac{\text{Contribution Margin}}{\text{Net Operating Income}}$$

Units			1000			2500			3000
Revenue	$25.00	100%	$25,000.00	$25.00	100%	$62,500.00	$25.00	100%	$75,000.00
VC	$10.00	40%	$10,000.00	$10.00	40%	$25,000.00	$10.00	40%	$30,000.00
CM	$15.00	60%	$15,000.00	$15.00	60%	$37,500.00	$15.00	60%	$45,000.00
FC			$12,000.00			$12,000.00			$12,000.00
NOI			$3,000.00			$25,500.00			$33,000.00
DOL			5.00			1.47			1.36

Fig. 3.12 DOL Calculation

Margin of Safety

	Breakeven Point			Actual/Targeted		
Units			800			2500
Revenue	$25.00	100%	$20,000.00	$25.00	100%	$62,500.00
VC	$10.00	40%	$8,000.00	$10.00	40%	$25,000.00
CM	$15.00	60%	$12,000.00	$15.00	60%	$37,500.00
FC			$12,000.00			$12,000.00
NOI			$0.00			$25,500.00

MOS in Sales $	=	Actual/Targeted Sales–Breakeven Sales		
	=	$62,500.00	–	$20,000.0
	=	$42,500.00		
MOS in %	=	MOS in Sales $ / Acual/Targeted Sales $		
	=	$42,500.00 / $62,500.00		
	=	68%		
MOS in Units	=	Actual/Targeted Units – Breakeven Units		
	=	2500	–	800
	=	1700		

Fig. 3.13 MOS Calculation

Margin of Safety in Percent

The margin of safety in percent is calculated by dividing the margin of safety in dollars by the actual/targeted amount of sales.

$$\text{Margin of Safety in Percent} = \frac{\text{Margin of Safety in Dollars}}{\text{Actual / Targeted Sales Dollars}}$$

Margin of Safety in Units

The concept of margin of safety can also be expressed in terms of unit volume by taking the same approach as using the margin of safety in dollars and finding the difference between the actual/total unit volume of sales and the breakeven point in unit volume.

Margin of Safety in Units = Actual/Target Unit Sales Volume – Breakeven Unit Sales Volume

Viewing margin of safety in terms of unit volume can be helpful for production personnel who operate and gauge their work in units of production.

Figure 3.13 illustrates how to calculate the margin of safety. The illustration includes the calculation for margin of safety in terms of both sales dollars and unit sales. The margin of safety is a two-step process: 1) calculate the dollar difference between the actual/targeted sales and the breakeven point in dollars, and then 2) calculate the margin of safety percentage.

Fig. 3.14 illustrates the concepts of both margin of safety and degree of operating leverage in terms of the traditional CVP graph.

Both margin of safety and degree of operating leverage are calculated at specific points, or levels, of activity. Both calculations must use activity levels past the breakeven point.

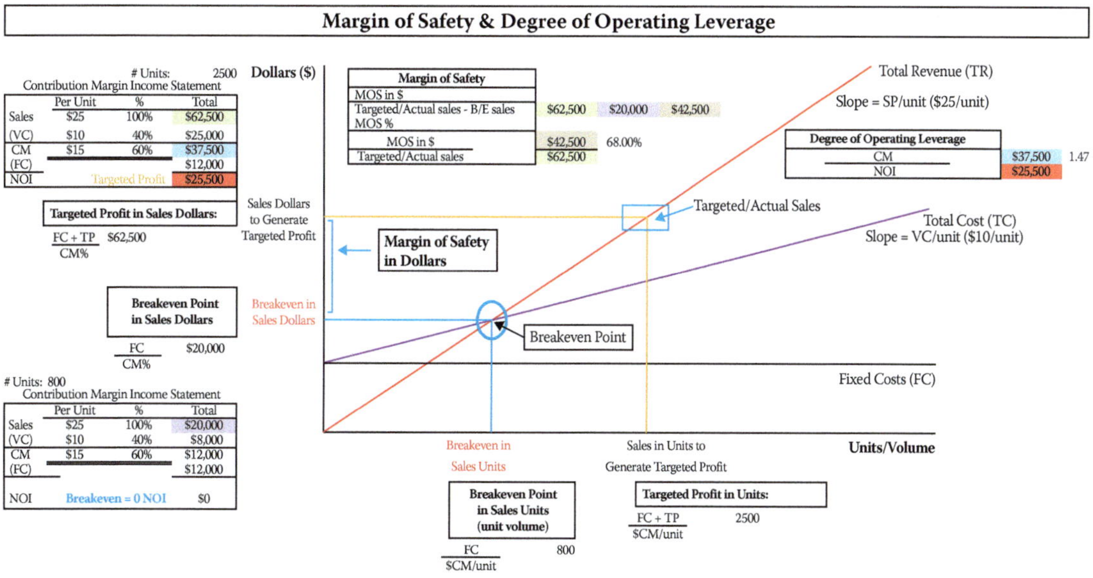

Fig. 3.14 MOS & DOL

4

COST FLOWS AND PRODUCT COSTING

How Much Does a Product Cost?

LEARNING OBJECTIVES

LO1: Identify and explain the general cost flow diagram.

LO2: Create the journal entries to record the cost flows through the accounts.

LO3: Identify the three product costs: direct materials, direct labor, and manufacturing overhead.

LO4: Prepare the journal entries to close the manufacturing overhead account(s).

LO5: Calculate a single, plant-wide predetermined overhead rate.

LO6: Describe and explain job-order costing.

LO7: Calculate the total job cost and the unit product cost using job-order costing.

LO8: Describe and explain activity-based costing.

LO9: Calculate the total product cost and the unit product cost using activity-based costing.

THE QUESTIONS WE TRY TO ANSWER

- What is the total cost to produce our expected unit volume this year?
- What is the total cost to produce a single unit?
- If we start making a second product, how should we allocate the manufacturing overhead to two different products?
- What price should we charge for our product(s)?
- Can we match a competitor's discounted price?

COST FLOWS AND THE COST FLOW DIAGRAM

Most operations have a certain flow of work and sequence of activities as they produce products and deliver services. To produce a product, employees might go to work in a factory and use various equipment and machinery in a certain order of activities to convert raw materials into a finished product. To make baseballs, employees process cork, rubber, leather, and string/yarn through a series of processes. Associates in a bank perform a series of activities when a customer opens a new checking account to provide the customer with the checking account, online banking access, a debit card, paper checks, and other services that meet the customer's individual needs. Whether producing baseballs or opening bank accounts, employees go to work to perform specific activities, using general and specialized equipment, to produce products, deliver services, and provide added value.

The costs associated with making baseballs include direct materials (cork, rubber, leather, and string/yarn), the direct labor wages paid to the employees, production of the baseballs, and the costs of the facility and equipment used to make those baseballs. The direct materials are first purchased, then the employees convert the direct materials into baseballs, which can then be sold and delivered to customers. The production process to create and sell baseballs is made up of a series of activities. The costs associated with the production activities also follow a flow through the accounts of the accounting system.

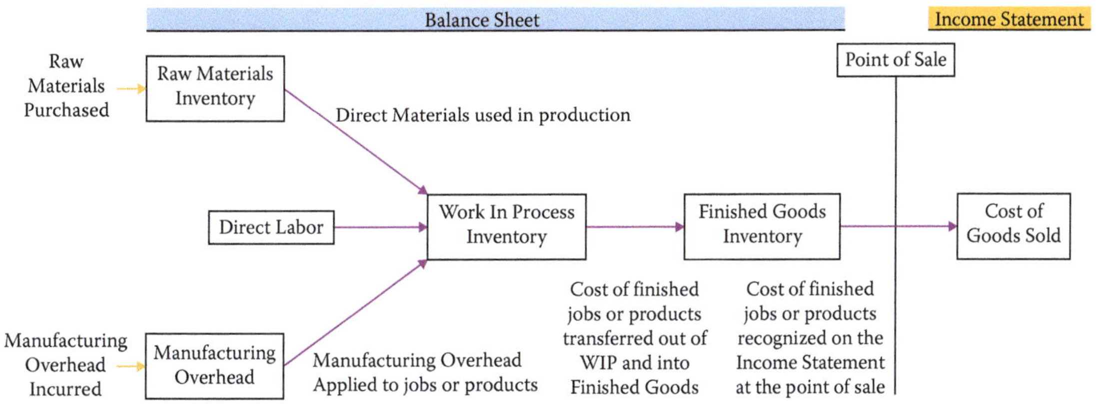

Fig. 4.1 General Cost Flow Diagram

The flow of costs through specific accounts in the accounting system generally reflect the movement of material through the production process as direct material is converted into products and then sold to a customer or services are provided. The accounts we will use in this chapter include raw materials inventory, manufacturing overhead, work-in-process inventory, finished goods inventory, and cost of goods sold. To visualize the accounts through which costs flow, Figure 4.1 illustrates the flow (or movement) of costs through the accounts:

The diagram begins at the left edge with purchases of the three basic product inputs: direct materials, direct labor, and manufacturing overhead. Raw materials are purchased and recorded in the raw material inventory account. When raw materials are requisitioned and put into the production process, the raw materials become direct materials (DM) and the cost for those materials is taken out of the raw materials inventory account and recorded in the work-in-process Inventory account—the cost flows (or moves) from one account to another account.

The time that employees spend working in the production process to convert the direct materials into finished products is called direct labor (DL). The costs for direct labor are recorded directly in the work-in-process inventory account. Direct labor does not have its own account because it is only incurred when employees are at work.

The third product cost is manufacturing overhead (MFG-OH), which includes all the various indirect overhead costs associated with production activities. When manufacturing overhead costs are incurred, they are recorded in one of the manufacturing overhead accounts. As production activity occurs, the manufacturing overhead costs are allocated to the work-in-process inventory account and included as one of the three (3) basic product costs. The manufacturing overhead account is a suspense account.

Note that we will refer to all of the manufacturing overhead costs collectively as manufacturing overhead. In practice, each individual manufacturing overhead cost will have its own account.

The work-in-process inventory account is the account wherein the three basic product costs (DM, DL, and MFGOH) are combined. The combination of direct material costs, direct labor costs, and manufacturing overhead gives us the total product cost.

Once the production process has been completed and the products are finished and ready to be sold or shipped to customers, the costs are taken out of the work-in-process inventory account and recorded in the finished goods inventory account. The costs remain in the finished goods inventory account until the products are purchased and shipped to the customer; at that point, they are taken out of finished goods inventory and recorded in the cost of goods sold account (COGS). When the product costs are moved or flow into the COGS account, those costs are recognized as an expense on the income statement and matched with the revenues generated by the sale of those products.

Now let's look at the flow of costs through the accounts in detail.

Raw Materials Inventory

The raw materials inventory account is a permanent account in the general ledger. As with all permanent accounts, raw materials inventory stays open and can carry a balance from one accounting period to another. For our purposes in this textbook, we simplify the issues regarding raw materials by referring to a single account in our diagram and in our discussions. In practice, a firm will have a separate raw materials inventory account (or sub-account) for each unique raw material carried in inventory. To produce baseballs, a firm may have separate inventory accounts for direct materials such as leather, cork, rubber, and each type of string/yarn, as well as indirect materials, such as adhesives they produce for each baseball based on of the quality and characteristic differences related to each ball.

The journal entry to record the purchase of $325,000 of direct and indirect raw materials might look like the following:

	Debit	Credit
Raw Materials Inventory	$325,000	
Accounts Payable		$325,000
(record the purchase of leather for baseballs)		

Indirect materials and supplies are also in raw materials inventory. This includes materials such as adhesives, solvents, lubricants, maintenance supplies, and other items used in some aspect of the production process. These kinds of materials are designated as raw materials, but because they are used in an indirect manufacturing activity or cannot be easily traced to a product they are commonly referred to as indirect materials. When indirect materials are used, the cost of the indirect materials must be taken out of the raw materials inventory account(s) and recorded in the manufacturing overhead account which is allocated based on a pre-determined rate.

The following journal entry records the use of $12,000 of indirect materials into one of the Manufacturing Overhead accounts:

	Debit	Credit
Manufacturing Overhead	$12,000	
Raw Materials Inventory		$12,000
(record the use of $12,000 of raw materials in repair and maintenance activities)		

To help us see the overall view of the raw materials inventory account, we can look at the account in total and look at the activity that occurs within the account over the course of an accounting period. To begin, let's review the general attributes and activities in an inventory account. At the beginning of the year, a firm will have some raw materials on hand, which we call beginning inventory, and is available to be used in production. As the year progresses, the firm will use raw material in

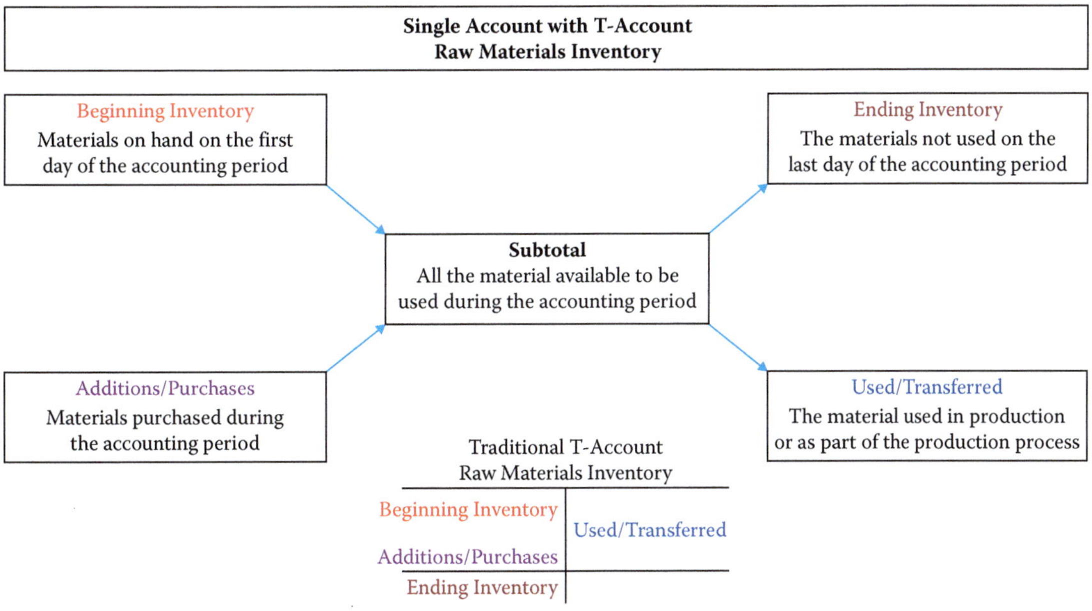

Fig. 4.2 Raw Materials Inventory Account

Adapted from: Katherine J. Silvester and John C. O'Neill, "Cost Flow Diagrams as an Alternative Method of External Problem Representation - A Diagrammatic Approach to Teaching Cost Accounting and Evidence of Its Effectiveness." Copyright © 2013 by Katherine J. Silvester and John C. O'Neill. Available at SSRN: https://ssrn.com/abstract=2306302 or http://dx.doi.org/10.2139/ssrn.2306302.

production, use some raw materials in activities like repairs and maintenance, and throughout the year will purchase additional raw materials.

As a summary from financial accounting, the following is a listing of the debit or credit nature of each of the attributes and activities in the raw materials inventory account:

Beginning Inventory	Debit
Purchases	Debit
Uses (indirect material or raw material used in production)	Credit
Ending Inventory	Debit

In Figure 4.2, the basic approach to summarizing the activity in an inventory account can be illustrated using both a five-box diagram and a traditional T-account. In the five-box diagram, the purchases for the period and beginning inventory are added and subtotaled to identify all the material that has been available during the period. From the subtotal of available material, the amount of material used as both direct material and indirect material is subtracted to identify the raw material on hand and available for use at the end of the period, ending inventory.

The T-account illustrates the same thing, only in a T-account format. The beginning inventory is a debit balance, the purchases are debited to the account, and the material used or transferred out is credited to the account. The ending inventory balance shows as a debit at the end of the period.

The following schedule illustrates the basic accounting approach to communicating the activity in an inventory account using a schedule format:

Beginning Inventory
<u>+ Purchases/Additions</u>
= Total Inventory Available

– Ending Inventory
= Transfers Out/Material Used

This format will be used to prepare a schedule of costs for all three (3) inventory accounts: raw materials, work in process, and finished goods.

One of the issues related to raw materials is the use of those materials both in the production process and in indirect activities like repairs and maintenance. Because raw materials can be used for both direct and indirect purposes, we need to communicate both uses of raw materials. To do so, we will prepare an expanded schedule.

Figure 4.3 illustrates the format of the schedule of cost of direct materials used. The schedule separates the amount of direct material used into both indirect materials used and direct materials used. The indirect materials used will have been debited to the manufacturing overhead account for indirect materials, and the direct materials used will have been debited to the work-in-process Inventory account during the period.

The costs of direct materials used from the schedule of cost of direct materials used will be added to the schedule of cost of goods manufactured.

Direct Labor

Direct labor is the wages paid to the employees who work in the production process. The skill and experience of the production employees are critical components of converting raw materials into finished products. Direct labor costs are accumulated with the other two product costs, direct materials and manufacturing overhead, in the work-in-process inventory account. Remember, direct labor does not have an account of its own; the direct labor costs are recorded in the work-in-process inventory account.

The following journal entry records $18,400 of direct labor wages into the work-in-process inventory account:

	Debit	Credit
Work-in-Process Inventory	$18,400	
Wages Payable		$18,400
(record the direct labor wages for production employees)		

The process of recording costs into an account that is reported on the balance sheet is called capitalization. The costs capitalized into an inventory account are also known as "inventoried costs." Salaries and wages are often thought of as period expenses, but when employees are working directly to make a product, the costs for those employees are one of the three basic product costs and are capitalized by recording them in the work-in-process Inventory account, which is reported on the balance sheet.

Manufacturing Overhead

Manufacturing overhead as an amalgamation of many different costs and expenses incurred is part of the production process. These costs and expenses relate to the production process and to materials that are difficult to trace to individual units of a product—hence, they are all indirect manufacturing costs. Here is a list of common costs and expenses that might be included and treated as manufacturing overhead:

- Rent for the production facility
- Depreciation on the production assets
- Insurance premiums to insure the production facility and work-in-process inventory
- Repair and maintenance of factory equipment
- Security for the production facility
- Property taxes paid on the production facility and equipment
- Utility costs for the production facility
- Indirect material used in repair and maintenance activities
- Indirect material that is difficult to trace to a product (such as adhesives/glue)
- Indirect labor used to support the production process (but not producing units)

All of the manufacturing overhead costs and expenses a firm incurs relate to maintaining its physical productive capacity. They are costs incurred for the physical facility or plant where products are made for the production equipment and machinery, for repairs and maintenance of production equipment, for security of the production facility, for utilities at the production facility, and for other items and activities that maintain and support the firm's capacity.

The following sample of journal entries record the incurrence of manufacturing overhead:

	Debit	Credit
Manufacturing overhead—indirect materials	$42,600	
Raw materials inventory		$42,600
(used raw materials when repairing production equipment)		
Manufacturing overhead—insurance	$2,450	
Insurance payable		$2,450
(received invoice for six-month premium for factory insurance)		
Manufacturing overhead—utilities	$8,750	
Utilities payable		$8,750
(recorded the monthly utility bill for the production facility)		

Note that many of these types of costs and expenses (insurance, utilities, depreciation, repairs and maintenance, etc.) may be incurred in other areas or departments (research and development, sales and marketing, corporate office, etc.) of the firm. Outside of the production process they are classified as period expenses because they relate to non-manufacturing activities and, as such, cannot be capitalized and must be expensed in the period in which they occur. These non-manufacturing activities incur costs because they are a function of a period of time in which the business operates.

Manufacturing overhead costs are critical to the process of producing a product or delivering a service and to maintaining the physical productive capacity of the firm. The difficulty manufacturing overhead costs stems from the relationship overhead costs have to the production process and not to individual units of product. For example, the utility costs for the production facility are crucial to making not only a single baseball but to making all the baseballs produced. If we were to cut a baseball in half, we would be able to see and touch the direct materials (rubber, cork, leather, and string/yarn), but we would not be able to identify how much of the heating and lighting and electricity were used or consumed to make that specific baseball. Because the manufacturing overhead costs are not directly related to or connected to a specific baseball or unit of product, we must find a way of allocating the overhead to the baseballs or units that are produced.

Another issue regarding manufacturing overhead is their complex cost behaviors. We refer to manufacturing overhead in total, but manufacturing overhead consists of many different costs, which include all three general types of behaviors: fixed, variable, and mixed. As we discussed in Chapter 3, we classify all costs as either fixed or variable and if a cost behaves like a mixed cost, we analyze the mixed costs and separate the total mixed cost into its variable portion and fixed portion. All the mixed costs related to the firm's physical productive capacity are indirect costs and part of manufacturing overhead.

As we work with manufacturing overhead in more detail, we will need to recognize that total manufacturing overhead (MFGOH) is a combination of variable manufacturing overhead (VOH) and fixed manufacturing overhead (FOH). In Chapter 1, we identified that the predominant difference between the absorption costing method (used for financial reporting purposes) and the variable costing method (used to support the contribution margin approach) is the way fixed manufacturing overhead was treated. As we continue, we will often see manufacturing overhead expressed in terms of both variable and fixed cost behaviors.

Manufacturing Overhead—Closing the Account(s)

At the end of each accounting period, the manufacturing overhead account(s) must be closed. Manufacturing overhead is a group of expense accounts that are closed so that the account(s) begins the next accounting period with a zero balance. We refer to manufacturing overhead as a total amount, or as a single account, to maintain simplicity.

For our purposes in this textbook, we will close manufacturing overhead into cost of goods sold (COGS). Manufacturing overhead consists of indirect product costs and any balance in manufacturing overhead relates to the manufacturing activity during the period and should be closed to the account where those costs flow: COGS.

If manufacturing overhead has a debit balance at the end of the period, the amount of manufacturing overhead has been under-applied. If manufacturing overhead has a $3,200 debit balance at the end of the period, the following entry increases the costs allocated to the COGS so that the account can be closed:

	Debit	Credit
Cost of Goods Sold	$3,200	
Manufacturing Overhead		$3,200

If manufacturing overhead has a credit balance at the end of the period, the amount of manufacturing overhead has been over-applied. If manufacturing overhead has a $2,800 credit balance at the end of the period, the following entry decreases the costs allocated to the COGS so that the account can be closed:

	Debit	Credit
Manufacturing Overhead	$2,800	
Cost of Goods Sold		$2,800

Work-in-Process Inventory

The work-in-process (WIP) inventory account is the account in which the three basic product costs (DM, DL, and MFGOH) are accumulated and combined into the total product cost when making a product. Our production employees go to the production facility and use their skills and expertise to convert direct materials and use the available equipment to create the finished products. Once a unit of product has been completed and is ready to be shipped to a customer, the costs are taken out of the work-in-process inventory account and recorded in the finished goods inventory account.

The following journal entries record $22,300 of direct materials used in production, $18,400 of direct labor, and $4,400 of manufacturing overhead applied to the work-in-process inventory account:

	Debit	Credit
Work-in-process Inventory	$22,300	
Raw Materials Inventory		$22,300
(record the requisition of materials used in production)		
Work-in-process Inventory	$18,400	
Wages Payable		$18,400
(recorded the wages for production employees)		
Work-in-process Inventory	$4,400	
Manufacturing Overhead		$4,400
(record the manufacturing overhead applied)		

If these were all of the costs to produce the products in a given month, then the combined amount of $45,100 ($22,300 + $18,400 + $4,400) would be the total product cost for the month. If 65,000 baseballs were produced during the month, then each baseball cost about $0.69 per baseball to make.

The work-in-process inventory account may appear transient because the cost of the direct materials, the direct labor, and the manufacturing overhead are all being included as part of our products and then transferred out of work-in-process inventory and into the finished goods inventory account when the units are completed. But the work-in-process inventory account will carry an amount of ending inventory from one accounting period to the next because a production process is ongoing and at least some units will be at some partial stage of completion at the end of the accounting period.

Schedule of Cost of Direct Material Used

Beginning Inventory—Raw Materials	
+	Purchase
	Raw Materials Available
–	Ending Inventory—Raw Materials
	Raw Materials Used
–	Indirect Materials
	Direct Materials Used

Fig. 4.3 Schedule of Cost of Direct Materials Used

Schedule of Cost of Goods Manufactured

As goods and products are completed and physically moved out of the production area and into the finished products area, the costs to make those products must be transferred out of the work-in-process inventory account and into the finished goods inventory account in the accounting records. The total costs accumulated to make the finished products are called the cost of goods manufactured. In a firm that makes products, the cost of goods manufactured is a similar number to inventory purchases in a distribution or retail firm.

To effectively account for the costs of the finished products that a firm makes and then sells, we generate a schedule of cost of goods manufactured as a tool to communicate the total costs that were taken out of the work-in-process inventory account and added to the finished goods inventory account during the accounting period. We need the schedule of cost of goods manufactured to summarize the costs of all the products completed during the account period and communicate information about the beginning and ending inventories in both the raw materials inventory and the work-in-process inventory accounts.

In the schedule of cost of goods manufactured, the basic approach is applied to both the raw materials inventory account and the work-in-process inventory account and combined into one schedule. The raw materials inventory account is straightforward, relatively uncomplicated, and follows this approach. The work-in-process inventory account is more complex because the additions to the account do not come from just a single purchasing activity, but from the combination of all three product costs: direct materials, direct labor, and manufacturing overhead.

The schedule of cost of goods manufactured (COG-MFG) uses the basic approach for analyzing an inventory account applied to the work-in-process inventory account. The work-in-process inventory account presents additional complexity because WIP has multiple types of additions: direct materials, direct labor, and manufacturing overhead. The WIP account is the account in which the three product costs are combined into a total product cost amount.

Figure 4.4 illustrates the schedule of cost of goods manufactured. Direct materials, direct labor, and manufacturing overhead applied are all added to the beginning WIP inventory and subtotaled to find the total amount of manufacturing costs for the period. The ending inventory is then subtracted to calculate the cost of goods manufactured.

	Beginning Inventory—Work In Process
+	Direct Materials Used
+	Direct Labor
+	Manufacturing Overhead Applied
	Total Manufacturing Costs
–	Ending Inventory—Work In Process
	Cost of Goods Manufactured

Fig. 4.4 Schedule of Cost of Goods Manufactured

The schedule of cost of goods manufactured is prepared at the end of the accounting period and reports the activity for the period in total. The actual flow of products is continuous during the period and the products are transferred from the production area into the finished goods area as they are completed. The costs for the completed units can also be transferred out of the WIP account and recorded in the finished goods inventory account throughout the account period, not just at the end of the period.

Finished Goods Inventory

The finished goods inventory (FG) account contains all the direct and indirect manufacturing costs incurred to make the products that have not yet been sold. When the products are completed, the total product cost for those units (all of the product costs: DM, DL, and MFGOH) are taken out of the WIP inventory account and recorded in the FG inventory account.

The following journal entry records moving the total product cost of $45,100 out of the WIP inventory account and into the FG inventory account when all 65,000 units have been completed and are ready to be sold:

	Debit	Credit
Finished Goods Inventory	$45,100	
Work-in-process Inventory		$45,100
(recorded the total product cost for 65,000 units completed and transferred)		

This entry also represents the cost of goods manufactured for the 65,000 units.

Schedule of Cost of Goods Sold

Because the finished goods inventory, like the other inventory accounts, starts the accounting period with a beginning inventory balance and also has a balance at the end of each accounting period, we prepare a schedule of cost of goods sold (COGS) to communicate the activity in the FG inventory account.

Figure 4.5 illustrates the schedule of cost of goods sold. Because the firm combines direct material, direct labor, and manufacturing overhead to create finished products, the additions to the

	Beginning Inventory—Finished Goods
+	Cost of Goods Manufactured
	Total Cost of Goods Available For Sale
–	Ending Inventory—Finished Goods
	Cost of Goods Sold

Fig. 4.5 Schedule of Cost of Goods Sold

finished goods inventory account are total costs to manufacture the products. We follow the same basic approach of an inventory account in the schedule of cost of goods sold as we did in both the schedule of costs of direct materials used and the schedule of cost of goods manufactured:

We have used a common format to analyze the three inventory accounts discussed in this chapter: raw materials inventory, work-in-process inventory, and finished goods inventory. Figure 4.6 presents the account analyses for all three inventory accounts.

Schedules of Costs

Schedule of Costs of Direct Materials Used

	Beginning Inventory—Raw Materials
+	Purchase
	Raw Materials Available
–	Ending Inventory—Raw Materials
	Raw Materials Used
–	Indirect Materials
	Direct Materials Used

Schedule of Cost of Goods Manufactured

	Beginning Inventory—Work In Process
+	Direct Materials Used
+	Direct Labor
+	Manufacturing Overhead Applied
	Total Manufacturing Costs
–	Ending Inventory—Work In Process
	Cost of Goods Manufactured

Schedule of Cost of Goods Sold

	Beginning Inventory—Finished Goods
+	Cost of Goods Manufactured
	Total Cost of Goods Available For Sale
–	Ending Inventory—Finished Goods
	Cost of Goods Sold

Fig. 4.6 Vertical Schedule of Costs

Schedules of Cost of Goods Manufactured

	Beginning Inventory – Work In Process
	Beginning Inventory – Raw Materials
+	Purchases
	Raw Materials Available
–	Ending Inventory – Raw Materials
	Raw Materials Used
–	Indirect Materials
+	Direct Materials Used
+	Direct Labor
+	Manufacturing Overhead Applied
	Total Manufacturing Costs
–	Ending Inventory – Work In Process
	Cost of Goods Manufactured

	Beginning Inventory – Raw Materials
+	Purchases
	Raw Materials Available
–	Ending Inventory – Raw Materials
	Raw Materials Used
–	Indirect Materials
+	Direct Materials Used
+	Direct Labor
+	Manufacturing Overhead Applied
	Total Manufacturing Costs
+	Beginning Inventory – Work In Process
–	Ending Inventory – Work In Process
	Cost of Goods Manufactured

Fig. 4.7 Combined Schedules of & Cost of Goods Manufactured

The schedule of cost of goods manufactured is sometimes presented in a format analyzing both the raw materials Inventory and the work-in-process Inventory accounts. Figure 4.7 illustrates two formats combining the analysis of both raw materials and work-in-process inventory accounts.

The two formats are color coded to assist in comparing the formats. They accomplish the same result, calculating the cost of goods manufactured. These combined formats are simply different ways of presenting what we have presented in the schedule of costs of direct materials used and the schedule of cost of goods manufactured. We have presented them separately to hopefully simplify the schedules and facilitate a better understanding of analyzing the inventory accounts.

Cost of Goods Sold

The finished products remain in the finished goods inventory account until they are sold to a customer. When a customer buys our products, the cost of those products must be recognized as an expense and matched with the revenue generated by the sale. Two entries must be made to record the two parts of the transaction: the revenue entry and the cost entry.

The following journal entries record the sale of 22,100 baseballs for $2.09 per baseball, and the total product cost of $15,249 to produce the baseballs:

	Debit	Credit
Cash (or accounts receivable)	$46,200	
Revenue		$46,200
(recorded the sale of 22,100 baseballs for $2.09/baseball)		
Cost of goods sold	$15,249	
Finished goods inventory		$15,249
(recorded the total product cost of the 22,100 baseballs sold)		

ALLOCATING MANUFACTURING OVERHEAD

Manufacturing Overhead Behavior

So far, we have discussed the difficulties presented by manufacturing overhead in general terms, such as manufacturing overhead is related to the production process, not to individual units of product, and that manufacturing overhead includes many different costs, which exhibit all three types of cost behavior: fixed, variable, and mixed. Because manufacturing overhead costs are all indirect costs, we allocate them into the production process and capitalize them in the work-in-process inventory account, along with direct materials and direct labor.

We will introduce and explore two methods of allocating manufacturing overhead to the production process: the traditional costing method and the activity-based costing method.

The traditional costing method allocates manufacturing overhead using a single predetermined overhead rate (POR). We use the traditional costing method in a job-order costing system. Moving forward, we will refer to manufacturing overhead as a single account when using the traditional costing method in a job-order costing system.

The activity-based costing method allocates manufacturing overhead using multiple allocation rates. Activity-based costing can be more accurate than job-order costing when a firm has multiple products (product lines) or multiple services (service lines).

Closing Out Manufacturing Overhead

At the end of the accounting period, any remaining amount in the manufacturing overhead account must be closed out to bring the balance in the manufacturing overhead account to zero. In this textbook, any remaining amount in manufacturing overhead at the end of the period will be closed into cost of goods sold. We will discuss the details of closing out manufacturing overhead later in the chapter.

Cost Drivers

A cost driver is an activity or event or function that causes manufacturing overhead to be incurred. An activity such as operating the machines on a production line requires electricity for the machines to operate. The number of hours the machines operate is a driver (or cause) of electricity costs. Identifying the root cause of an overhead cost can be difficult because incurring overhead costs is not necessarily a direct consequence of producing specific units of product or delivering specific instances of services.

In this textbook, we will not determine the appropriate cost drivers as these will vary in practice. Instead, we will use activities that are commonly considered to be cost drivers in many firms:

Customer orders
Material orders
Machine setups
Product lines
Parts administration
Material deliveries
Repairs and maintenance

Some of the common ways of measuring the cost drivers that we use in this textbook include the following:

Direct labor hours
Machine hours
Number of customer orders
Number of material orders
Number of machine setups
Number of products (product lines)
Number of parts (individual parts)
Number of material deliveries

To use a cost driver effectively, we need to know how much of the cost driver (activity) will be used by each product or service and the amount of overhead related to the cost driver.

Cost drivers are used in both traditional costing and activity-based costing. Traditional costing uses a single (1) cost driver, which is referred to as the allocation base. Activity-based costing uses multiple cost drivers, which are referred to as activities.

Traditional Costing—Single Predetermined Overhead Rate

Traditional costing allocates manufacturing overhead to the work-in-process inventory account using one allocation rate, commonly referred to as a single predetermined overhead rate. Here is the generic formula for calculating a single predetermined overhead rate (POR):

$$\text{Predetermined Overhead Rate (POR)} = \frac{\text{Total Estimated Annual Manufacturing Overhead}}{\text{Total Estimated Annual Allocation Base}}$$

The predetermined overhead rate is calculated before the start of the accounting period (usually the financial year).

Estimated Total Manufacturing Overhead

When calculating the predetermined overhead rate, a firm's management will review the total amount of overhead spent during the past year, and possibly previous years, then estimate how much total overhead they expect to spend in the following year. Management may factor into their estimates expected price increases, expected amounts of labor, expected changes in general economic conditions, and other items they feel may affect the total amount of overhead they will pay in the following year.

As we discussed in Chapter 3, our goal is to classify all costs as either fixed costs or variable costs, based on the behavior of the cost related to changes in unit volume. Some manufacturing overhead costs exhibit a mixed-cost behavior with both a variable-cost and a fixed-cost portion. When we worked through the analysis of a mixed cost, we found we could use the formula Y = a + bX (Total Mixed Cost = fixed cost + variable cost per unit [total unit volume]) to express the behavior of a specific cost item (such as utilities or maintenance).

We can combine the fixed and variable portions of all the various manufacturing overhead costs to generate a single formula that would help us predict the total amount of manufacturing overhead for various levels of production. The single formula for total manufacturing overhead can now be used as a tool to help estimate the total amount of manufacturing overhead when calculating the predetermined overhead rate.

Allocation Base – Cost Driver for Traditional Costing

Calculating the predetermined overhead requires an allocation base. The allocation base used in the POR is a single cost driver for the firm's manufacturing overhead. As we discussed in Chapter 3, a firm may have many different activities that drive the incurrence of manufacturing overhead, but for our purposes of calculating the POR, we will limit the options of one of three commonly used allocation bases:

Direct-labor hours (DLH)
Direct-labor dollars (DL$)
Machine hours (MH)

Management will also estimate how much allocation base they expect to use in the following year. The allocation base can be thought of as the measure of the activity that causes the firm to incur overhead. When a unit of allocation base is used (or consumed) during the year, it triggers an estimated amount of overhead to be incurred.

Selecting an allocation base suggests a relationship between the base and manufacturing overhead. Therefore, the allocation base used should be a cause for incurring the overhead. For example, if we use direct-labor hours as our allocation base when producing baseballs, then manufacturing overhead should increase in some proportion to an increase in the number of hours our production employees work.

Figure 4.8 illustrates the calculation of a predetermined overhead rate using direct-labor hours (DLH) as the allocation base. Both the numerator, total estimated annual manufacturing overhead, and the denominator, total estimated annual allocation base (DLH). In this textbook, our job is not to determine the estimated amount of manufacturing overhead nor the allocation base; we will use the estimated overhead and the estimated base as provided by owners or managers.

Predetermined Overhead Rate (POR) Example

Predetermined Overhead Rate Formula

		fixed costs		vc/unit	volume			
Total Estimate Manufacturing Overhead	=	125,000	+	$0.25	1,200,000	=	$425,000	

Example 1–Direct Labor Hours

Total Estimated Annual Manufacturing Overhead	$425,000	
Total Estimated Annual Allocation Base (DLH)	220,000	DLH

Predetermined Overhead Rate	=	Total Estimated Annual Manufacturing Overhead / Total Estimated Annual Allocation Base	$425,000 / 220,000	=	$1.9318 per DLH

Fig. 4.8 POR Example using Direct Labor Hours (DLH)

In this example, a firm's management has estimated that they will spend $425,000 for manufacturing overhead during the following (next) year and estimate they will use 220,000 direct-labor hours during the year. The POR is calculated by dividing the $425,000 of estimated overhead by the 220,000 estimated DLH, resulting in a rate of $1.93 (rounded) for every direct-labor hour.

In the following year, every time a direct-labor hour is used, $1.93 of manufacturing overhead is added to the work-in-process inventory account.

The following two exhibits, Figures 4.9 and 4.10, illustrate how the same amount of overhead might be allocated using the two other allocation bases, total direct-labor costs or machine hours.

Predetermined Overhead Rate (POR) Examples

Predetermined Overhead Rate Formula

		fixed costs		vc/unit	volume		
Total Estimate Manufacturing Overhead	=	125,000	+	$0.25	1,200,000	=	$425,000

Example 2–Direct Labor Dollars/Direct Labor Payroll

Total Estimated Annual Manufacturing Overhead	$425,000		
Total Estimated Annual Allocation Base (DLC)	$4.620,000	DLS	(this is usually identified as the total amount of payroll for the production employees)
Wage rate: $21			

Predetermined Overhead Rate	=	Total Estimated Annual Manufacturing Overhead	$425,000	=	$0.0920 per direct-labor dollar
		Total Estimated Annual Allocation Base	$4.620,000		

Fig. 4.9 POR Example Using Direct Labor Dollars (DL$)

Predetermined Overhead Rate (POR) Examples

Predetermined Overhead Rate Formula

		fixed costs		vc/unit	volume		
Total Estimate Manufacturing Overhead	=	125,000	+	$0.25	1,200,000	=	$425,000

Example 3–Machine Hours

Total Estimated Annual Manufacturing Overhead	$425,000	
Total Estimated Annual Allocation Base (MH)	340,000	MH

Predetermined Overhead Rate	=	Total Estimated Annual Manufacturing Overhead	$425,000	=	$1.2500 per MH
		Total Estimated Annual Allocation Base	340,000		

Fig. 4.10 POR Example using Machine Hours (MH)

These examples illustrate how the use of different allocation bases generates very different predetermined overhead rates.

Job-Order Costing System

A job-order costing system is a costing approach that uses a single predetermined overhead rate to allocate manufacturing overhead to each specific job completed for each customer. The job-order costing approach works exceptionally well for businesses that are hired by customers or clients to perform specific jobs. Businesses that use Job-Order Costing include the following:

General contractors	Plumbing contractors	Electrical contractors
HVAC contractors	Cabinet contractors	Painting contractors
Remodeling contractors	Roofing contractors	Landscape contractors
Accounting/CPA firms	Law firms	Architectural firms
Engineering firms	Consulting firms	Automobile dealers
Custom jewelry makers	Yacht builders	

These businesses perform one or more specific jobs or services for each customer or client, but each individual job differs from any other job in terms of scope of work, time to complete the job, and complexity of the customer's or client's needs.

For example, a cabinetmaker builds and installs cabinets for customers, and each job is different from another. One customer job may include replacing the cabinets in a home kitchen, while another customer job may be to install all the cabinetry at a new retail store or automobile dealership. Every job the cabinetmaker receives, the cabinetmaker performs the same functions of making and installing cabinets, but each job will have a different number of cabinets, different sizes of cabinets, and will have different requirements for the material used to make the cabinets (metal, oak, pine, bamboo, etc.).

Job-order costing also works well for service firms such as accounting firms, law firms, and architectural firms. Service firms often refer to their job-order costing system as a time-and-billing system. Time-and-billing systems are job-order costing systems with two fundamental differences: Time-and-billing systems must capture out-of-pocket-type costs instead of tracking direct materials and they must capture the time spent by attorneys for specific services. A law firm doesn't use direct materials; they must capture costs such as filing fees, costs incurred during discovery, costs for expert witnesses, costs for specialized research and information sources, along with others. A law firm must also capture the time and work provided to clients for specific services.

Job-Order Costing and Work-in-process Inventory

In a job-order costing system, each job performed for a customer has its own work-in-process inventory account represented by a physical job cost sheet, a job cost folder, or a digital job cost folder in an accounting software. The job cost sheet is used to accumulate all the costs incurred to complete a specific job, along with other relevant job information.

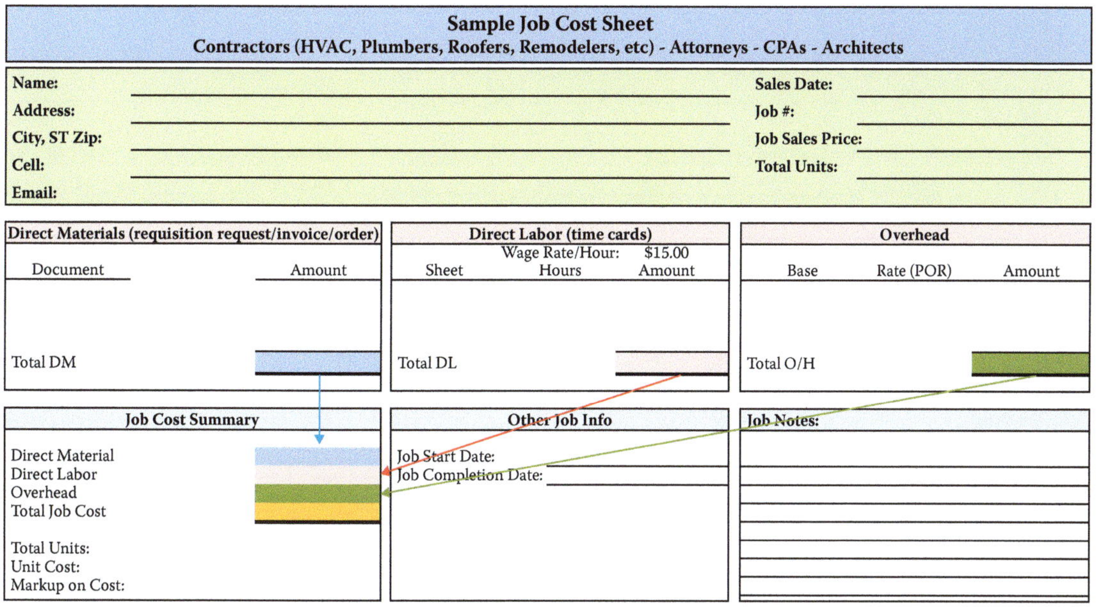

Fig. 4.11 Job Cost Sheet

Figure 4.11 is a sample job cost sheet. Along the top of the job cost sheet is a section for general customer and job information such as location, contact information, start date, contract amount, and number of units. Across the middle of the job cost sheet are three sections to record and track the three basic product costs: direct material, direct labor, and manufacturing overhead.

In the direct materials section, the cost of the direct materials used in the job will be recorded, along with the type of documentation for the cost. Some firms use internal requisition orders because they keep a large inventory of materials on hand. Some firms use invoices or product order forms to document the costs of the materials purchased from external vendors or suppliers. If miscellaneous supplies are purchased for a specific job, the receipts for those costs will be included with the job cost sheet as documentation, and the cost is included with the other direct material items.

In the "Direct Labor" section, the wages and compensation paid to the employees working on the specific job will be recorded using the time cards from the employees working on that job. Some firms use paper time cards to record and track the time employees work, while other firms use various types of digital time and billing systems.

In the "Overhead" section, the amount of manufacturing overhead allocated to the specific job is calculated and recorded. For overhead allocation, the firm will use their single predetermined overhead rate to calculate an amount based on how much of the allocation base is used in the job.

The total amounts for direct materials, direct labor, and applied manufacturing overhead are carried from their respective sections into the bottom left section titled "Job Cost Summary." The total amounts of direct materials, direct labor, and applied manufacturing overhead are combined for the total cost of that specific job. Each job is unique because each job has different amounts of material needed and different amounts of labor required, and the amount of applied manufacturing overhead will vary depending on how much of the application base is used in the specific job.

The total job cost is divided by the total units used in the job to calculate the total unit product cost. Although each job is unique, the differences between each job are caused by the differences in scope or complexity of the project.

NuView Windows
Job Cost Sheet

Name:	Smith Home	**Sales Date:**	3/14/2xxx
Address:	111 Fir Drive	**Job:**	Smith Windows
City, ST Zip:	Your Town, Oregon 97000	**Job Sales Price:**	$72,516.00
Cell:	555-555-5555	**Total Units:**	38
Email:	customersemail@email.com		

Direct Materials

Req #	Amount
1006	$6,500.00
1008	$7,500.00
Total DM	$14,000.00

Direct Labor (Wage Rate/hour: $15.00)

Sheet	Hours	Amount
2795	1350	$20,250.00
2802	520	$7,800.00
Total DL		$28,050.00

Overhead

Base	Rate (POR)	Amount
1350	$1.75	$2,362.50
520	$1.75	$910.00
Total O/H		$3,272.50

Job Cost Summary

Direct Material	$14,000.00
Direct Labor	$28,050.00
Overhead	$3,272.50
Total Job Cost	$45,322.50
Total Units:	38
Unit Cost:	$1,192.70
Markup on Cost:	60%

Other Job Info

Job Start Date:	4/20/2xx
Completion Date:	4/30/2xxx
Revenue	$72,516.00 (Total Job Cost * 1.6)
Cost	$45,322.50
Job Profit/(Loss)	$27,193.50

Job Notes:

Customer wants street-facing windows installed first.
Installers use south side of customer driveway.
Customer will make final pmt at job completion.

Job pricing formulat:
Job sales price = total job cost × (1 + markup on cost %)

Fig. 4.12 Completed Job Cost Sheet

A firm offering a consistent product or service must have a method of estimating the cost of a specific customer job that allows for the differences in scope and complexity between jobs. The historical experience a firm generates from tracking the total job cost and the total unit product cost of previously completed jobs can provide a basis for determining the sales price of future jobs.

Figure 4.12 illustrates a completed job cost sheet for a firm, NuView Windows, that sells and installs replacement windows. The total amounts from the direct materials, direct labor, and overhead sections are carried down to the job cost summary section (note the arrows and color coding) and added together for the total job cost. The total job cost is divided by the number of units (total number of windows) to calculate the unit cost.

The price of the job is calculated using a 60 percent markup on cost. The markup on cost formula is as follows:

$$\text{Job Price} = \text{Total Job Cost} \times (1 + \%\ \text{markup on cost})$$
$$\$72{,}516 = \$45{,}322.50 \times (1 + .6)$$

The "Other Job Info" section and the "Job Notes" section are both used by NuView Windows to communicate and track information they feel is important.

Activity-Based Costing

Activity-based costing is an approach to allocating manufacturing overhead using multiple allocation rates, called activity rates, in place of a single predetermined overhead rate. Using multiple activity rates is an effective approach for a firm that produces multiple products or delivers multiple services.

The following are common product pairings firms might manufacture and sell:

Softballs and baseballs
Two-seat watercraft and three-seat watercraft
Hardcover books and paperback books
12" laptops and 15" laptops
Smartphones and tablets

As we proceed with our discussion of activity-based costing, we will refer to complete product lines simply as products. A firm might have two products, softballs and baseballs, and produce thousands of units of each product. This is an important concept because in activity-based costing, manufacturing overhead is allocated to the product and then the manufacturing overhead is divided by the number of units to calculate the manufacturing overhead per unit.

Using activity-based costing requires a number of steps to allocate the manufacturing overhead and calculate the total product cost and the total unit product cost. We will work through the following steps when allocating manufacturing overhead when using the activity-based costing method:

1. Identify the activities/cost drivers
2. Identify the measures of the activities/cost drivers
3. Identify the cost pools for each activity/cost driver
4. Identify the measure of activity for each activity/cost driver
5. Add the activity measure of each product or service to find the total expected measure of activity
6. Calculate the activity rates
7. Allocate the cost pool to each product or service
8. Calculate the amount of the cost pool allocated to each expected unit
9. Add the direct materials and direct labor costs per unit to the amount of overhead allocated to each unit

Activities—Cost Drivers for ABC

For a firm making baseballs and softballs, the amount or volume of the cost driver used to make baseballs must be added to the amount or volume of the cost driver used to make softballs to find the total level of activity. In the following illustration, the measurement of the activity, or volume of cost driver, for baseballs and softballs is identified for each individual cost driver or activity.

Baseballs and softballs are products that share similar types of production equipment, processes, and employee skill sets, while also requiring different amounts of processing time, different qualities or quantities of materials, or different processing sequences. When multiple products or multiple services use a common overhead item, the allocation of the overhead item should be guided or

Expected Activity								
	Activity	Expected Activity						
Activity	Measure	Softballs	+	Baseballs	=	Total		
Labor-related	DLH	35,100	+	87,500	=	122,600	DLH	
Machine Setups	# setups	3,000	+	2,000	=	5,000	Setups	
Parts Administration	# parts	11	+	9	=	20	Parts	
Production Orders	# orders	275	+	650	=	925	Orders	
Material Receipts	# receipts	150	+	600	=	750	Receipts	
General Factory	MH	12,000	+	28,000	=	40,000	MHs	

Fig. 4.13 Activity Measures

driven by the specific activity that causes specific amounts of overhead to be incurred and not based solely on the number of units produced.

In Figure 4.13, each activity/cost driver is listed in the Activity column. The measurement of activity is then identified and listed in the Activity Measure column. The expected volume of each activity is listed by product or service in their respective Expected Activity columns, then added together to find the total level of expected activity. The Activity Measure columns identify how the activity (cost driver) will be measured while the Expected Activity columns present the amount or volume of the activity measurement.

The objective of the Expected Activity section is to find the total amount of expected activity for each activity. The expected activity of each product must be added together when finding the total amount of expected activity.

We will use the total amount of expected activity to calculate the activity rate. We will then use the activity rate to allocated the manufacturing overhead to each of the individual product lines.

Cost Pools

Cost pools are the estimated total amounts of overhead each activity (cost driver) is expected to incur. The objective in this step is to identify the total amount of overhead that will be allocated to each product or service.

With ABC, we use multiple cost pools. With traditional costing, we use a single cost pool. This is the key difference between the two methods of allocating manufacturing overhead.

Activity Rates

Activity rates are similar to the predetermined overhead rate discussed earlier in this chapter and serve the same purpose: allocating manufacturing overhead. Activity rates are the amounts of a cost pool that will be allocated to each product or service based on how much of the cost driver each one uses or consumes. The activity rates are expressed as a dollar amount per activity measure, such as per direct labor hour, per machine hour, or per machine setup.

Manufacturing Overhead—Activity Rates											
	1	2	3	4		5		6	(3/6)		
	Activity	Activity		Expected Activity					7		
Activity	Level	Measure	Cost Pool	Soft-balls	+	Baseballs	=	Total	Activity Rate		
Labor-related	Unit	DLH	$80,000	35,100	+	87,500	=	122,600	$0.65	per	DLH
Machine Setups	Batch	# setups	$150,000	3,000	+	2,000	=	5,000	$30.00	per	Setup
Parts Administration	Product	# parts	$160,000	11	+	9	=	20	$8,000.00	per	Part
Production Orders	Batch	# orders	$70,000	275	+	650	=	925	$75.68	per	Order
Material Receipts	Batch	# receipts	$90,000	150	+	600	=	750	$120.00	per	Receipts
General Factory	Facility	MH	$250,000	12,000	+	28,000	=	40,000	$6.25	per	MH
			$800,000								

Fig. 4.14 Activity Rates

We calculate an activity rate by dividing the dollar value of the cost pool by the measurement of the related cost driver used in total.

Activity Rate = Cost Pool / Total Expected Activity Level

Figure 4.14 illustrates how the activity rates are calculated. The cost pool for each activity is divided by the total expected activity. For the labor-related activity, the $80,000 cost pool is divided by the 122,600 total DLH to generate the labor-related activity rate of $0.65/DLH. For the machine setups activity, the $150,000 cost pool is divided by the 5,000 total setups to generate the activity rate of $30.00/setup.

Manufacturing Overhead Allocation—ABC

The next step is to allocate the manufacturing overhead to each individual product or service. Each activity rate is linked to each individual product or service to allocate the overhead from the cost pool to the individual product or service. When an activity rate is applied to the expected activity of a product or service, the manufacturing overhead for that activity is being allocated to the product or service as a total amount of manufacturing overhead related to that activity used to make all the individual units of products or instances of services delivered.

In Figure 4.14, the total cost pool for the labor-related activity is allocated to baseballs ($0.65 × 87,500 DLH) and to the softballs ($0.65 × 31,500 DLH). Each cost pool is allocated in an identical manner. The $800,000 of total manufacturing overhead is allocated to the two products: $485,285 allocated to the baseballs and $314,715 allocated to the softballs.

The amounts allocated to each product are then divided by the total expected number of units to be produced. The firm expects to make 1,750,000 baseballs and 450,000 softballs. The total manufacturing overhead allocated to baseballs of $485,285 is divided by the 1,750,000 baseballs expected to be made, which generates an allocated overhead of $0.28 for every baseball the firm anticipates they will make in the following year.

The firm expects to make 450,000 softballs. The total manufacturing overhead allocated to the softballs of $314,715 is divided by the 450,000 softballs expected to be made, which generates an allocated manufacturing overhead of $0.70 for every softball the firm anticipates they will make in the following year.

Figure 4.15 shows the process of how a firm might apply activity-based costing. The example uses the information from Figures 4.13 and 4.14, along with additional information regarding estimated annual sales and estimated direct material and direct labor costs.

Activity-Based v. Traditional Costing

Estimated Annual Sales	Softballs	Baseballs	
Estimated Annual Sales in units	450,000	1,750,000	
DM per unit	$3.75	$2.90	
DLH per unit	0.078	0.05	$18.00

The Process

1) Identify activities
2) Identify activity measures
3) Determine cost pools
4) Find total estimated activity
5) Calculate activity rates
6) Allocated MFG-OH using activity rates
7) Calculate allocated MFG-OH per unit
8) Calculate total unit product cost (DM+DL+MFGOH)

Estimated Annual Sales in DLH	# Units	Total DLH
Softballs	450,000	35,100
Baseballs	1,750,000	87,500
Total DLH		122,600

DM & DL Costs per unit	Softballs	Baseballs
Direct Materials	$3.75	$2.90
Direct Labor	$1.40	$0.90

Manufacturing Overhead–Activity R

Activity	1 Activity Level	2 Activity Measure	3 Activity Cost Pool	4 Expected Activity Softballs	+	5 Expected Activity Baseballs	=	6 Total	?? 7 Activity Rate		
Labor-related	Unit	DLH	$80,000	35,100	+	87,500	=	122,600	$0.65	per	DLH
Machine Setups	Batch	# setups	$150,000	3,000	+	2,000	=	5,000	$30.00	per	Setup
Parts Administration	Product	# parts	$160,000	11	+	9	=	20	$8,000.00	per	Part
Production Orders	Batch	# orders	$70,000	275	+	650	=	925	$75.68	per	Order
Material Receipts	Batch	# receipts	$90,000	150	+	600	=	750	$120.00	per	Receipt
General Factory	Facility	MH	$250,000	12,000	+	28,000	=	40,000	$6.25	per	MH
			$800,000								

Single Predetermined Overhead Rate	Est. MFG-OH	$800,000	=	$6.53	per	DLH
DLH allocation base	Est. DLH	122,600				

Softballs	ABC	Traditional
Direct Material	$3.75	$3.75
Direct Labor	$1.40	$1.40
Total DM +DL	$5.15	$5.15
Manufacturing Overhead		
Labor-related	$22.904	
Machine Setups	$90.000	
Parts Administration	$88.000	
Production Orders	$20.811	
Material Receipts	$18.000	
General Factory	$75.000	
Total Manufacturing Overhead	$314.715	
Total # units	$50.000	
MFG-OH per unit	$0.70	$0.51
Total Unit Product Cost	$5.85	$5.66
35% MU-C	$2.05	$1.98
Selling Price	$7.90	$7.65

For ABC – the MFG-OH is allocated to each product IN TOTAL and then divided by the # units.

Baseballs	ABC	Traditional
Direct Material	$2.90	$2.90
Direct Labor	$0.90	$0.90
Total DM + DL	$3.80	$3.80
Manufacturing Overhead		
Labor-related	$57,096	
Machine Setups	$60,000	
Parts Administration	$72,000	
Production Orders	$49,189	
Material Receipts	$72,000	
General Factory	$175,000	
Total Manufacturing Overhead	$485.285	
Total # units	$750,000	
MFG-OH per unit	$0,277	$0.33
Total Unit Product Cost	$4.08	$4.13
35% MU-C	$1.43	$1.44
Selling Price	$5.50	$5.57

Fig. 4.15 ABC v. Traditional POR

In the box in the middle of Figure 4.15, we present the calculation of the single predetermined overhead rate if the firm used the traditional costing method. In the bottom section of Figure 4.15, both the traditional costing method and the activity-based costing method are presented, side-by-side, for the two products, softballs and baseballs. The only difference between the two methods is the method of allocating the manufacturing overhead.

The total unit product costs for the two methods, using both methods, are summarized in the following table. The total amount of manufacturing overhead allocated to the baseballs is greater than the amount allocated to softballs, using the activity-based costing method, $485,285 versus $314,715. Although more manufacturing overhead is allocated to baseballs, the total unit product cost is lower for baseballs than softballs, $4.08 versus $5.85.

	Softballs	Baseballs
Total unit cost—traditional	$5.66	$4.13
Total unit cost—ABC	$5.85	$4.08

Furthermore, under the traditional costing method, the softballs have a lower total unit product cost than baseballs, while under the ABC method, baseballs have a lower total unit product cost than softballs. These differences highlight the effect that often occurs when changing from a traditional costing method to an activity-based costing method: The total unit product cost decreases for the higher volume product while the total unit product cost increases for the lower volume product.

To continue our discussion of product costs, we will now address the issue of using consistent costs that can be used in both planning activities and performance evaluation activities.

STANDARD COSTS

A standard cost is the cost a firm expects to pay for a product's inputs (direct materials, direct labor, manufacturing overhead) in the near future. A standard cost exhibits a relatively stable price for a typical quantity of an input that can be relied upon for planning purposes. The direct material and direct labor amounts are helpful when forecasting and planning for various market and volume scenarios because they have an amount per unit that remains relatively consistent.

Manufacturing overhead can be treated as a standard cost for both its fixed and variable portions. The variable portion of manufacturing overhead is more easily used and evaluated as a standard cost. The fixed portion of manufacturing overhead is already a standard cost because it is fixed and can't be changed easily in the near term without significant consequences.

Standard costs require both the standard prices paid for the inputs as well as the standard quantities of the input used in making each unit of product or instance of service. In many cases the standard cost is quoted or identified based on the unit of measurement for the input (which is different from a unit of product).

Direct materials	Costs per square inch of leather, meter of yarn, and other measures such as ounces, pounds, kilos, feet, tons, and yards
Direct labor	Cost per hour or minute of paid time
Manufacturing overhead	Costs based on another measure of input, such as direct labor hours or machine hours

Because standard costs are identified and communicated in terms of the input, the standard quantity required for each unit of product must be identified or calculated. Therefore, the standard cost per unit of measure of input must be multiplied by the standard quantity of the input used per unit of product or service. Standard costs are used to not only forecast the cost to each product or service, but also to evaluate how the actual results compare to the forecasted performance. Standard costs allow for more streamlined accounting processes when large quantities of materials, labor, and overhead are used in the production process. All the journal entries can be made based on standard costs throughout the accounting period.

Management accountants work to capture all the costs related to direct materials: direct labor, and manufacturing overhead. Direct materials, direct labor, and manufacturing overhead are incurred continuously throughout an accounting period and usually in larger transactions in which large quantities of raw materials are purchased or utility bills for a factory are paid. These large amounts are a result of purchasing and paying for inputs in large quantities that facilitate the production of large quantities of final product.

Industry Application

Standard costs are used effectively by firms that produce a product or deliver a service that are essentially identical for every unit or instance. Products such as pencils, baseballs, and automobiles are good candidates for using standard costs. Each unit of product requires the same amount of inputs (DM, DL, and MFGOH), and each unit of product produce is substantially similar to, if not identical to, another unit.

In our baseball example, the same amount of direct materials, direct labor, and manufacturing overhead is required to make each baseball. Firms that manufacture baseballs have historical information and experience that allows them to develop and use standard costs for direct materials, direct labor, and manufacturing overhead with reasonable precision, which allows for efficient accounting for and management of the production process.

Standard costs are also used extensively in process costing systems. Process costing is a method of accounting for direct materials, direct labor, and manufacturing overhead for homogeneous products that are manufactured in multiple stages: paper towels, fabric, oil and gas, agricultural products, and others. In this textbook, we will not present the process costing system but will leave the method to more advanced textbooks and courses.

Forecasting Application

A powerful and effective use of standard costs can be demonstrated in the forecasting future production. When standard costs for direct material, direct labor, and manufacturing overhead remain relatively stable, they can be used to forecast a wide range of production levels based on management's expectation of future market conditions. Forecasting the potential results from a range of production levels provides valuable information that managers can use to make decisions concerning material purchases, labor needs, facility expansion or contraction, operational efficiency, and others.

The work we performed in Chapter 2 relied heavily on standard costs to project future results. By standardizing the costs, the unit volume drives the changes in all the variable costs, providing effective estimates of expected results created by changing volumes.

Standard Quantities

The concept of standard quantity applies equally well to direct materials, direct labor, and manufacturing overhead, which are all inputs or resources used to produce a product or deliver a service. Standard direct material quantities include the physical components that are transformed from separate items into a finished product in the conversion process. Standard direct labor quantities include the time employees spend converting the various physical components into a finished product. Standard manufacturing overhead quantities include all the various indirect manufacturing costs that are incurred to maintain, support, and repair the manufacturing environment and processes.

Developing Standard Quantities per Unit

Developing standard quantities of direct material, direct labor, and manufacturing overhead requires all the input to be included to produce each unit of finished product. The basic approach is to divide the total estimated volume of the input needed by the total estimated number of units to be produced.

$$\text{Standard Quantity per Unit} = \frac{\text{Total Estimated Volume of the Input to Be Used}}{\text{Total Estimated Number of Units to Be Produced}}$$

The total volume of the input for the three basic product inputs might include some of the following:

- Direct Materials—amount/number of raw materials and components that should be used to make the product
- Direct Labor—amount of time employees should spend making the product
- Manufacturing overhead—amount of overhead that should be incurred to maintain the production facility and processes

STANDARD QUANTITY—DIRECT MATERIALS

To use a standard costing system effectively, the standard quantity must also be known. The standard quantity is the amount of direct materials, the time of direct labor, and the amount of manufacturing overhead that each unit of product or instance of service requires to be completed.

For example, a baseball might require nine (9) square inches of leather. In addition to the nine (9) square inches of leather used to make a baseball, some quantities of leather may be used in the manufacturing process that do not become part of a finished baseball, such as rework, machine failure, human error, poor quality leather, and other issues inherent in a manufacturing environment.

Some businesses completely exclude the costs resulting from these kinds of problems, while others may include some type of estimate for these issues.

Total Direct Materials = Standard Quantity of Direct Material per Unit x Number of Units to Be Produced

Remember, standard quantities refer to the typical amount of an input (direct materials, direct labor, manufacturing overhead) needed to produce one individual unit of product or service.

Developing Standard Cost per Unit

The approach for calculating the standard cost per unit is generated by multiplying the standard price per unit of input by the amount of the input required to produce one unit of product. This approach is applied to direct materials, direct labor, and manufacturing overhead.

DIRECT MATERIALS

Direct materials for a baseball consist of cork, rubber, string/yarn, leather, and seam string. The standard price paid for any of these items includes not only the purchase price charged by the supplier, but also any additional costs to transport, insure, and obtain and deliver the material to the production facility. Common terms for the total amount for all the costs are total cost, all-in cost, fully loaded cost, and other industry-specific terms.

Figure 4.16 illustrates the standard costs for direct materials used in baseball production.

DIRECT LABOR

Direct labor for a baseball consists of the total amount of time employees spend converting the cork, rubber, string/yarn, leather, and seam string into a finished baseball, multiplied by the wage rate per hour paid to the employee. Standard costs for direct labor can be confusing because the wage rate paid to employees is generally shown as a per-hour wage rate (e.g., employees earn $14.50/hour), while the time employees spend to make a unit of product will be more than or less than a single hour. Employees may spend a total of 20 minutes to make a single baseball. If the averaged rate employees are paid is $14.50 per hour, either the wage rate needs to be changed to a per-minute rate or the time to make a baseball needs to be changed to an hourly basis.

In Figure 4.17, the total number of labor hours needed to make the expected number of baseballs is multiplied by the wage rate to find the total wages expected to be paid. Then employment taxes and employee benefit costs are added to find the total employment cost, or total payroll costs. The total employment cost must then be divided by the total number of baseballs the firm expects to produce to calculate the standard cost of direct labor per baseball.

Standard Costs for Direct Materials										
Estimated Number of Baseballs to be Produced:				138,000						
				Cork	Rubber	Wool String	Adhesive	Leather	Seem String	Total Materials
Unit of Measure				ounces	ounces	meters	gallons	square inches	meters	
Units of Measure Purchased				12,500	22,500	10,000	1,500	1,250,000	7,500	
Cost per unit of measure purchased				$0.030	$0.065	$0.650	$2.250	$0.150	$0.700	
Total/Extended Purchase Price	a			$375.00	$1,462.50	$6,500.00	$3,375.00	$187,500.00	$5,250.00	
Sales/VAT Tax	b	tax rate:	3.25%	$12.19	$47.53	$211.25	$109.69	$6,093.75	$170.63	
Transportation/ Shipping	c			75	145	475	600	7500	400	
Insurance	d		0.150%	$0.56	$2.19	$9.75	$5.06	$281.25	$7.88	
Total Costs				$462.75	$1,657.23	$7,196.00	$4,089.75	$201,375.00	$5,828.50	
Standard Cost of DM per Baseball				$0.0034	$0.0120	$0.0521	$0.0296	$1.4592	$0.0422	$1.5986

Notes:

a The total/extended purchase price is found by multiplying the amount purchased by the cost per unit of measure purchased.
b The sales/VAT tax is assessed at 3.25% of the total/extended purchase price.
c The transportation/shipping costs are negotiated with individual firms that provide the service.
d Insurance is charge at a fixed rate of 0.15% of the total/extended purchase price.

Fig. 4.16 Standard Costs for DM Example

MANUFACTURING OVERHEAD

Manufacturing overhead is the accumulation of many individual indirect overhead costs into a single amount. To calculate the standard cost for manufacturing overhead, both the variable portion and the fixed portion must be added together. The challenge with manufacturing overhead is that the relationship of MFGOH to volume is not constant, because the fixed portion does not change when volume changes.

Figure 4.18 illustrates the standard costs for manufacturing overhead. For manufacturing overhead, both the variable portion and the fixed portion must be included because manufacturing overhead consists of many different individual costs and expenses, which exhibit all three types of cost behaviors: variable cost, fixed cost, and mixed cost.

Standard Costs for Direct Labor				
Estimated Number of Baseballs to be Produced:	138,000			
				Time
Unit of Measure				hour
Total Number of Hours				8,750
Wage Rate per Hour				$14,500
Total Wages	a			$126,875.00
Employment taxes	b	tax rate:	7.65%	$9,705.94
Employee benefits	c	wage rate	30%	$38,062.50
				$174,643.44
Total Employment/Payroll Costs				
Standard Cost of DL per Baseball				$1.2655

Notes:

a The total/extended purchase price is found by multiplying the wage rate per hour by the total number of hours.
b The sales/VAT tax is assessed at 3.25% of the total/extended purchase price.
c The transportation/shipping costs are negotiated with individual firms that provide the service.

Fig. 4.17 Standard Costs for DL Example

Standard Costs for Manufacturing Overhead		
Estimated Number of Baseballs to be Produced:	138,000	
		Manufacturing Overhead
Unit of Measure		direct-labor hours
Total Number of DLH		8,750
Variable MFGOH per DLH		$2,350
Total Variable MFGOH		$20,562.50
Fixed MFGOH	a	$45,000.00
Total MFGOH		$65,562.50
Standard Cost of MFGOH per Baseball		$0.4751

Notes:

a Total variable MFGOH is calculated by mulitplying the total number of DLH by the Variable MFGOH per DLH

Fig. 4.18 Standard Costs for MFGOH Example

5

FLEXIBLE FORECASTING

Evaluating what we have done

THE QUESTIONS WE TRY TO ANSWER

- Did we do a good job earning revenue?
- Did we do a good job controlling costs?
- Can we identify costs that were unexpectedly higher or lower than we anticipated?

LEARNING OBJECTIVES

LO1: Describe and explain the flexible forecast and its relationship to the operating forecast.

LO2: Calculate the volume variance, the revenue variance, and the spending variances.

LO3: Describe and explain the quantity/efficiency variances and the price/rate variances.

LO4: Calculate the quantity variance and the price variance for direct materials.

LO5: Calculate the efficiency variance and the rate variance for direct labor.

LO6: Calculate the efficiency variance and the rate variance for variable manufacturing overhead.

FLEXIBLE FORECASTS

In this chapter, we introduce the concept of the flexible forecast. A flexible forecast is created at the close of an accounting period and used to compare the actual results of the period to expected performance. The value added by the flexible forecast is that the flexible forecast is calculated using the actual unit volume of the period, not the unit volume in the original forecast. The flexible forecast is essentially a recalculation of the original forecast using the actual unit volume sold during the period. This is because many costs are variable and using the unit volume of the original forecast does not enable a good analysis of the variable costs actually incurred.

The weakness of the original forecast, as we discuss in Chapter 2, is the estimated unit volume used to calculate the original forecast. The original forecast is created before the start of the accounting period as we need it to allocate fixed costs to products during the year. When the original forecast is created, no one knows how many units will be sold during the period. Thus, the forecast unit sales volume is only an estimate at the time of the original forecast.

Because the original forecast estimated unit sales volumes, the estimate volumes will be different from the actual number of units sold. The difference between the estimated and actual units sold creates what is called a volume variance. The volume variance will have an effect on every line item in the forecast because each line of the forecast is calculated using the unit volume. If the original forecast estimated 20,000 units sold in June but the actual sales

Comparison of the Original and Flexible Forecasts			
Forecast	**Use**	**Preparation**	**Unit Volume Used**
Original	Planning	Before the start of a period	Estimated unit volume
Flexible	Evaluation	Close of a period	Actual unit volume

Fig. 5.1 Original v Flexible Comparison

in June were 21,500 units, the volume variance of 1,500 units will affect both the revenue and all of the expenses.

The strength of the flexible forecast is its use of the actual unit volume sold during the period. The actual unit volume isn't known until the period closes, which can be somewhat confusing because the term "forecast" is generally used to refer to future estimates, but a flexible forecast is actually created after the close of an accounting period to evaluate the performance in the period.

Both the original forecast and the flexible forecast can provide useful information, but the information they provide is used for very different purposes. The original forecast is used as a planning tool for future accounting periods. The flexible forecast is used as an evaluation tool to evaluate the performance in an accounting period.

Figure 5.1 provides a comparison between the original forecast and the flexible forecast to highlight their uses, the timing of their preparation, and the unit volume used to create each forecast.

CREATING THE FLEXIBLE FORECAST

To create the flexible forecast the original forecast is recalculated based on the actual volume of production. The flexible forecast is then compared to the actual results to evaluate the performance.

In Chapter 2 we discussed the operating forecast. This forecast was based on the specific number of units the firm's owners and managers believed would be produced each month and quarter, and for the year. The original forecast was developed in the previous year, and during the time between when the original forecast was created and the current accounting period/month, many things can change that will affect the actual results. Because the original forecast was created before the current year began, the unit volume used to create the original forecast will not be the same as the actual unit volume experienced. The original forecast used the estimated number of units sold as the basis to calculate all the individual forecasts for production, direct materials, direct labor, manufacturing overhead, and sales and general administration. Throughout the original forecast, we used a revenue or cost formula to generate every amount in the original forecast.

The flexible forecast simply recalculates the forecast using the actual unit volume, using the same revenue and cost formulas.

Forecast Formulas

The formulas used in both the original forecast and the flexible forecast are the same. The forecast formulas for revenues and expenses are the expression of both the fixed and variable portions of those revenues and expenses. Generally, revenues are variable because no revenue is generated

Forecast Formulas Beaver Baseball For the Month Ended May 31. 20xx				
				Original Forecast
		Baseball Volume in Units		25,000
		Fixed	Variable	
Revenue:				
$17.00 per baseball			$17.00	$425,000
Expenses:	Cost Behaviors			
Direct Materials	VC		$3.75	$93,750
Direct Labor	VC		$0.90	$22,500
Variable Manufacturing Overhead	VC		$0.1750	$4,375
Wages & Salaries	MC	$67,500	$2.10	$120,000
Electricity	MC	$4,500	$0.02	$5,000
Rent	FC	$28,650		$28,650
Liability Insurance	FC	$7,645		$7,645
Employee Health Insurance	FC	$9,450		$9,450
Miscellaneous	MC	$750	$0.15	$4,500
Total Expenses				$295,870
Net Operating Income				$129,130

Fig. 5.2 Forecast Formulas

unless something is sold. The expenses can exhibit either fixed or variable behavior, or a combination of both fixed and variable behaviors if the expense is a mixed expense.

Figure 5.2 presents the forecast formulas and the operating forecast for May, 20xx. The formulas were used in the prior year to plan for May, 20xx using the estimated unit sales volume of 25,000 units. The amount of each line item in the original forecast was calculated by using the 25,000-unit sales volume in the formula for that line item. The 25,000 units is an estimate and the actual results for May will almost certainly be different. The amount of revenue was calculated by multiplying the sales price per unit of $17.00 by the 25,000 units expected to be sold. The amount of direct materials was calculated by multiplying the variable cost of $3.75 per unit by the 25,000 units expected to be sold. The amount for electricity was calculated by multiplying the 25,000 units expected to be sold by the $0.02 per unit and then added to the $4,500 fixed portion of electricity. The fixed costs (rent, liability insurance, employee health insurance) do not vary with unit sales volume as they are a cost of capacity.

Revenue Variance

The original forecast is based on 25,000 units expected to be sold in May. Because the unit sales volume is estimated and the actual unit sales volume will be different, the actual results in May will be affected. We will see that the actual number of units sold in May will be 32,000 units. If the amount of revenue in the original forecast was calculated by multiplying 25,000 units by the $17/unit sales price for a total of $425,000 of revenue, the fact that 7,000 more units were sold in May will significantly affect the amount of revenue actually generated in May. The actual revenue for May is $530,750.

The question we need to answer is if we sold 32,000 units in May, did we do a good job generating revenue if we generated $530,750?

The purpose of the flexible forecast is to provide information to help us understand what we should have done in the period. In the case of May's revenue, did we do a good job generating $530,750 of revenue? Remember, we originally planned to sell 25,000 units to generate $425,000 of revenue. If we sold 32,000 units, then at $17/unit we should have generated $544,000 of revenue.

Unit	Volume Revenue
25,000 (original forecast last year)	$425,000
32,000 (actual units in flexible forecast)	$544,000
32,000 (actual results for the month)	$530,750

The volume difference of 7,000 should cause revenues to go up by $119,000. This is the effect of the volume variance that we eliminated by using the flexible forecast. To effectively evaluate the results of May, we need to compare what actually happened in May to what SHOULD HAVE happened in May. For revenues, what should have been generated in May was $544,000 when only $530,750 was generated; so, we did not do a very good job generating revenue in May, and the $13,250 unfavorable revenue variance indicates we should investigate the difference and find out what happened.

For the remainder of this chapter, we will evaluate the costs of a firm using the flexible forecast to compare to the actual results. It is useful to start with a review of how the forecast was made and to do that we need to understand the use of standard costs (which were introduced in Chapter 2 to develop the original forecast and used in Chapter 4 to cost a product).

STANDARD COSTS

Standard costs are comprised of the standard quantities and standard prices of our product inputs, and selling expenses and are key components to creating and using a flexible forecast. The standard quantities help identify the amount of direct material, direct labor, and manufacturing overhead we SHOULD HAVE **used** to produce the actual number of units (i.e., actual volume or actual results). The standard prices help us identify the amount we SHOULD HAVE **paid** or incurred to produce the actual number of units or achieve the actual volume.

Figure 5.3 illustrates the two parts of the standard cost for each product input and which variance evaluates each part—a map of the standard cost components to the variances. This diagram links the standard cost component with the associated variance. We will discuss the relationships of the standard cost components to the variances in much more detail later in the chapter.

Where the Flexible Forecast and Variances Fit

In Figure 5.4, the flexible forecast fits between the original forecast and the actual results. When the original forecast, the flexible forecast, and the actual results are compared from left to right, we can see where the variances fit and see the different associated relationships.

Inputs	Standard Cost Components	Related Variances	Concept
Direct Materials	Quantity of material	Quantity Variance	Were the materials effectively & efficiently used, or not?
	Price of material	Price Variance	Were the materials purchased at an advantageous price, or not?
Direct Labor	Number of hours	Efficiency Variance	Were the employees effective at their production activities, or not?
	Wage rate per hour	Rate Variance	Were the wages paid to employees in-line with expectations, or not?
Variable Overhead	Allocation base	Efficiency Variance	Were the various overhead items effectively and efficiently used, or not?
	Prices paid	Rate Variance	Were the prices paid for overhead items in-line with expectations, or not?
Fixed Overhead	Fixed overhead variance analysis is a tool to evaluate the method of allocating fixed manufuring overhead. FOH variance analysis will be discussed in more advanced management or cost accounting courses.		

Fig. 5.3 Standard Cost Diagram

The original forecast was prepared before the current period and used an estimated unit volume to calculate all of the revenue and expenses. The flexible forecast uses the actual unit volume with the revenue and expense formulas from the original forecast to calculate the flexible forecast so that actual results can be effectively evaluated.

Most of the differences between the original forecast and the actual results are caused by the difference between the estimated unit volume used in the original forecast and the actual unit volume in the current period. This difference in units between the original forecast and actual results is called the volume variance. When the flexible forecast is calculated with actual unit volume, the effect of the volume variance is removed. Once the effects of the volume variance are removed, the flexible forecast can be effectively compared to the actual results to provide useful information about the remaining differences: the revenue variance and the spending variances.

Variance Relationship Diagram						
Timing	Last Year			Current Period		Current Period
	Original Forecast			**Flexible Forecast**		**Actual Results**
Unit Volume	Estimated Unit Volume	**Volume Variance** (different between estimated unit volume and actual unit volume)		Actual Unit Volume		Actual Unit Volume
	Estimated Revenue		Revenue	Actual Unit Volume X Sales Price/Unit	**Revenue Variance** (difference between flexible forecast revenue and actual revenue)	Actual Revenue Generated
	Estimated Expenses		Expenses	Actual Unit Volume X Standard Cost/Unit	**Spending Variances** (difference between flexible forecast expenses and actual expenses)	Actual Expenses Incurred

Fig. 5.4 Variance Relationship Diagram

The revenue and spending variances between the flexible forecast and the actual results can be considered the first level of variance analysis. Further analysis of the spending variances can be carried out. This is essentially drilling into the information to better understand the firm's revenues and expenses. The comparison between the flexible forecast and the actual results is more effective because the flexible forecast is communicating what SHOULD HAVE BEEN DONE at the actual unit volume level. The difference in revenue between the flexible forecast and the actual results is the revenue variance. The differences in expenses between the flexible forecast and the actual results are the spending variances. Once the spending variances have been identified, we can evaluate them to ascertain how the spending variance was generated. Analyzing the spending variances for direct materials, direct labor, and variable manufacturing overhead (VOH) separates the results of spending into the causes of the spending variance. The objective is to understand why the spending variance occurred, not just that a difference in the expense occurred. The spending variance can be caused by one, or both, of the following:

1. More or less of the quantity of input was used at the actual level of unit volume than what should have been used. The difference or variance in the quantity of input used is called
   a. direct material quantity variance;
   b. direct labor efficiency variance; and
   c. variable overhead efficiency variance.

2. More or less was paid for the input than should have been paid. The difference or variance in the price paid for the input is called
   a. direct material price variance;
   b. direct labor rate variance; and
   c. variable overhead rate variance.

To facilitate the further analysis of the spending variances for the three product inputs (direct materials, direct labor, manufacturing overhead), we must be able to isolate the effect of how the quantity of the input was used from the price paid for the input.

VARIANCES

Variances are analysis tools used by owners and managers to understand how actual revenue and expenses differ from revenue the firm should have generated and from the expenses the firm should have incurred at the actual level of unit sales volume. The revenue variance is relatively straightforward, while some of the spending variances will require additional analysis.

A key factor in spending variance analysis is the use of standard costs. For revenues, a firm will have a price per unit that should be paid by every customer. This is the standard selling price.

For expenses, a firm will have a standard quantity of input (direct materials, direct labor, variable overhead) that should be used or consumed to make one unit of product. A firm will also have a standard price for the input (direct materials, direct labor, variable overhead) that should be paid to make and sell one unit of their product.

Figure 5.6 presents the flexible forecast and the actual results for the month of May. The revenue and expense formulas used the 32,000 actual units sold to generate the flexible forecast for May. The flexible forecast is compared to the actual results to find the revenue variance and the spending variances. Note, there is no volume variance when comparing the flexible forecast with actual results because both are based on the actual units sold.

Revenue Variance

The revenue variance is the difference between the amount of revenue that should have been generated at the actual unit volume in the flexible forecast revenue and the amount of actual revenue.

Flexible Forecast to Actual Results
Beaver Baseball
For the Month Ended May 31, 20xx

				Flexible Forecast	Actual Results	Variances		
		Baseball Volume in Units		32,000	32,000			
Revenue:		Fixed	Variable					
$17.00 per baseball			$17.00	$544,000	$530,750	($13,250)	Unfavorable	Revenue Variance
Expenses:	Cost Behaviors							
Direct Materials	VC		$3.75	$120,000	$126,450	($6,450)	Unfavorable	Spending Variance
Direct Labor	VC		$0.90	$28,800	$28,500	$300	Favorable	Spending Variance
Variable Manufacturing Overhead	VC		$0.1750	$5,600	$6,000	($400)	Unfavorable	Spending Variance
Wages & Salaries	MC	$67,500	$2.10	$134,700	$131,200	$3,500	Favorable	Spending Variance
Electricity	MC	$4,500	$0.02	$5,140	$5,150	($10)	Unfavorable	Spending Variance
Rent	FC	$28,650		$28,650	$28,500	$150	Favorable	Spending Variance
Liability Insurance	FC	$7,645		$7,645	$7,600	$45	Favorable	Spending Variance
Employee Health Insurance	FC	$9,450		$9,450	$9,500	($50)	Unfavorable	Spending Variance
Miscellaneous	MC	$750	$0.15	$5,550	$5,100	$450	Favorable	Spending Variance
Total Expenses				$345,535	$348,000	($2,465)		
Net Operating Income				$198,465	$182,750	$15,715		

Fig. 5.5 Flexible Forecast to Actual Results

The revenue variance could be caused by activities such as discounting prices or issuing coupons. Managers will mostly likely have some type of revenue expectations based on the pricing decisions made during the accounting period.

In Figure 5.6, the spending variance is the difference between the $544,000 of revenue that should have been generated from the sale of 32,000 actual units and the $530,750 of revenue actually generated.

Spending Variances

The spending variances are the differences between the expenses that should have been incurred at the actual level of unit sales volume, as shown in the flexible forecast and the actual expense incurred. Spending variances are generated for all costs, both manufacturing costs and non-manufacturing expenses. The spending variances for the non-manufacturing expenses are evaluated at this level: wages and salaries, electricity, rent, liability insurance, employee health insurance, and miscellaneous.

The spending variances for direct materials, direct labor, and variable manufacturing overhead can be further separated because they each have both quantities and prices that determine the cost incurred for each input. The issue of standard costs was addressed at length in Chapter 4, and the same concepts will now be applied to analyzing the spending variances for direct materials, direct labor, and variable overhead.

It can be confusing when using standard costs in the flexible forecast. The cause for the confusion is the standard quantity used to calculate the amount of direct materials, direct labor, and variable manufacturing overhead included in the flexible forecast. The standard quantity used in the flexible forecast is the standard quantity of the input required for each unit of product. The standard quantity per unit is multiplied by the actual units sold. When we use the spending variance grid to separate the spending variance into its quantity and price components, the standard quantity used for the flexible forecast is that standard quantity of input that should be used to make the actual units sold.

Figure 5.5 presents the comparison between the flexible forecast and the actual results for the month of May with the differences created by the comparisons in the Variances column. The flexible forecast is the recalculation of the forecast using the actual unit volume of 32,000 baseballs from the month of May. The actual results are taken from the general ledger. The variances are the differences between the what the firm should have done (flexible forecast) and actual performance of the firm in May.

Figure 5.5 contains the information we will need as we proceed to the next level in analyzing the spending variances for direct materials, direct labor, and variable manufacturing overhead. The spending variance is the difference between the flexible forecast and actual results. The spending variance will be separated into two parts: 1) the quantity or efficiency variance and 2) the price or rate variance.

Favorable/Unfavorable Variance Designations

All the variances calculated and analyzed in this chapter are identified as either favorable or unfavorable. Each variance must be evaluated independently from all other considerations for its effect on net operating income. A favorable variance is a variance that has a positive effect on net operating income. An unfavorable variance is one that has a negative effect on net operating income. If the actual revenue is lower than the revenue shown on the flexible forecast, then the revenue variance is an unfavorable variance.

For a revenue variance, when the actual revenue is greater than the flexible forecast revenue, the difference has a favorable effect on net operating income, such that the actual revenue, alone and without considering anything else, will cause the net operating income to be higher than the net operating income shown in the flexible forecast. Actual revenue less than the flexible forecast revenue would have an unfavorable effect on net operating income.

For a spending variance, the differences in expenses have the opposite effect on net operating income than revenue. When the actual expense is greater than the expense shown on the flexible forecast, the variance has an unfavorable effect on net operating income. When the actual expense is less than the expense shown on the flexible forecast, the variance has a favorable effect on net operating income. The favorable and unfavorable designations are used when calculating the revenue variance and the spending variances, as well as when separating the spending variances into their quantity/efficiency variances and their price/rate variances. To facilitate the analysis of these variances we have developed the spending variance grid as a tool to assist in both setting up a variance problem and identifying the favorable/unfavorable nature of the variance.

Spending Variance Analysis Grid and Formulas

We will use two related tools to separate the spending variances for direct materials, direct labor, and variable overhead into their component parts of quantity and price: the spending variance analysis grid and spending variance formulas. The spending variance analysis grid is a graphical tool we can use to place all the given information into specific locations in the grid and then work to find or solve for any missing pieces. We will also use the formula approach to calculate the variances; this formula can also be derived from the spending variance grid.

The spending variance analysis grid and the spending variance formulas are laid out in a similar manner. The spending variance formulas can be derived from the layout of the spending variance grid. The design of the spending variance grid layout to match the spending variance formulas is intended to provide an effective method to both disaggregate the spending variances and verify the disaggregated variances. The spending variance analysis grid is a tool to facilitate spending variance analysis. When looking at the left-to-right layout shown earlier in the chapter, the flexible forecast is at the far left of the grid and the actual results are at the far right of the grid. The grid is then rotated 90 degrees to the right (clockwise) so that the spending variance grid flows from top (the flexible forecast) to bottom (actual results). We rotate the grid to help facilitate the calculation of the quantity/efficiency variances as well as the price/rate variances.

An important aspect of the spending variance grid is that we move from top to bottom, subtracting amounts as we move down the grid. This result reflects the effect of the difference (variance) on the net operating income. Positive results in the spending variance grid are favorable variances, while negative results in the spending variance grid are unfavorable variances.

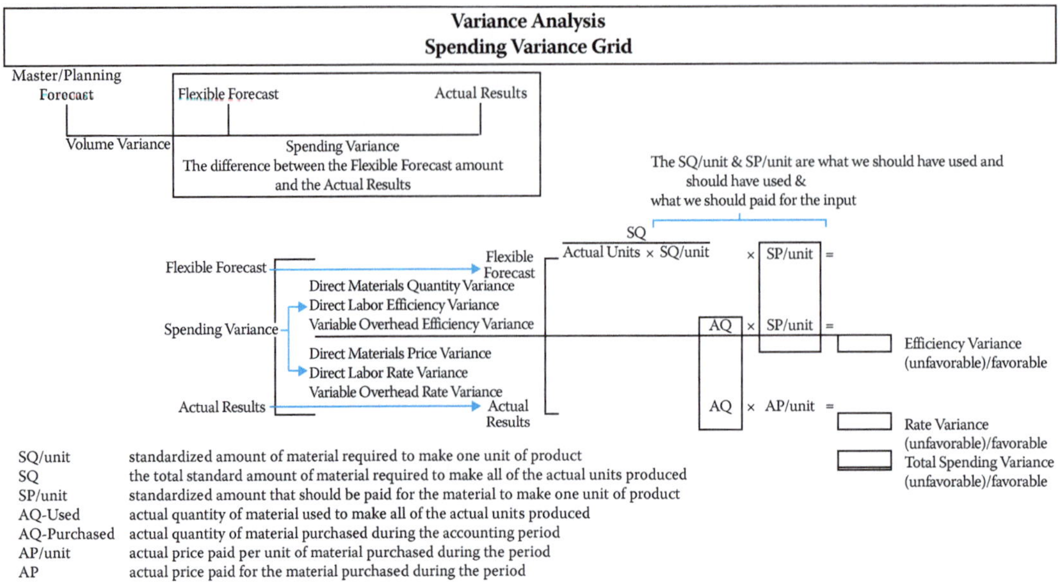

Fig. 5.6 Spending Variance Grid

Figure 5.6 presents a diagram of the spending variance analysis grid, which flows from top to bottom. At the top of the grid we begin with the flexible forecast. Below the flexible forecast we calculate the amount that we should have spent for the actual amount of the input we used. At the bottom of the grid we place the actual amount paid for the input.

The middle position in the grid is where we calculate the amount that should have been spent for the actual amount of input used by multiplying the actual quantity of input used by the standard price of the input. This isolates the effect the quantity of input used on the top half of the grid and the effect of the price paid for the quantity of input used on the bottom half of the grid.

Spending Variance Formulas

The variances shown on the spending variance grid can also be calculated using a formula approach. To facilitate writing the formulas, we use a number of abbreviations that we will define here:

Standard quantity (SQ) = Standard quantity per unit of product
Standard price (SP) = Standard price per unit of input
Actual quantity (AQ) = Actual quantity of input used or purchased
Actual price (AP) = Actual price paid for the input
Actual labor (AL) = Actual direct labor used

QUANTITY/EFFICIENCY VARIANCES

The top half of the spending variance grid analyzes the quantity of the input used:

Direct materials quantity variance
Direct labor efficiency variance
Variable overhead efficiency variance

For direct materials, we use a quantity of materials as an input, and the variance in quantity is be evaluated.

For direct labor and variable overhead, we use a quantity of labor and a quantity of overhead as inputs; the variance is denoted as the direct labor efficiency variance because the effective use of both direct labor and variable manufacturing overhead is referred to as the efficiency with which the inputs are being used.

Whether the analysis on the top half of the grid is for direct materials, direct labor, or variable overhead, the core concept is to analyze the use of the input to generate the actual unit volume and actual results: Were the quantities of the materials used effectively? Were the employees working efficiently? Was the overhead used effectively? Although the variance has different names, the same question is being asked: Was the input properly and effectively used in production?

PRICE/RATE VARIANCES

The bottom half of the spending variance grid analyzes the price paid for the input purchased:

Direct materials price variance
Direct labor rate variance
Variable overhead rate variance

For direct materials, we pay a specific price for the materials purchased and that price is being evaluated.

For direct labor and variable overhead, we pay a specific rate for labor and overhead; the variance is found by evaluating the rate paid for the inputs.

Whether the analysis on the bottom half of the grid is for direct materials, direct labor, or variable overhead, the core concept is to analyze the price paid for the input used to generate the actual unit volume and results: Was the price paid for the material fair? Were the employees paid the appropriate amount? Was the price paid for overhead items expected? Although the variance has different names, the same question is being asked: Was the price paid for the input fair, appropriate, and expected?

DIRECT MATERIALS QUANTITY VARIANCE

Direct Materials Quantity Variance = Standard Price/unit of material (standard quantity of material – actual quantity of material used)

DM Quantity Variance = SP/unit(SQ – AQ)

The direct materials quantity variance evaluates the quantity of material used in production compared to the quantity of direct material that should have been used in production for the volume that was produced. Manufacturing and production processes are not perfectly efficient because inefficiencies and waste are inherent in such processes and cannot be eliminated completely. Some firms target a zero variance for the direct materials quantity variance, which will cause the calculation to identify any inefficiency or waste. Some firms allow for some amount of inefficiency or waste, which will cause the variance calculation to identify a level or degree of inefficiency or waste only above the amounts included in the standard quantity for waste. The approach a firm takes to establishing standard quantities, standard prices, and standard costs should reflect its strategic approach to those items, so the results of any variance analysis will generate information that will reflect and support the firm's strategic and operational philosophies.

The direct materials used in production are the responsibility of the production manager. The production manager oversees and coordinates the production process to meet the demand for the product. The production manager is responsible for the materials used in the production process and hence the production manager is usually responsible for the direct materials quantity variance.

DIRECT MATERIALS PRICE VARIANCE

Direct Materials Price Variance = Actual quantity of material purchased (standard price per unit of material – actual price per unit of material)

DM Price Variance = AQ (SP/unit – AP/unit)

The direct materials price variance evaluates the price paid for the materials purchased during the period compared to the price that should have been paid for them. Planning and forecasting input prices is a key function within a business that affects production scheduling, inventory management, purchasing activities, and other functions because input price changes can significantly alter how and when a firm produces its products.

Direct materials differ from direct labor and manufacturing overhead because direct materials can be inventoried. The function of purchasing materials is commonly separated from the production function. The purchasing department is usually responsible for obtaining the best possible price for direct materials that meet or exceed the required levels of quality. Hence, the purchasing manager is responsible for the direct materials price variance.

The ability to store direct materials in inventory creates a unique feature that does not exist with direct labor or manufacturing overhead. Materials can be purchased in quantities much larger than required for immediate production. When large quantities are purchased, the price variance is calculated at the time of purchase (the quantity variance is calculated at the time the materials are used in production). Therefore, while a large quantity of materials could be purchased, only a portion of those materials might be used in production. The remaining quantity purchased is then stored in inventory for future production needs.

DIRECT LABOR EFFICIENCY VARIANCE

Direct Labor Efficiency Variance = Standard price (wage)/unit (standard quantity of labor hours – actual labor hours)

DL Efficiency Variance = SP/unit (SL – AL)

The direct labor efficiency variance evaluates the efficiency of the direct labor force, in essence evaluating the quantity (in hours) of the direct labor input used in the production process. Many products and services have a standard amount of time an employee should spend to create a finished product or deliver a service.

Employees are not all equally efficient, and they are not all equally skilled. The direct labor efficiency variance captures and evaluates the cost difference between the amount of time employees should have spent producing the actual unit volume and how much time was actually spent for the units produced.

DIRECT LABOR RATE VARIANCE

Direct Labor Rate Variance = Actual labor hours (standard price (wage) per hour – actual price (wage) per hour)

DL Rate Variance = AL/unit (SP/unit – AP/unit)

The direct labor rate variance evaluates the wages paid (actual price) for the amount of time (actual quantity) used to achieve the actual unit volume. The difference between the standard wage rate (standard price) that the firm has developed and the actual wages paid reflects the changes in the wage rate and employee benefit cost changes in the current labor market. The standard wage rate includes not only the wage rate per hour paid to the employees but also employer-borne employment taxes and fringe benefits provided to employees, which creates a full-cost per hour for direct labor personnel.

VARIABLE MANUFACTURING OVERHEAD EFFICIENCY VARIANCE

Variable Overhead Efficiency Variance = Standard price (POR)/unit (standard quantity of allocation base – actual quantity of allocation base)

VOH Efficiency Variance = SP/unit (SQ – AQ)

The variable manufacturing overhead (VOH) efficiency variance evaluates the efficiency (quantity) of the variable overhead used in the production process. The efficiency of variable manufacturing overhead is gauged by the amount of the allocation base used to achieve the actual unit volume.

Because the allocation base is the quantity being evaluated, the results help a firm understand how well the allocation base reflects the incurrence of variable manufacturing overhead.

VARIABLE MANUFACTURING OVERHEAD RATE VARIANCE

Variable Overhead Rate Variance = Actual quantity of allocation base (standard POR – actual price paid per unit of allocation base)

VOH Rate Variance = AQ (SP/unit – AP/unit)

The variable manufacturing overhead rate variance evaluates the variable overhead incurred (actual price) to achieve the actual unit volume. The VOH rate variance is an evaluation of the firm's predetermined overhead rate (standard price) used to allocate the variable overhead.

Spending Variance Analysis—Baseball Example

To show how the direct materials, direct labor, and variable manufacturing overhead variances fit together, we will use our baseball manufacturing example. Figure 5.6 shows the flexible forecast, the actual results, the revenue variance, and the spending variances from a single month of producing baseballs.

Notice that the revenue and spending variances are calculated using the flexible forecast. The original forecast was used to compare to actual results and identify the volume variance. When the flexible forecast is generated using the actual unit volume, no volume variance exists because the effect of the volume variance has been eliminated by using actual unit volume in the flexible forecast instead of an estimate unit volume.

Using the forecast formulas that express the fixed and variable cost behaviors of each line item results in a better predictive value for the forecast. If each item (especially expenses) has been accurately separated into its fixed and variable parts, then the forecast should better predict what the performance should be at a given level of unit volume.

The fixed and/or variable nature of each of the revenue and expense line items is expressed in the formulas used to calculate the original forecast using the original unit volume estimate, and in the flexible forecast using the actual unit volume for the month. The two forecasts use the same forecast formulas using different unit volumes. The original forecast used 25,000 units, while the flexible forecast used 32,000 units. The flexible forecast is calculated by applying the actual unit volume of 32,000 baseballs to the forecast formulas for both revenue and expenses. The flexible forecast communicates what the performance ***should have*** been at the actual unit volume.

The actual results are taken from the accounting and operating records of the firm. The unit volume comes from sales information. The expense amounts come from the general ledger, usually in the form of a trial balance.

The revenue variance is the difference in revenue between the flexible forecast and the actual results. The spending variances are the differences between the flexible forecast and the actual results for each expense line item. The spending variances for direct materials, direct labor, and variable

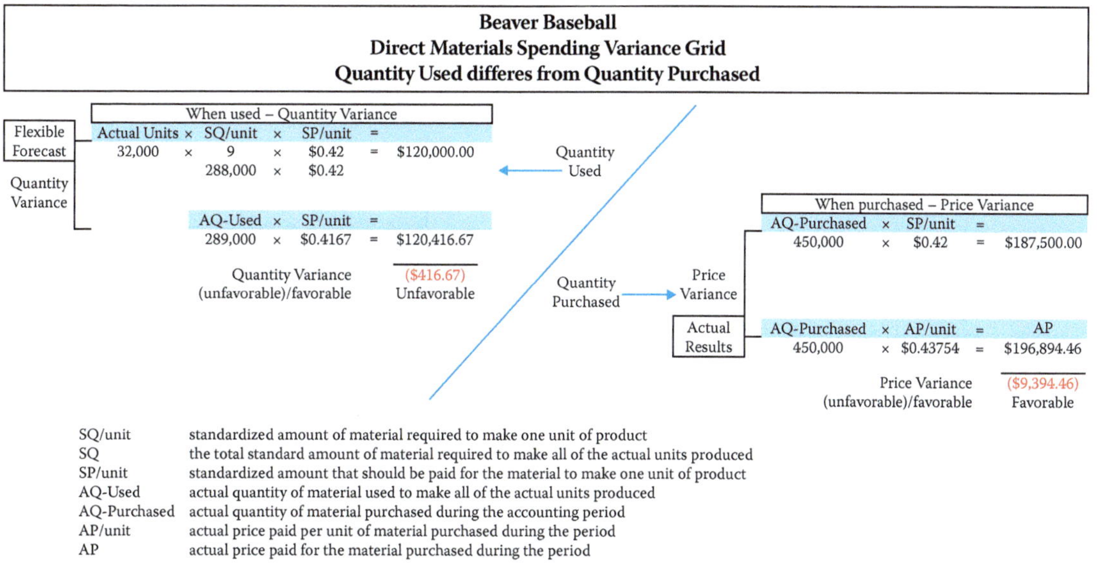

Fig. 5.7 Beaver Baseball Direct Materials Split Grid

manufacturing overhead are the only three, which will be further analyzed into the two component variances, as discussed previously in this chapter.

Direct Material Variances

All of the materials used to produce a baseball will be considered together as a unit of direct material (cork, rubber, leather, string/yarn) to simplify the example and the explanations, and we will use nine square inches as the standard quantity of direct materials for each baseball.

From the figure, we can see that the actual quantity of direct material used in the period to produce and sell 32,000 baseballs was 289,000 square inches. During the same month, the purchasing department ordered 450,000 square inches of leather for less than the standard price.

When the amount of direct material used is different from the amount of direct material ordered, the spending variance grid will use two different actual quantities: actual quantity used, and actual quantity purchased. The reasons for using the two different actual quantities are that the activity of purchasing materials is separate from the activity of using materials, each of which are managed by different managers, and materials can be inventoried and stored from one period to the next.

Figure 5.8 illustrates the direct materials variance analysis using the spending variance analysis grid when the amount of raw materials purchased differs from the amount of raw materials used in production in the month of May. The analysis shows an unfavorable direct materials quantity variance of $416.67, while showing an unfavorable direct materials price variance of $9,394.46. Remember, the actual quantity used was 289,000 square inches, while the actual quantity purchased was 450,000. The difference in the actual quantities precludes this format of the variance analysis from explaining the current direct materials spending variance between the flexible forecast and the actual results.

Figure 5.9 presents the spending variance analysis grid for direct materials when the amount of direct materials purchased and the amount of direct materials used are the same. The format of the spending variance grid can also be simplified when the actual quantity used is the same as the

Beaver Baseball
Direct Materials Spending Variance Grid
Quantity Used = Quantity Purchased

Flexible Forecast	Actual Units	×	SQ/unit	×	SP/unit	=				
	32,000	×	9	×	$0.42	=	$120,000.00	a		
			288,000	×	$0.42					
Quantity Variance			AQ/Used	×	SP/unit	=				
			289,000	×	$0.42	=	$120,416.67	b		
Price Variance								a-b	($416.67) Unfavorable	Quantity Variance (unfavorable)/favorable
Actual Results			AQ-Purchased	×	AP/unit	=				
			289,000	×	$0.44	=	$126,450.00	c		
								b-c	($6,033.33) Unfavorable	Price Variance (unfavorable)/favorable
								a-c	($6,450.00) Unfavorable	Spending Variance (unfavorable)/favorable

SQ/unit standardized amount of material required to make one unit of product
SQ the total standard amount of material required to make all of the actual units produced
SP/unit standardized amount that should be paid for the material to make one unit of product
AQ-Used actual quantity of material used to make all of the actual units produced
AQ-Purchased actual quantity of material purchased during the accounting period
AP/unit actual price paid per unit of material purchased during the period
AP actual price paid for the material purchased during the period

Fig. 5.8 Beaver Baseball Direct Materials Spending Variance Grid

actual quantity purchased. Because different actual quantities are used in the spending variance analysis grid, the current period spending variance for direct materials cannot be fully explained in this format. To fully explain the direct materials spending variance for the current period, the actual quantity used can be used to calculate the direct materials price variance.

From the direct materials spending variance analysis grid, the quantity and price variance formulas can be identified. For the direct materials quantity variance, the standard price per unit is held constant, while subtracting the actual quantity used from the standard quantity.

Direct Materials Quantity Variance = SP/unit (SQ – AQ)
Direct Materials Quantity Variance = $.4167 (288,000 sq.in. – 289,000 sq.in.)

For the direct materials price variance, the actual quantity purchased is held constant, while subtracting the actual price paid per unit from the standard price.

Direct Materials Price Variance = AQ (SP/unit – AP/unit)
Direct Materials Price Variance = 450,000 sq in. ($0.42– $0.4375)

Direct Labor Variances

The direct labor efficiency variance evaluates the number of labor hours used to generate the actual unit volume compared to the standard number of labor hours that should have been used for the actual unit volume.

Beaver Baseball
Direct Labor Spending Variance Grid

	Standard Quantity				Standard Price					
Flexible Budget	Actual Units	×	SQ/unit	×	SP/unit	=				
	32,000		0.05	×	$18.00	=	$28,800.00	a		
	1,600									
Efficiency Variance			AQ	×	SP/unit	=				
Rate Variance			1,650	×	$18.00	=	$29,700.00	b		
								a-b	($900.00) unfavorable	Efficiency Variance (unfavorable)/favorable
Actual Results			AQ	×	AP/unit	=				
			1,650	×	$17.27	=	$28,500.00	c		
								b-c	($1,200.00) favorable	Rate Variance (unfavorable)/favorable
								a-c	($300.00) favorable	Total Spending Variance (unfavorable)/favorable

SQ/unit	standardized amount (time) of labor hours required to make one unit of product
SQ	the total standard amount (time) of labor hours required to make all of the actual units produced
SP/unit	standardized amount (wage rate) that should be paid for the labor hours to make one unit of product
AQ-Used	actual quantity (time) of labor hours used to make all of the actual units produced
AQ-Purchased	actual quantity (time) of labor hours purchased during the accounting Period
AP/unit	actual price paid (wage rate)per unit of direct labor hours purchased during the period
AP	actual price paid (wage rate) for the direct labor hours purchased during the period

Fig. 5.9 Beaver Baseball Direct Labor Spending Variance Grid

Figure 5.10 illustrates the direct labor variance analysis using the spending variance analysis grid. The employees worked 1,650 hours compared to the 1,600 hours that should have been worked to produce 32,000 baseballs.

The direct labor rate variance evaluates the amount paid to the employees to generate the actual unit volume compared to the amount that should have been paid for the actual unit volume. The actual payroll amount for the month was $28,500 for the 1,650 hours worked and a total of $29,700 should have been paid for the same 1,650 hours.

Beaver Baseball
Variable Manufacturing Overhead Spending Variance Grid

Flexible Forecast	Actual Volume		SQ/unit	×	SP/unit	=			
	32,000	×	0.05	×	$3.50	=	$5,600.00		
	1,600								
VOH Efficiency Variance			AQ	×	SP/unit	=			
			1,650	×	$3.50	=	$5,775.00		
VOH Rate Variance								($175.00) unfavorable	Efficiency Variance (unfavorable)/favorable
Actual Results			AQ	×	AP	=			
			1,650	×	$3.64	=	$6,000.00		
								($225.00) unfavorable	Rate Variance (unfavorable)/favorable
								($400.00) unfavorable	Total Spending Variance (unfavorable)/favorable

Fig. 5.10 Beaver Baseball Variable MOH Spending Variance Grid

From the direct labor spending variance grid, the efficiency and rate variance formulas can be identified. For the direct labor efficiency variance, the standard price per unit is held constant while subtracting the actual quantity of labor hours from the standard number of direct labor hours.

Direct Labor Efficiency Variance = SP/unit (SQ – AQ)
Direct Labor Efficiency Variance = $18.00 (1,600 DLH – 1,650 DLH)

For the direct labor rate variance, the actual quantity of labor hours is held constant, while the actual wage rate per hour is subtracted from the standard wage rate.

Direct Labor Rate Variance = AQ/unit (SP/unit – AP/unit)
Direct Labor Rate Variance = 1,650 DLH ($18.00 – $17.27)

Variable Manufacturing Overhead Variances

Figure 5.11 presents the spending variance analysis grid for variable manufacturing overhead. The variable overhead efficiency variance evaluates the allocation base, in this case direct labor hours (DLH). Beaver Baseball incurred 1,650 DLH during the month when 1,600 DLH should have been incurred. The firm actually paid $6,000 for the variable overhead costs and they should have allocated $5,775 of VOH during the month.

Remember, the VOH efficiency and rate variances evaluate the allocation base and the predetermined overhead rate, respectively.

From the variable overhead spending variance grid, the efficiency and rate variance formulas can be identified. For the variable overhead efficiency variance, the standard price per direct labor hour (POR) is held constant, while the actual quantity of direct labor hours is subtracted from the standard quantity of direct labor hours.

Variable Manufacturing Overhead Efficiency Variance = SP/unit (SQ – AQ)
Variable Manufacturing Overhead Efficiency Variance = $3.50 (1,600 DLH – 1,650 DLH)

Beaver Baseball Direct Materials Journal Entries
Quantity Used = Quantity Purchased

	Debit	Credit
Work In Process Inventory	$120,000.00	
Direct Materials Quantity Variance	$416.67	
Raw Materials Inventory		$120,416.67
Raw Materials Inventory	$120,416.67	
Direct Materials Price Variance	$6,033.33	
Accounts Payable		$126,450.00

Fig. 5.11 Beaver Baseball Direct Materials Journal Entries

For the variable overhead rate variance, the actual quantity of direct labor hours is held constant, while the actual wage rate per hour is subtracted from the standard wage rate per hour.

Variable Manufacturing Overhead Rate Variance = AQ (SP/unit – AP/unit)
Variable Manufacturing Overhead Rate Variance = 1,650 DLH ($3.50 – $3.64)

Fixed Manufacturing Overhead Variances

The fixed manufacturing overhead efficiency and rate variances are used to evaluate the allocation base and predetermined overhead rate for the fixed manufacturing overhead. These can be significant costs to the firm, but for our purposes we'll leave the fixed overhead variances to be examined in future managerial or cost accounting courses.

Journal Entries for Variances

The journal entries associated with the direct materials, direct labor, and variable overhead variances are based on the standard costing system to account for product costs. The standard costing system records the standard cost of the direct materials, direct labor, and variable overhead, and then the variances are recorded to capture the difference between what should have been paid for the product inputs and the actual cost incurred for those inputs.

For any of the direct materials, direct labor, or variable overhead variances, the unfavorable variance is recorded as a debit and the unfavorable variance is recorded as a credit.

	Debit	Credit
Direct materials quantity variance	Unfavorable	Favorable
Direct materials price variance	Unfavorable	Favorable
Direct labor efficiency variance	Unfavorable	Favorable
Direct labor rate variance	Unfavorable	Favorable
Variable overhead efficiency variance	Unfavorable	Favorable
Variable overhead rate variance	Unfavorable	Favorable

The spending variances are variances in expenses, specifically the variable product costs, and if a spending variance (or one of the component variances) is unfavorable, then the amount incurred for a specific cost is greater than the amount that should have been incurred; the higher expense thus has the effect of lowering net operating income and the unfavorable variance is, in effect, adding more expense to the standard cost, so the actual cost is reflected in the financial statements. This is accomplished by recording the unfavorable variance as a debit, which also balances the associated journal entry.

The opposite occurs with favorable variances. A favorable variance occurs when the actual costs are less than the costs that should have been incurred. A favorable variance, in effect, reduces the standard cost to reflect the lower actual costs. The favorable variance is recorded as a credit to reduce the standard cost, so the lower actual cost is reflected in the financial statements.

The following figures show both the diagrams and the journal entries for the direct materials and direct labor for Beaver Baseball. The spending variance grids have been simplified by showing only the amounts for each position on the grid that allow us to see both the grid and the journal entries for each spending variance.

Beaver Baseball
Direct Labor Journal Entry

Work In Process Inventory	$28,800.00	
Direct Labor Efficiency Variance	$900.00	
Direct Labor Rate Variance		$1,200.00
Wages Payable		$28,500.00

Fig. 5.12 Beaver Baseball Direct Labor Journal Entry

EVALUATION

6

How do we evaluate our performance?

LEARNING OBJECTIVES

LO1: Explain quality performance measurement and calculate the cost of quality.

LO2: Explain and identify key performance indicators.

LO3: Explain and identify internal and external benchmarks.

LO4: Explain and identify operating segments, cost centers, revenue centers, profit centers, and investment centers.

LO5: Explain and calculate segment margin.

LO6: Explain and identify traceable fixed costs and common fixed costs.

LO7: Explain and identify the components of a balance scorecard.

THE QUESTIONS WE TRY TO ANSWER

- How can we know if a firm, division, store, product line, or activity is performing well?
- Are the resources of the firm being used effectively and efficiently?

In this chapter, we address the issue of performance evaluation. We will look at issues related to improvement and quality, strategy, and operational activities. The aim is to learn how to evaluate performance using measures such as cost of quality, profitability, return on investment, residual income, and the balanced scorecard.

Quality Performance Measurement Using Cost of Quality

Quality is an ever-present issue for both manufacturing and service firms. This is because firms face quality issues whether they are working to maintain a minimum standard of quality required to compete in a price-sensitive market or they are working to create a high standard of quality to differentiate their product and be able to charge a higher price. A firm can also face quality issues because of actions taken by external regulatory groups or agencies.

In the 1950s, Edward Deming championed the quality movement in an effort to not only improve quality but also to reduce costs. Dr. Deming found many Japanese firms were eager to improve the quality of their products and have since enjoyed tremendous market success. Dr. Deming's efforts launched what is commonly known as the total quality movement. A number of frameworks have been developed to implement total quality principles such as Total Quality Management (TQM) and Six Sigma. The objective of these frameworks is to measure the firm's quality improvement and cost reduction efforts. In this chapter, we will focus on one aspect of TQM: quality measurement and in particular the measurement of cost of quality.

Managerial accounting information plays a critically important role in a firm's efforts to measure the cost of quality so that it can improve business processes and strategic decision making. The information gathered by the accounting and information systems in a firm is the basis for much of the analyses decision makers need to make well-informed decisions. The management accountant combines accounting information with knowledge of business operations to create valuable analyses that decision makers can use to plan, evaluate, and make necessary business decisions at both the tactical and strategic levels.

Cost of Quality

Cost of quality is a tool used to evaluate the amount a firm spends on preventing poor quality with the amount that is lost due to poor quality. To prevent poor quality requires a firm to invest in prevention and appraisal processes to avoid or detect poor quality goods or services (see Fig. 6.1).

Prevention costs—avoid poor quality goods or services
- Employee training
- Improved materials
- Preventive maintenance

Appraisal costs—detect poor quality goods or services
- Inspection throughout production
- Inspection of final product
- Product testing

If poor quality goods or services are detected either during the manufacturing or service process or after the product or service has been delivered, the firm incurs additional costs and potentially the loss of future potential revenues.

Internal failure costs—avoid poor quality goods or services *before* delivery to customers
- Production loss caused by downtime
- Rejected product units

External failure costs—incurred *after* defective product is delivered
- Lost profits from lost customers
- Warranty costs
- Service costs at customer sites
- Sales returns due to quality problems

This information is then combined to construct a cost of quality report, which identifies, categorizes, and quantifies all the costs it incurs relating to quality. Using this information, management accountants can calculate the percentage of total costs of quality that are incurred in each cost category. Managers can then use the report for evaluating business operations.

	Costs Incurred	COQ	%
Prevention costs			
None			
Appraisal costs			
Inspection of raw materials	$51,000	$51,000	23%
Internal failure costs			
Rework and spoilage	$65,000	$65,000	29%
External failur costs			
Lost profits	$92,000		
Warranty costs	$16,000	$108,000	48%
Total Cost of Quality	$224,000		

Fig. 6.1 Cost of Quality Report

Key Performance Indicators

Key performance indicators (KPIs) are measurable activities, actions, or events that relate to the performance of an organization. The critical attribute for any KPI is a direct correlation of the measure to the ultimate results a firm may experience. Each firm develops its own KPIs based on its business model, the products and services it offers, the activities and processes in which it engages, and other factors related to their operations as well as to their industry. A manufacturer of heavy machinery is very different from a large retail operation, and the KPIs each firm uses must reflect the industry in which it competes as well as its own unique operations.

STRATEGY AND GOALS TO KEY PERFORMANCE INDICATORS

As we discuss key performance indicators, we need some perspective of how firms use KPIs. The owners (or board of directors) and managers are responsible for setting the strategic objectives of a firm as well as for making any changes to the strategic objectives as needed. The chosen strategic objectives will require the firm to develop, enhance, and maximize a set of core strategies that directly relate to the firm's specific strategic objectives. The firm should identify a set of critical success factors to execute its core strategies, enabling it to continue to meet its strategic objectives. The firm must identify its key performance indicators to provide a way to measure and monitor how well and how effectively the activities in the firm are related to the critical success factors that support the core strategies that are designed to meet the firm's strategic objectives.

Strategic Objectives→Core Strategies→Critical Success Factors→Key Performance Indicators

STRATEGIC OBJECTIVES

A strategic objective is a main, central, or overarching objective an organization has chosen to pursue. Strategic objectives might include market share targets, research and development goals, product quality, customer satisfaction levels, geographic reach, or product breadth. Strategic objectives communicate the direction in which the firm and its employees desire to move.

CORE STRATEGIES

Core strategies are the particular strengths, methods, or areas the firm and its employees have or can develop that drive progress toward achieving a strategic objective. The core strategies are the areas in which the firm has or will develop a competitive advantage in the marketplace.

CRITICAL SUCCESS FACTORS

Critical success factors are the activities a core strategy requires for success in that strategy. The critical success factors must be measurable to be able to determine whether a core strategy is working.

LEADING AND LAGGING INDICATORS

Key performance indicators are usually grouped as either leading indicators or lagging indicators. Lagging indicators are "output" oriented and show how the business has performed in the past, while leading indicators are "input" oriented and are thus focused on what takes place before a product or service is sold. Most financial indicators such as revenue growth, net operating income, and return on assets are lagging indicators as they are the result of the activities of the firm. Leading indicators are about business processes, which are directly correlated to the production and delivery of a firm's products or services. Because leading indicators are predictive, they do not guarantee the success of products or services. A lagging indicator without a leading indicator will give no indication as to how a good financial result can be achieved and provide no early warnings about progress toward strategic goals. Thus, a combination of leading and lagging indicators is necessary for a firm to get a good understanding of its business performance.

BENCHMARKING

Benchmarking is a method of evaluating an organization's current performance by comparing current performance to its own prior performance, the performance of other firms, industry standards or averages, or predetermined performance standards or targets. The objective of benchmarking is to evaluate current performance using a consistent point of reference. The benchmarks used for comparison can come from both internal and external sources such as mission or vision statements, customer and client surveys, performance metrics, SWOT (strength, weaknesses, opportunities, threats) analyses, industry standards, target standards or metrics, previous performance levels, and many others.

External Benchmarking

External benchmarking entails using a standard or target generated outside the enterprise. Many external benchmarking standards can be used: customer and client survey information, industry standards, or averages.

The limitations of external benchmarking include using abstract benchmarks, such as those derived from surveys or industry averages, or using industry performance metrics that don't necessarily apply to the specific firm's operations or situation. Surveys and averages can contain results that aren't comparable to the firm's activities or situation.

The benefits of external benchmarking are derived from comparing the firm's activity and performance to measurements that come from outside the firm. Information from outside the firm has the potential of providing a view of what might be possible for the firm to achieve, especially measurements recognized as those that are best practices. These measurements can show the results from the most effective performance, which allows a firm to compare itself to the highest known performance levels.

Internal or Historical Benchmarking

Internal and historical benchmarking use internally generated information from prior periods to create benchmarks for evaluating current performance. Internal benchmarking can provide valuable insights, revealing results of previous operational decisions, the effect of process changes, or other internal decisions.

The limitation of internal benchmarks is its inability to include potential performance results, which inhibit the firm to push current and future performance past prior performance. If prior performance has been poor, then comparing current performance to such a benchmark will not provide any information or insight of value because the benchmark communicates only what the firm has already achieved and not what it could potentially achieve.

The benefits of internal benchmarking include identifying historical performance and measuring the effect of changes and modifications the firm has made to its processes and activities. The historical nature of internal benchmarking also provides the opportunity to identify trends in performance over long periods of time.

When both external and internal benchmarking are used together, firms can evaluate internal improvements as well as how current performance compares to other firms in its industry.

Beaver Pizza Segment Reporting

	Consolidated Beaver Pizza		=	East Campus		+	North Campus	
Revenue	$1,000,000	100%		$400,000	100%		$600,000	100%
Variable Costs	$220,000	22%		$100,000	25%		$120,000	20%
Contribution Margin	$780,000	78%		$300,000	75%		$480,000	80%
Fixed Costs–Traceable	$670,000	67%		$280,000	70%		$390,000	65%
Segment Margin	$110,000	11%		$20,000	5%		$90,000	15%
Fixed Costs–Common	$60,000	6%		××			××	
Net Operating Income	$50,000	5%						

	Consolidated		East Campus		North Campus	
Profitability	$50,000 / $1,000,000	5.0%	$20,000 / $400,000	5.0%	$90,000 / $600,000	15.0%

Fig. 6.2 Beaver Pizza Profitability Report

PROFITABILITY

Profitability is a measurement to evaluate the ongoing operations of a firm. Profitability can be expressed in a variety of terms and for our work in this textbook, we'll use net profit margin as our measurement of profitability. The net profit margin is a financial statement ratio and presented as follows:

$$\text{Net Profit Margin} = \frac{\text{Net Income}}{\text{Total Net Revenue}}$$

As we move forward, we will refer to net profit margin simply as profitability.

The income statement reports the revenues and expenses of an activity, or firm, for a given period of time. The goal is to maximize revenues and minimize expenses to generate as much net income as possible. The level with responsibility for the ongoing operations of a firm is sometimes referred to as a profit center. Another way to describe the responsibility over both revenues and expenses of an activity is to have income statement responsibility, or profit and loss responsibility.

A manager with income statement responsibility of a profit center can influence both the revenue and expenses. He or she can influence the revenues by deciding what to sell, determining the selling price, and choosing any type of discounting, such as volume discounts, coupons, etc. He or she can influence the expenses by deciding who the firm employs and the expenses it incurs.

With control over revenue and expenses, a manager with income statement responsibility can influence its net income. One effective way to evaluate net income is to measure net income in terms that can be easily expressed and effectively compared to past performance or other benchmarks. The net income profit margin or profitability calculation provides a percentage that is easily expressed and can be compared to an internal historical benchmark, such as profitability in prior periods, and an external benchmark, such as an industry standard for profitability.

Figure 6.3 presents the profitability calculations for Beaver Pizza. Profitability is calculated for both the business as a consolidated entity as well as each of the operating segments. At the consolidated level, we use net operating income as our measure of profit. At the segment level, we use segment margin as our measure of segment profit. The calculation of consolidated profitability includes the common fixed costs that provide benefits to both segments and the consolidated common fixed costs are included in total at the consolidated level of the business.

RETURN ON INVESTMENT

Return on investment (ROI) is another way to monitor and evaluate the performance of a business or its individual segments. There are two commonly used ROI ratios:

$$\text{When evaluating new investments ROI} = \frac{\text{Net Income}}{\text{Investment}}$$

$$\text{When evaluating continuing operations ROI} = \frac{\text{Net Operating Income}}{\text{Average Operating Assets}}$$

The ROI ratio evaluates the amount of net operating income generated from the assets employed in a business or an operating segment. Net operating income reflects the profit an organization has generated during a given period. Average operating assets include cash, accounts receivable, inventory, plant and equipment, and other productive assets.

In large organizations, responsibility for both operations and investments is referred to as an investment center. Responsibility for both the operations and the investment in an activity can also be

Beaver Pizza Segment Reporting

	Consolidated Beaver Pizza	=	East Campus	+	North Campus	
Revenue	$1,000,000	100%	$400,000	100%	$600,000	100%
VC	$220,000	22%	$100,000	25%	$120,000	20%
CM	$780,000	78%	$300,000	75%	$480,000	80%
FC-Traceable	$670,000	67%	$280,000	70%	$390,000	65%
SM	$110,000	11%	$20,000	5%	$90,000	15%
FC-Common	$60,000	6%	xx		xx	
NOI	$50,000	5%				
Average Operating Assets	$1,400,000		$600,000		$750,000	

Return on Investment

Net Operating Income / Average Operating Assets

	Consolidated		East Campus		North Campus	
Return on Investment	$50,000 / $1,400,000	3.6%	$20,000 / $600,000	3.3%	$90,000 / $750,000	12.0%

Fig. 6.3 Beaver Pizza ROI Report

described as balance sheet responsibility. A manager with balance sheet responsibility can influence the revenues, expenses, assets, and liabilities of an investment center. In addition to influencing profitability, he or she can influence the amount invested in the assets of the activity, and most likely the liabilities as well. In our discussion of ROI, we will focus on the revenues, expenses, and assets and disregard the issues of liabilities at this point. We will include liabilities, and the effect of liabilities, when we address the issue of creating value in Chapter 10.

With control over both the income statement and the balance sheet of an activity, any evaluation tool should include measures from both statements. For our purposes, we use ROI as an evaluation tool because ROI includes the net income measure from the income statement and the investment/average operating assets measure from the balance sheet. The ROI calculation provides a percentage that is easily expressed and effectively compared to past performance or other benchmarks.

Figure 6.4 presents the ROI calculation for Beaver Pizza for both the consolidated business as well as for each operating segment. In addition to the net operating income presented, we need to

Residual Income Formula

		Firm Performance		Investment in Activity		Minimum Performance Level
Residual Income	=	Operating Income	–	[Total Operating Assets	*	Required Rate of Return]

Fig. 6.4 Residual Income Formula

Beaver Pizza Segment Reporting

	Consolidated Beaver Pizza		=	East Campus		+	North Campus	
Revenue	$1,000,000	100%		$400,000	100%		$600,000	100%
Variable Costs	$220,000	22%		$100,000	25%		$120,000	20%
Contribution Margin	$780,000	78%		$300,000	75%		$480,000	80%
Fixed Costs–Traceable	$670,000	67%		$280,000	70%		$390,000	65%
Segment Margin	$110,000	11%		$20,000	5%		$90,000	15%
Fixed Costs–Common	$60,000	6%		xx			xx	
Net Operating Income	$50,000	5%						
Average Operating Assets	$1,400,000			$600,000			$750,000	
Required Rate of Return	15.0%			15.0%			15.0%	

Residual Income

Net Operating Income – (Average Operating Assets × Required Rate of Return)

$50,000 – [$1,400,000 × 15.0%]

Residual Income ($160,000)

Fig. 6.5 Beaver Pizza RI Report

know the average operating assets of the consolidated business and for each operating segment. In the example, the average operating assets are given. In some cases, the beginning and ending amounts of operating assets might be given, and the average must be calculated by adding the beginning and ending operating assets together and dividing the total by two.

RESIDUAL INCOME

Residual income (RI) is a method of evaluating the performance of a business or an operating segment by comparing performance to a minimum standard of required performance. The firm's performance is net income for the period; the minimum standard of required performance is expressed as a minimum required rate of return on the assets employed for the activity. Residual income is calculated using the following formula:

Residual income can be viewed as extra or excess profit from an activity that indicates the activity is creating extra or excess value to the firm and its shareholders, in addition to the minimum required rate of return.

Figure 6.6 presents the residual income calculation for the consolidated results of Beaver Pizza. By multiplying the average operating assets required rate of return, we are calculating a minimum amount of income that the owners and managers require for use of the money invested in the business. Residual income is an amount of operating income that is generated over the required return on the assets.

280-10-50-1

An operating segment is a component of a public entity that has all of the following characteristics:

a. It engages in business activities from which it may earn revenues and incur expenses (including revenues and expenses relating to transactions with other components of the same public entity).

b. Its operating results are regularly reviewed by the public entity's chief operating decision maker to make decisions about resources to be allocated to the segment and assess its performance.

c. Its discrete financial information is available.

Exhibit 6.1 GAAP Definition—Segment
Source: https://www.sec.gov/Archives/edgar/data/1137204/000143209311000133/filename1.htm

SEGMENTS

IFRS 8.2

An operating segment is a component of an entity:

- that engages in business activities from which it may earn revenues and incur expenses (including revenues and expenses relating to transactions with other components of the same entity)
- whose operating results are reviewed regularly by the entity's chief operating decision maker to make decisions about resources to be allocated to the segment and assess its performance and
- for which discrete financial information is available.

Exhibit 6.2 IFRS Definition–Segment
Source: https://www.sec.gov/Archives/edgar/data/1137204/000143209311000133/filename1.htm

GAAP and IFRS Segment Reporting

Both GAAP and IFRS require some level of segment reporting as part of the additional disclosures found in the notes to the financial statements. These additional segment disclosures add information about individual segments of a consolidated group based on minimum thresholds of assets and income. The following is the GAAP definition of a segment:

The following is the IFRS definition of a segment:

Despite the differences and nuances between the two definitions, the intent of both is to provide some level of segmented information to the external financial statement user that gives the user some insight into how the company views and manages its operations. While the segment disclosures increase the amount of information available to external users, the disclosures still allow for a significant amount of aggregation, which makes the disclosures difficult for internal users to make forward-looking decisions.

The following illustrations come from the Walt Disney Company's form 10-k, as filed with the United States Securities and Exchange Commission in 2016. Figure 6.9 depicts the operating segments reported by the Walt Disney Company in their December 31, 2016 Form 10-k. Figure 6.10 lists all 63 subsidiaries owned, wholly or in part, by the Walt Disney Company, as disclosed in their December 31, 2016 Form 10-k.

The Walt Disney Company
Reporting Segments

Media Networks	Parks and Resorts	Studio Entertainment	Consumer Products	Interactive

The Walt Disney Company, Form 10-K, December 31, 2016, page 70.

Exhibit 6.3 The Walt Disney Company Reporting Segments

Name of Subsidiary	Country of Incorporation
ABC Cable Networks Group	United States
ABC Enterprises, Inc.	United States
ABC Family Worldwide, Inc.	United States
ABC Holding Company, Inc.	United States
ABC Kids SPC1, Inc.	United States
ABC, Inc.	United States
American Broadcasting Companies, Inc.	United States
Buena Vista Home Entertainment, Inc.	United States
Buena Vista International, Inc.	United States
Buena Vista Pay Television, Inc.	United States
Buena Vista Television, LLC	United States
Buena Vista Theatrical Group, Ltd.	United States
Buena Vista Video On Demand	United States
Cable LT Holdings, Inc.	United States
Circle Location Services, Inc.	United States
Disholder 3, Inc.	United States
Disney Enterprises, Inc.	United States
Disney Online	United States
Disney Vacation Club Management Corp.	United States
Disney Vacation Development, Inc.	United States
Disney Worldwide Services, Inc.	United States
Disney/ABC International Television, Inc.	United States
EDL Corporation S.A.S.	France
EDL S.N.C. Corporation	United States
ESPN Classic, Inc.	United States
ESPN Enterprises, Inc.	United States
ESPN, Inc.	United States
ESPN Productions, Inc.	United States
Euro Disney Investments S.A.S.	France
Euro Disney Investments, Inc.	United States
Euro Disney S.A.S.	France
Hong Kong Disneyland Management Limited	Hong Kong
Imprint, Inc.	United States
International Family Entertainment, Inc.	United States
Jetix Europe Properties S.a.r.l.	Luxembourg
Lucasfilm Entertainment Company Ltd. LLC	United States
Lucasfilm Ltd. LLC	United States
Magical Cruise Company, Limited	United Kingdom
Maker Studios Holding	United States
Marvel Characters B.V.	Netherlands
Marvel Entertainment, LLC	United States
Marvel Studios, LLC	United States
MVL Film Finance LLC	United States

MVL International C.V.	Netherlands
Pixar	United States
Playdom, Inc.	United States
Shanghai International Theme Park Associated Facilities Limited	China
Shanghai International Theme Park Company Limited	China
Steamboat Ventures Asia, L.P.	United States
The Walt Disney Company (Japan) Ltd.	Japan
The Walt Disney Company (Southeast Asia) Pte Ltd.	Singapore
The Walt Disney Company Limited	United Kingdom
Touchstone Television Productions, LLC	United States
UTV Software Communications Limited	India
Walt Disney Parks & Resorts U.S., Inc.	United States
Walt Disney Pictures	United States
Walt Disney Pictures Productions, LLC	United States
Walt Disney Travel Co., Inc.	United States
Wedco Global Ventures One LP	United Kingdom
Wedco Global Ventures Two LP	United Kingdom
Wedco Global Ventures Three LP	United Kingdom
Wedco International Holdings, Inc.	United States
Wedco One (Luxembourg) S.a.r.l. Participations S.C.A.	Luxembourg

Exhibit 6.4 Disney Subsidiaries 10k 2015
Source: DIS Exhibit 21 Subsidiaries 10 3 2015. Copyright © by Disney.

Disney lists 63 subsidiaries, but its segment disclosure identifies only five (5) operating segments, which leads to a high level of aggregation. With 63 entities and five (5) operating segments, each segment averages 12.6 entities, maintaining significant aggregation even at the operating segment level. For example, Walt Disney Parks & Resorts U.S., Inc. most likely includes Disneyland and California Adventure parks in California as well as The Magic Kingdom EPCOT, Disney's Hollywood Studios, Disney's Animal Kingdom, Pandora, Disney's Typhoon Lagoon, and Disney's Blizzard Beach in Florida. These are most likely aggregated with the other Disney parks in France, Hong Kong, China, and Japan.

Segments are individual operating divisions, units, departments, service lines, or subsidiaries of a combined or consolidated group of businesses that sell products or provide services to outside customers and can report their own financial statements. Publicly traded companies, and many privately held firms, operate multiple businesses, multiple locations, multiple service lines, or other operating entities that are combined and consolidated for financial reporting purposes.

For financial reporting purposes, GAAP requires a firm to report its performance according to the operating segments to the firm that manages its operations. In the consolidation process, the 63 legal entities are grouped into five operating segments, plus the corporate parent.

Figure 6.11 is the GAAP required segment disclosure filed by the Walt Disney Company in their Form 10-K. The Walt Disney Company manages its operations using five operating segments (Media Networks, Parks and Resorts, Studio Entertainment, Consumer Products, and Interactive):

TABLE OF CONTENTS

Interactive

The Company creates and distributes branded entertainment and lifestyle content for interactive media platforms. The primary operations include the production and distribution of multi-platform games, the licensing of our properties for games and mobile devices, and the development of branded online services.

In June 2015, the Company announced the combination of its Consumer Products and Interactive segments into a single segment. The Company will begin reporting the financial results of the combined segment in fiscal 2016.

SEGMENT INFORMATION

The operating segments reported below are the segments of the Company for which separate financial information is available and for which segment results are evaluated regularly by the Chief Executive Officer in deciding how to allocate resources and in assessing performance.

Segment operating results reflect earnings before corporate and unallocated shared expenses, restructuring and impairment charges, other expense, interest income/(expense), income taxes and noncontrolling interests. Segment operating income includes equity in the income of investees. Corporate and unallocated shared expenses principally consist of corporate functions, executive management and certain unallocated administrative support functions.

Equity in the income of investees included in segment operating results is as follows:

	2015	2014	2013
Media Networks			
Cable Networks	$ **896**	$ 895	$ 788
Broadcasting	**(82)**	(39)	(46)
Parks and Resorts	—	(2)	—
Equity in the income of investees included in segment operating income	$ **814**	$ 854	$ 742

In fiscal 2013, the Company recorded a $55 million charge for our share of expense related to an equity redemption at Hulu LLC (Hulu Equity Redemption). This charge is recorded in Equity in the income of investees in the Consolidated Statement of Income but has been excluded from segment operating income. See Note 3 for further discussion of the transaction.

The following segment results include allocations of certain costs, including information technology, pension, legal and other shared services costs, which are allocated based on metrics designed to correlate with consumption. These allocations

Source: https://www.sec.gov/Archives/edgar/data/1001039/000100103915000255/fy2015_q4x10k.htm

are agreed-upon amounts between the businesses and may differ from amounts that would be negotiated in arm's length transactions. In addition, all significant intersegment transactions have been eliminated except that Studio Entertainment revenues and operating income include an allocation of Consumer Products and Interactive revenues, which is meant to reflect royalties on revenue generated by Consumer Products and Interactive on merchandise based on intellectual property from certain Studio Entertainment films.

	2015	2014	2013
Revenues			
Media Networks	$ 23,264	$ 21,152	$ 20,356
Parks and Resorts	16,162	15,099	14,087
Studio Entertainment			
Third parties	6,838	6,988	5,721
Intersegment	528	290	258
	7,366	7,278	5,979
Consumer Products			
Third parties	5,027	4,274	3,811
Intersegment	(528)	(289)	(256)
	4,499	3,985	3,555
Interactive			
Third parties	1,174	1,300	1,066
Intersegment	—	(1)	(2)
	1,174	1,299	1,064
Total consolidated revenues	$ 52,465	$ 48,813	$ 45,041
Segment operating income (loss)			
Media Networks	$ 7,793	$ 7,321	$ 6,818
Parks and Resorts	3,031	2,663	2,220
Studio Entertainment	1,973	1,549	661
Consumer Products	1,752	1,356	1,112
Interactive	132	116	(87)
Total segment operating income	$ 14,681	$ 13,005	$ 10,724
Reconciliation of segment operating income to income before income taxes			
Segment operating income	$ 14,681	$ 13,005	$ 10,724
Corporate and unallocated shared expenses	(643)	(611)	(531)
Restructuring and impairment charges	(53)	(140)	(214)
Other expense, net	—	(31)	(69)
Interest income/(expense), net	(117)	23	(235)
Hulu Equity Redemption charge	—	—	(55)
Income before income taxes	$ 13,868	$ 12,246	$ 9,620
Capital expenditures			
Media Networks			
Cable Networks	$ 127	$ 172	$ 176
Broadcasting	71	88	87
Parks and Resorts			
Domestic	1,457	1,184	1,140

	2015	2014	2013
International	2,147	1,504	970
Studio Entertainment	107	63	78
Consumer Products	76	43	45
Interactive	11	5	13
Corporate	269	252	287
Total capital expenditures	$ 4,265	$ 3,311	$ 2,796

	2015	2014	2013
Depreciation expense			
Media Networks	$ 245	$ 238	$ 238
Parks and Resorts			
Domestic	1,169	1,117	1,041
International	345	353	327
Studio Entertainment	55	48	54
Consumer Products	57	59	57
Interactive	12	10	20
Corporate	249	239	220
Total depreciation expense	$ 2,132	$ 2,064	$ 1,957
Amortization of intangible assets			
Media Networks	$ 21	$ 12	$ 13
Parks and Resorts	3	2	2
Studio Entertainment	84	88	107
Consumer Products	102	109	89
Interactive	12	13	24
Corporate	—	—	—
Total amortization of intangible assets	$ 222	$ 224	$ 235
Identifiable assets(1)			
Media Networks	$ 30,638	$ 29,566	
Parks and Resorts	25,510	23,297	
Studio Entertainment	15,334	15,162	
Consumer Products	7,591	7,526	
Interactive	2,087	2,199	
Corporate(2)	7,022	6,391	
Total consolidated assets	$ 88,182	$ 84,141	
Supplemental revenue data			
Affiliate Fees	$ 12,029	$ 10,632	$ 10,018
Advertising	8,499	8,094	8,006
Retail merchandise, food and beverage	5,986	5,598	5,185
Theme park admissions	5,483	5,114	4,704
Revenues			
United States and Canada	$ 40,320	$ 36,769	$ 34,021
Europe	6,507	6,505	6,181
Asia Pacific	3,958	3,930	3,333
Latin America and Other	1,680	1,609	1,506
	$ 52,465	$ 48,813	$ 45,041
Segment operating income			
United States and Canada	$ 10,820	$ 9,594	$ 7,871
Europe	1,964	1,581	1,361
Asia Pacific	1,365	1,342	1,016
Latin America and Other	532	488	476
	$ 14,681	$ 13,005	$ 10,724

		2015		2014
Long-lived assets(3)				
United States and Canada	$	53,976	$	52,909
Europe		8,254		8,733
Asia Pacific		6,817		5,084
Latin America and Other		182		217
	$	69,229	$	66,943

(1) Identifiable assets include amounts associated with equity method investments, goodwill and intangible assets. Equity method investments by segment are as follows:

		2015		2014
Media Networks	$	2,454	$	2,321
Parks and Resorts		9		28
Studio Entertainment		2		2
Consumer Products		1		1
Interactive		—		—
Corporate		17		124
	$	2,483	$	2,476

Goodwill and intangible assets by segment are as follows:

		2015		2014
Media Networks	$	18,186	$	18,270
Parks and Resorts		376		379
Studio Entertainment		8,538		8,679
Consumer Products		6,118		6,187
Interactive		1,650		1,670
Corporate		130		130
	$	34,998	$	35,315

(2) Primarily fixed assets, cash and cash equivalents, deferred tax assets and investments

(3) Long-lived assets are total assets less the following: current assets, long-term receivables, deferred taxes, financial investments and derivatives

2 ***Summary of Significant Accounting Policies***

Principles of Consolidation

The consolidated financial statements of the Company include the accounts of The Walt Disney Company and its majority-owned and controlled subsidiaries. Intercompany accounts and transactions have been eliminated in consolidation.

The Company enters into relationships or investments with other entities that may be a variable interest entity (VIE). A VIE is consolidated in the financial statements if the Company has the power to direct activities that most significantly impact the economic performance of the VIE and has the obligation to absorb losses or the right to receive benefits from the VIE that could potentially be significant to the VIE (as defined by ASC 810-10-25-38). Disneyland Paris, HKDL and Shanghai Disney Resort (collectively the International Theme Parks) are VIEs. Company subsidiaries (the Management Companies) have management agreements with the International Theme Parks, which provide the Management Companies, subject to certain protective rights of joint venture partners, with the ability to direct the day-to-day operating activities and the development of business strategies that we believe most significantly impact the economic performance of the International Theme Parks. In addition, the Management Companies receive management fees under these arrangements that we believe could be significant to the International Theme Parks. Therefore, the Company has consolidated the International Theme Parks in its financial statements.

Exhibit 6.6 Walt Disney Company Segment Disclosure 12-31-2015

This process of aggregation provides a view of the entire company while obscuring the operating results of individual entities or activities. An outside investor or creditor cannot compare the operating results of Disneyland in California to the operating results of Tokyo Disney because all of the Disney theme parks and resorts appear to be grouped together into the Parks and Resorts operating segment.

An outside investor or creditor may be concerned with how the Walt Disney Company performs as a whole, but such aggregated information is not useful to internal decision makers. Company directors and managers are responsible for allocating the capital throughout the various segments and entities within the Walt Disney Company, but to effectively allocate capital and resources, they need much more detailed, disaggregated, information.

This section will deal with individual operating segments that sell to outside customers and can report their own financial statements. If we were a manager inside the Walt Disney Company, we would not refer to the Parks and Resorts segment because the segment is highly aggregated, but we would need information from individual theme parks, hotels, or cruise ships. One of our purposes in working at such a detailed organizational level is to determine and evaluate the performance of each operating activity. By determining and evaluating the performance of each operating activity, such as each individual theme park in the Walt Disney Company (Disneyland, California Adventure, Downtown Disney, the Magic Kingdom, Epcot Center, Animal Kingdom, Hollywood Studios, Tokyo Disney, Shanghai Disney, Hong Kong Disneyland, Disneyland Paris), managers can more effectively allocate capital and resources to where they think the greatest benefits might be achieved.

Segment Reporting

Segment reporting is the reporting of multiple operating segments within a business.

In this section, we will be working with operating activities that are separate from each other such as different locations, different buildings and equipment, different service lines, and not just different legal entities. Later in the chapter we will examine department reporting, which is similar to the segment-reporting concept except it is an organization with a single location operating multiple departments that share some common resources like building space, utilities, etc.

Segment reporting communicates the performance of an organization by showing the performance of each individual segment and the organization as a whole. Reporting the organization as a whole along with individual segments is the result of disaggregating the organization's performance information. Owners and managers need specific, detailed information regarding specific, individual operating activities (no matter if they are called units, service lines, branches, divisions, subsidiaries, etc.). To facilitate segment reporting, we need to analyze the fixed costs and introduce the concept of segment margin.

Fixed Cost Analysis

The fixed costs of a firm create some complications and can cause some confusion in reporting segment activity and performance. The difficulty with fixed costs arises from the way the fixed costs are used to benefit more than one segment. When a segment has its own physical location, such as a separate branch, store, warehouse, or production facility, then the fixed costs of those specific locations are directly related to those facilities and the corresponding business activities.

If we think of fixed costs as those costs that represent land, building, equipment, or other assets or activities, we need to understand the relationship between the fixed cost and the operating segment. The process of identifying the relationship of fixed costs to operating segments is called fixed-cost analysis. To help us in this analysis, we must introduce two new terms to describe fixed costs: traceable fixed costs and common fixed costs.

Traceable Fixed Costs

Traceable fixed costs are also referred to as avoidable fixed costs. When working with operating segments we will use the term "traceable fixed costs." Traceable fixed costs are the fixed costs that are directly related to an operating segment, and they can be traced to the operating segment's physical location or to the segment's specific activities.

The land, building(s), and equipment physically located at the site of an operating segment are assets traceable to (i.e., attached to) the operating segment. If the segment were to be sold, then the land, buildings, and equipment at the segment's physical location, and the fixed costs associated with those assets, would also be sold so the new owners could continue to operate the segment.

Common Fixed Costs

Common fixed costs are also referred to as committed or unavoidable fixed costs. When working with operating segments we will use the term "common fixed costs." Common fixed costs are the fixed costs that are indirectly related to an operating segment and cannot be traced to an operating segment's physical location or solely to a segment's specific activities. The benefits of common fixed costs are shared among at least two segments.

If a segment is sold and a fixed cost remains, then that fixed cost represents assets or activities that are not directly related to the segment that was sold, and we classify that fixed cost as a common fixed cost. An important aspect of fixed cost analysis to remember is that at one level of an organization a specific fixed cost may be classified as traceable to a segment, but at the next level down in the organization some of those traceable fixed costs may become common fixed costs. The classification of a fixed cost as traceable or common is dependent on the degree to which the fixed cost is related to the operating activity, and that relationship can change depending on which level of the organization the fixed cost analysis is being performed.

Segment Margin

Separating fixed costs into traceable fixed costs and common fixed costs requires us to expand our analysis to accommodate the two types of fixed costs. The basic contribution margin format of the income statement must be expanded to show both traceable fixed costs and common fixed costs separately. The basic format and the expanded format of the contribution margin income statement are as follows:

Basic	Format Expanded Format
Revenue	Revenue
(Variable Costs)	(Variable Costs)
Contribution Margin	Contribution Margin
(Fixed Costs)	(Traceable Fixed Costs)
Net Operating Income	Segment Margin
	(Common Fixed Costs)
	Net Operating Income

The segment margin is calculated by subtracting the traceable fixed costs from the contribution margin of the operating segment. Each segment has its own revenue generated from its own sales, and each segment has its own variable cost for the products it produces. The revenues of a segment, minus the variable costs of a segment, equal the contribution margin of that segment. Then the segment's traceable fixed costs are subtracted from segment's contribution margin to generate the segment's margin.

Segment margin can be viewed as the net operating income for a segment. Segment margin is used to delineate the results of the operating segments from the net operating income, which is the result of the firm as a whole.

Figure 6.12 shows two levels of segment reporting for Beaver Pizza.

At the first (or top) level, Beaver Pizza is shown as a consolidated business in the first column, then its two segments in the next two columns, which represent the two operating pizza shops on the left half of the figure.

Each segment, the East Campus shop and the North Campus shop, reports its own revenues and its own variable costs, and its own contribution margin. The segment revenues and segment variable costs are added together for the consolidated revenue and consolidated variable costs. In this scenario, the revenue and variable costs of the two segments are the total revenue and variable costs for Beaver Pizza.

From the contribution margin of each segment, the traceable fixed costs of each segment are subtracted to generate the segment's margin. The segment margin from the two segments represents the total segment margin for all of Beaver Pizza.

The traceable fixed costs are the fixed costs for assets and activities that are directly related to specific operating segments. In the Beaver Pizza example, the traceable fixed costs consist of rent, property taxes, insurance, equipment, cars, and other items for each specific segment. Each segment is a different location so each segment has its own building, its own equipment, its own cars, etc. In this example, each segment is a different physical location, which helps us visualize the traceable fixed costs.

If Beaver Pizza were to sell the North Campus shop, the traceable fixed costs of $390,000 shown in the North Campus segment column would become the responsibility of the new owners as they continue to operate the pizza shop. We could say that the $390,000 of North Campus traceable fixed costs are attached to, or belong to, the North Campus shop. When the North Campus shop is sold, the new owners are purchasing the pizza ovens, the walk-in coolers and freezers, the preparation tables, the counters, the improvements, the delivery cars, and all the other assets of the North Campus shop so that they can continue to make and sell pizzas.

The right half of Figure 6.12 shows the second level of reporting. The North Campus reports its total activity by showing is two divisions or department—delivery and dine-in—that comprise all the activity of the North Campus shop. From the first level of reporting to the second level of reporting, the $390,000 of traceable fixed costs related to the North Campus shop must be

Beaver Pizza Segment Reporting

	Consolidated Beaver Pizza	=	East Campus	+	North Campus	
Revenue	$1,000,000	100%	$400,000	100%	$600,000	100%
VC	$220,000	22%	$100,000	25%	$120,000	20%
CM	$780,000	78%	$300,000	75%	$480,000	80%
FC-Traceable	$670,000	67%	$280,000	70%	$390,000	65%
SM	$110,000	11%	$20,000	5%	$90,000	15%
FC-Common	$60,000	6%	XX		XX	
NOI	$50,000	5%				

This is the process of disaggregating or separating into operating/ segmented units

Separating the traceable FC

	North Campus	=	Delivery	+	Dine-In	
Revenue	$600,000	100%	$250,000	100%	$350,000	100%
VC	$120,000	20%	$50,000	20%	$70,000	20%
CM	$480,000	80%	$200,000	80%	$280,000	80%
FC-Traceable	$310,000	52%	$160,000	64%	$150,000	43%
SM	$170,000	28%	$40,000	16%	$130,000	37%
FC-Common	$80,000	13%	XX		XX	
NOI	$90,000	15%				

Fig. 6.6 Segments—Beaver Pizza

separated into the traceable and common fixed costs when moving from the consolidated level of reporting to the North Campus segment level. At the second level, the $390,000 of originally traceable fixed costs are separated into $310,000 of traceable fixed costs related to the delivery and dine-in segments, while $80,000 is classified as common fixed costs at the North Campus segment level.

If we were to drive out to the North Campus shop, we would be able to find all the assets and activities that generate the $390,000 of fixed costs that are traceable to the North Campus shop. Once at the North Campus shop, we would be able to trace $160,000 of fixed costs to the delivery activity, and we would be able to trace $150,000 of fixed costs to the dine-in activity. We would also find that $80,000 of the fixed costs traceable to the North Campus shop are now classified as common fixed costs at the segment level because they relate to all of the activities at the North Campus shop but not directly to either the delivery activity or the dine-in activity.

The traceable fixed costs related to the delivery activity might include such things as delivery vehicles, warming bags, and lighted vehicle signs. We can also readily identify the traceable fixed costs related to the dine-in activity such as the dining booths, eating bars, chairs, stools, soda dispenser, lighting, décor, public bathrooms, flooring, and cash register.

We also find the common fixed costs that benefit both the delivery activity and the dine-in activity such as pizza ovens, walk-in coolers and freezers, preparation tables, and ventilation equipment, which are all required to make pizza, no matter whether the pizza is delivered to the customer or eaten at the shop.

The same approach to identifying fixed costs that we applied at the consolidated level of Beaver Pizza can be applied to classifying fixed costs at the North Campus segment level. If North Campus decided to stop delivering pizza, then the fixed costs related to delivering pizza would not be incurred. Beaver Pizza could sell the delivery vehicles and dispose of the lighted vehicle signs and delivery bags. The fixed costs traceable to delivery would be eliminated.

If the delivery activity was stopped, the common fixed costs at the North Campus shop would continue to be incurred. If North Campus stopped delivering pizzas, they would continue to need the pizza ovens, walk-in coolers and freezers, preparation tables, ventilation, and other equipment to continue making pizza for their dine-in customers.

Segment Decisions

Segment reporting also provides the performance information that can be used to evaluate a segment when deciding whether a segment should continue to be operated or sold. When evaluating whether to keep or sell a segment, its segment margin is the key piece of information. When a segment has a positive segment margin, then the segment is a profitable activity and the segment is providing money to help pay for the common fixed costs. In other words, the segment is providing excess cash after covering its own variable and fixed costs. If a segment has a negative segment margin, then the segment is unprofitable and not covering its own fixed costs and not providing any money to cover common fixed costs.

Balanced Scorecard

A balanced scorecard is a comprehensive tool that can be used to evaluate a firm's performance based on multiple criteria that include both financial and nonfinancial measurements. The idea is to help organization members align their activities with the strategies and goals of the firm. One of the great challenges in any organization is getting people to perform the work that relates directly toward strategic goals and objectives. If organization members do not know the firm's strategy or goals, then they cannot effectively work in a way that is in line with those strategies and goals; they must not only know and recognize the firm's strategies and goals, but they also must understand how their work and activities relate to those strategies and goals. If employees know the strategies and goals of the firm and if they are clear as to how their work and their activities relate to accomplishing those strategies and goals, then they have the ability and power to make conscious choices and expend their efforts in ways that best support the firm.

The balanced scorecard has four general areas, or perspectives, to evaluate current performance. The four areas or perspectives are financial, customer, learning and growth, and internal processes. For each area, a firm would have up to five specific items or metrics against which performance would be compared and evaluated. The following illustration depicts an example of a typical balanced scorecard.

For each goal or measurement listed, a benchmark or standard for that area will be identified and included. The performance for each goal will be entered into the balanced scorecard, then the actual performance will be compared to the benchmark or standard at regular intervals, such as quarterly or annual. The firm will work to identify areas of strength and weakness and to develop appropriate plans or goals for the future.

Some of the benchmarks in a balanced scorecard are based on leading indicators and some are based on lagging indicators. Financial metrics are commonly lagging indicators, providing feedback of the results of business activities. Customer metrics can be based on both leading and

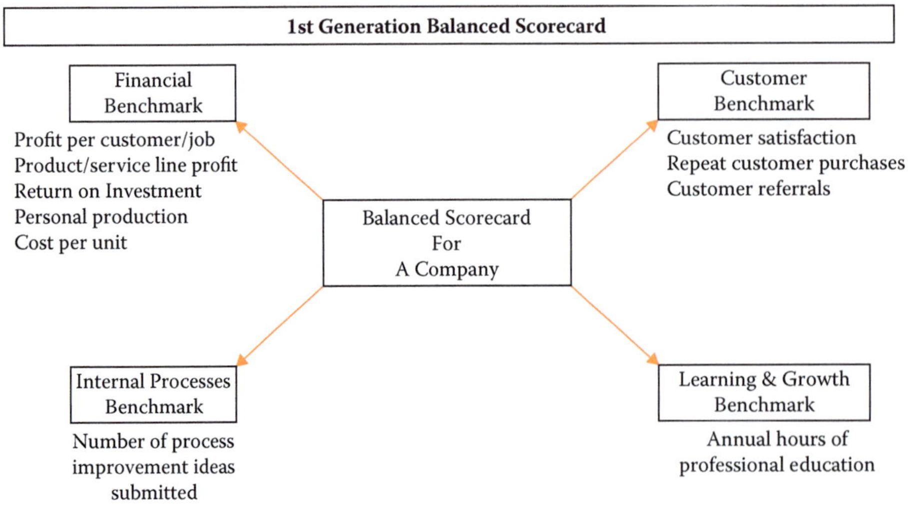

Fig. 6.7 Balanced Scorecard Example

lagging indicators. Customer satisfaction is a lagging indicator, but customer referrals are a leading indicator. The learning and growth metrics are all leading indicators because all the activities take place before goods and services are sold to customers. The internal processes metrics are generally all based on leading indicators because any work related to internal processes happens before productive work.

The balanced scorecard approach provides multiple areas and items in which a firm can be evaluated across a broad array of metrics. Often evaluations are based on a narrow, or even on a single, item or metric, such as revenue per customer or margin per product. Narrow evaluation criteria are often not representative of the actual performance of the firm.

7

SHORT-TERM DECISIONS

How do we best use our current capacity?

LEARNING OBJECTIVES

LO1: Describe and explain incremental costs and incremental benefits.

LO2: Describe and explain relevant and irrelevant costs and benefits.

LO3: Identify the various types of capacities within a firm.

LO4: Explain and describe a bottleneck/constrained resource.

LO5: Calculate the contribution margin for a bottleneck/constrained resource.

LO6: Calculate the net operating income of a special order.

LO7: Calculate the incremental net operating income to determine whether to sell at the split-off point or process further.

THE QUESTIONS WE TRY TO ANSWER

- Should we accept a special order from a customer asking for some customization at a discounted price?
- Should we sell our material or product now or continue to process it into something else?
- How can we manage a bottleneck most profitably?

In this chapter, we will discuss various decisions owners and managers must make as part of their ongoing operations. These decisions are usually evaluated in a relatively short time frame and are commonly referred to as short-term decisions. We believe that the general reference to short-term decisions can be misleading. Decisions such as those covered in this chapter (special orders, sell or process further, keep or close a department, and constrained resources) might address issues in a short time horizon; however, these decisions are not only driven by the time frame, they are also driven by the capacity of the firm and how they can use that capacity most effectively. The decisions we discuss in this chapter all relate to the effective use of current capacity and working within the current limits of capacity.

As we start to understand the decisions that are constrained by current capacity in this chapter, we will make a couple of important assumptions that facilitate our analyses. One important assumption we make in this chapter is that the firm is operating profitably; specifically, the firm is operating past the breakeven point. The other assumption is that the firm is operating at or below its productive capacity. These two assumptions will allow us to structure the analyses in more simplified formats, which will be easier to produce and use for decision making purposes.

As already stated, our focus in this chapter is on current capacity decisions, which include special orders, selling or processing further, keeping or closing a department, and managing a constrained resource or bottleneck. Special orders and selling or processing further are decisions that managers face on a regular basis and which are evaluated based on current cost and cash flow information. Keeping or closing a department is a decision that requires the analysis of the avoidable and unavoidable fixed costs and is evaluated on a department's segment margin. Managing a constrained resource is evaluated on the most productive use of the constrained resource.

WORKING WITHIN PHYSICAL CAPACITY

We have grouped special order, sell/process further, keep/close a department, and constrained resource decisions together as current capacity decisions for two predominant reasons. First, these types of decisions are made within a relatively short time horizon. A business might receive a special order from a current or prospective customer and the customer needs the order filled quickly, sometimes within only a few weeks. Second, these types of decisions are evaluated and made without the ability to change the total productive capacity of the firm. The decisions on special orders, to sell/process further, to keep/close a department, and managing a constrained resource do not affect the overall productive capacity of the firm. Therefore, we will refer to these decisions as either current capacity or short-term decisions.

Figure 7.1 presents the traditional CVP graph, which provides some context to better understand and identify how current capacity decisions not only include decisions that must be made within a short time, but also how current capacity decisions must be made within the current productive capacity, even though the effect of those decisions may extend over many years.

The diagram shows the fixed costs, total costs, and total revenue of an organization in a traditional CVP graph or diagram. The breakeven point is identified using the orange circle. The portion of the total revenue line circled in blue identifies the current level of activity of the firm as it relates to both its breakeven point and its current physical capacity. As we discussed in Chapter 3, the traditional CVP diagram can be described as a short-term marginal analysis tool. The graph is a short-term tool because it shows only the immediate, constant relationship between costs,

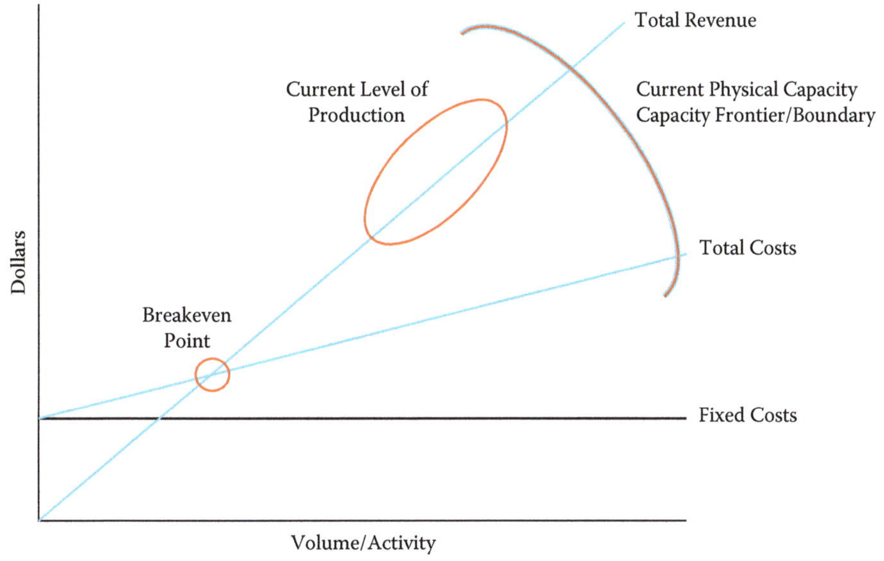

Fig. 7.1 Current Capacity Decisions

revenues, and volume, which is grounded in our assumption of linearity. The graph also depicts current capacity because the edges of the graph might be viewed as an implied boundary of the firm's current physical capacity.

All of the short-term decisions we discuss in this chapter assume that the firm is producing within the area identified by the blue circle, which is past the breakeven point and within the firm's current physical capacity. Current capacity decisions are short-term, marginal cost-based decisions because they must be made relatively quickly and because they are made in relation to the total use of the firm's productive capacity. By recognizing that current production is at a level past the breakeven point, we can exclude the fixed costs when evaluating special orders and sell/process further decisions. As we can assume that fixed costs have already been covered, we can structure our analysis of special orders and sell/process further decisions as variable costing analyses.

Capacities

A firm has many different types of capacities that it must manage. A firm may have capacity limits on product materials and inputs, financial resources, skilled or trained labor, and transportation of its products, regulations, and physical production. Although not an exhaustive list, these various capacities are a good representation of the kinds of limits or boundaries a firm might face.

Our work with capacity decisions in this textbook will focus on the physical production capacities. The physical productive capacities of a firm are relatively concrete capacities that allow us to visualize them as we work through the analysis and decision tools. Physical productive capacities relate to the production volume of a firm's land, buildings, equipment, employees, and other such tangible assets and resources of a firm. The concepts and tools with which we work when analyzing productive capacity issues can also be used when analyzing issues dealing with other types of capacities.

Bottlenecks

The current physical productive capacity of a firm is the actual total output that can be generated. Total physical output is the result of all the physical assets and resources of the firm, and the limit of total output is governed by the individual asset or resource that operates at the lowest volume. A bottleneck is the asset or resource or operation that generates the lowest level of volume within the total production process.

If marshmallow production requires three different operations, such as mixing, cutting, and packaging, then the slowest of the three operations is considered the bottleneck.

Figure 7.2 illustrates the various productive capacities in the marshmallow-making process.

The mixing operation can produce 20,000 pounds of marshmallows in a month, while the cutting operation can process 27,000 pounds and the packaging process can accommodate 25,000 pounds. In this example, the mixing operation can produce only 20,000 pounds, which becomes the limit, or bottleneck, of the complete marshmallow-making process, even though the cutting and packaging operations can both handle more than 20,000 pounds each month. The mixing operation is the bottleneck.

Marshmallow Monthly Capacity			
	Mixing Process	Cutting Process	Packaging Process
Machine Count	Two machines	Three machines	Five machines
Capacity per Machine	10, 000 pounds/machine	9,000 pounds/machine	5,000 pounds/machine
Total Capacity	**20,000 total pounds**	27,000 total pounds	25,000 total pounds

Fig. 7.2 Bottleneck within Operations Example

Bottlenecks, occur because of a limitation of one or more of the inputs or processes of a product or service. Remember, the inputs include the three basic product costs of direct materials, direct labor, and manufacturing overhead. One or more of the direct materials may be in short supply, which will limit total production. The firm may need employees with specialized training or skills that are either difficult to find or costly to develop, and a lack of these employees could limit overall production. Manufacturing overhead consists of the indirect costs of manufacturing for resources such as land, building, and equipment, and if the firm does not have enough land, building, or equipment, then overall production could be limited.

Special Orders

Special orders are orders from either current customers or prospective customers, where the customer requests specific modifications or some type of customization to the product along with a discounted price. Special orders are often for a significant quantity. When a special order is received, the manager must evaluate the profitability of the special order and determine whether the special order should be accepted or rejected. Our analysis will be the potential net operating income generated by the special order.

When evaluating special orders, we will make a couple of assumptions to assist in our analysis:

1. The firm is operating past its breakeven point.
2. The firm is operating within its physical productive capacity.
3. The fixed costs have already been covered.

Once the fixed costs have been covered, the fixed costs become irrelevant to the decision of accepting or rejecting a special order because no matter whether we accept or reject the special order, the fixed costs have already been paid and won't change as a result of our decision regarding the special order.

Figure 7.3 illustrates a special order received from a customer requesting specific product modifications and a discounted price.

Ridgeline Backpacks
Special Order Analysis

Premium Daypay Unit Information

Sales Price per Unit	$175	100%
Direct Materials	$105.00	60.00%
Direct Labor	$15.58	8.90%
Manufacturing Overhead	$21.00	12.00%
Unit Product Cost	$141.58	
Contribution Margin per Daypack	$33.43	
Unit Product Cost Detail		
Direct Materials	$105.00	
Direct Labor	$15.58	
Variable Overhead (VOH)	$5.25	25.00%
Fixed Overhead (FOH)	$15.75	75.00%
Unit Product Cost	$141.58	

Ridgeline Backpacks manufactures a premium daypack specifically designed to accommodate laptop computers and other electronic devices such as tablets, cameras, etc. while travelling.

The information to the left shows the current sales price and product costs for the premium daypacks. The direct materials, direct labor, and manufacturing overhead are first shown as totals. The second grouping shows the same direct materials and direct labor, but the manufacturing overhead is separated between its variable and fixed portions.

Special Order Information and Analysis

Ridgeline received a special order from a potential customer for 100 premium daypacks at a discounted prices of $140/daypack. The order includes a request for an event patch to be sewn on to each daypack. Each patch would cost $2.50 and require Ridgeline to purchase a specialized sewing machine for $450. The specialized sewing machine would not be used with any other current production process.

Special Order Price	$140
Special Order Unit Volume	100
Special Order Modification Costs per Unit	$2.50
Additional Fixed Costs for Special Order	$450

	Per Unit	Total
Special Order Sales Price	$140	$14,000
Less Variable Costs:		
Direct Material	$105.00	$10,500.00
Direct Labor	$15.58	$1,557.50
VOH	$5.25	$525.00
Modification Costs	$2.50	$250.00
Total Variable Costs	$128.33	$12,832.50
Additional Fixed Costs for Special Order		$450.00
Total Special Order Cost		$13,282.50
Special Order Net Operating Income		$717.50

Looking at the revenue & costs related to just the special order is a form of INCREMENTAL ANALYSIS

Fig. 7.3 Special Order Example

To evaluate the special order, Ridgeline gathered the special order information and prepared the analysis specifically for the product manager and sales manager to review. In the analysis, the direct materials and direct labor are included at the same amounts for both the regularly produced daypacks and the special-order daypacks, but for manufacturing overhead, the only amount included in the analysis is for the variable manufacturing overhead. Only the VOH needs to be included because we are assuming that Ridgeline is operating at a unit volume level past their breakeven point and that the fixed costs are already covered. The modification costs for adding the custom patch are included as additional variable costs.

For this special order, Ridgeline would also need to purchase a specialized sewing machine to sew the patch onto the daypacks. Ridgeline does not have plans to immediately use the sewing machine in any other operation. Because the specialized sewing machine would be used only for the special order, the special order by itself must generate enough revenue to pay for both the total variable cost for the special order and the price of the specialized equipment purchased for this job, and also generate a positive net operating income. In essence, the specialized equipment is treated as an additional fixed cost and added to the total cost for the special order because it will be used only for the special order.

In this analysis, the special order appears to generate enough revenue to pay for all the variable and fixed costs associated with it and generates the additional net operating income of $717.50. The special order should be accepted because it will generate positive net operating income.

The fixed manufacturing overhead can be disregarded in the analysis because it has already been covered once the breakeven point has been reached. The additional fixed costs related specifically to the special order must be included in the analysis.

Sell or Process Further

Some firms operate in an industry that is characterized by creating multiple products from a common raw material. Industries such as oil and gas and agriculture are good examples wherein firms must make decisions about when to sell and when to continue to process the raw material. The firm may be able to process a raw material in multiple stages, and at the end of each stage the firm may have the ability to sell it on the open market.

The raw material is purchased and usually has some cleaning, preparation, or separating costs called joint costs to prepare the raw material to either be sold or processed further into a specific end product. In this example, the joint costs are incurred in the initial process and are applied to all of the raw material to separate the raw material into two or more groups of similar size, quality, or some other characteristic.

The end of each processing stage that generates at least two different groupings or products from a single input is called a split-off point. A split-off point is the point at which the material can be sold on the open market for value. A split-off point can occur at the end of either a joint process that separates the material into multiple sub-groups or at the end of a specific process applied to just one of the material categories or groups.

The firm must analyze the value of selling the material on the open market at each split-off point versus the value of continuing to process the material. The firm will typically decide to continue to process the material as long as the additional revenue generated by the additional processing is greater than the additional processing costs.

Figure 7.4 shows the analysis of how Potato Planet Cooperative, an agricultural cooperative, might evaluate the option of selling the potatoes at the split-off point or continuing to process the potatoes into an end product.

The Potato Planet Cooperative purchases potatoes from its members. When the potatoes arrive, they are cleaned and separated according to size. Once the potatoes have been separated, they can be either sold to grocery stores as bags of raw potatoes or processed into various end products such as hash browns, French fries, or tater tots. In our example, we assume that potato size is the determining factor for the specific end product.

All the potatoes must be cleaned and separated, incurring total joint costs of $110,000: $100,000 to purchase the potatoes and $10,000 to clean and separate them. At the point the potatoes are

Potato Planet Cooperative
Sell or Process Further Analysis

	Joint Costs
Raw Material Cost	$100,000
Cleaning & Prep Costs	$10,000
Total Joint Costs	$110,000

For the cost of $110,000 the potatoes are purchased, washed and separated according to size.

	(hashbrowns) Small	(french fries) Medium	(tater tots) Large	Total	
Sales Value @ split off	$40,000	$45,000	$55,000	$140,000	
Additional Processing Costs	$50,000	$80,000	$105,000	$235,000	
Final Sales Value	$95,000	$150,000	$175,000	$420,000	
Incremental Sales Value	$55,000	$105,000	$120,000	$280,000	(Final Sales Value–Split Off Sales Value)
Incremental Processing Costs	$50,000	$80,000	$105,000	$235,000	(Additional Processing Costs)
Incremental NOI	$5,000	$25,000	$15,000	$45,000	

Fig. 7.4 Sell or Process Further Example 1

separated, the split-off point, the small potatoes could be sold for $40,000, the medium potatoes for $45,000, and the large potatoes for $55,000 on the open market to places like grocery stores. At the split-off point the total $110,000 of joint costs cannot be traced to the three individual categories of potatoes; the joint costs are a common cost to the complete batch of all the potatoes originally purchased, regardless of size. The sales value for each size of potato at the split-off point is crucial to evaluate the profitability of processing each potato size into an end product.

An important aspect at the split-off point is that the total sales value at the split-off point is greater than the total joint costs. This indicates that all the potatoes could be sold as raw potatoes at the split-off point and generate a profit.

Once the potatoes have been separated, the processing costs for each potato size must be identified, along with the final sales value for each end product. For the small potatoes that could be processed into hash browns, the additional processing costs total $50,000 while the final sales value for the hash browns would be $95,000. The analysis includes comparing the additional, or incremental, processing costs of making hash browns out of small potatoes to the incremental increase in sales value the hash browns generate over their original sales value.

In Figure 7.4, the hash browns generate $95,000 of sales value (revenue) while the raw small potatoes would generate $40,000 of sales value. Therefore, processing small potatoes into hash browns would increase the revenue by $55,000. The cost to process the small potatoes into hash browns totals $50,000. The incremental revenue of $55,000 and the incremental cost of $50,000 to process small potatoes into hash browns generates a net operating income of $5,000. The decision to continue processing a material or product depends on generating a positive net operating income from the specific process. In the case of the small potatoes, the firm would decide to process them into hash browns because hash browns generate a positive $5,000 net operating income.

For Potato Planet, all three end products (hash browns, French fries, and tater tots) generate positive net operating income and all three potato sizes should be processed into their respective end products.

In contrast, Figure 7.5 presents a scenario in which Potato Planet would incur a loss to process small potatoes into hash browns.

Potato Planet Cooperative
Sell or Process Further Analysis

	Joint Costs
Raw Material Cost	$100,000
Cleaning & Prep Costs	$10,000
Total Joint Costs	$110,000

For the cost of $110,000 the potatoes are purchased, washed and separated according to size.

	(hashbrowns) Small	(french fries) Medium	(tater tots) Large	Total	
Sales Value @ split off	$40,000	$45,000	$55,000	$140,000	
Additional Processing Costs	$50,000	$80,000	$105,000	$235,000	
Final Sales Value	$85,000	$150,000	$175,000	$410,000	
Incremental Sales Value	$45,000	$105,000	$120,000	$270,000	(Final Sales Value–Split Off Sales Value)
Incremental Processing Costs	$50,000	$80,000	$105,000	$235,000	(Additional Processing Costs)
Incremental NOI	($5,000)	$25,000	$15,000	$35,000	

Fig. 7.5 Sell or Process Further Example 2

If the hash browns were to generate only $85,000 of final sales value while still requiring $50,000 of additional processing costs, then processing small potatoes into hash browns would generate a $5,000 net operating loss ($45,000 of incremental sales value – $50,000 of additional processing costs) and the firm would be better off to sell the small potatoes at the split-off point.

KEEP OR CLOSE A DEPARTMENT—SINGLE LOCATION

Departments are different from divisions or subsidiaries or segments. For our purposes, departments are operating activities of a single business in a single location. A grocery store or a small department store in a rural area might have a single location with multiple departments operating within it. An enterprise with multiple departments in a single location must also evaluate the performance of each department. One of the difficulties of an operation with a single location is in knowing how to treat the fixed costs.

In a single location, we'll refer to traceable fixed costs as avoidable fixed costs, and we'll refer to common fixed costs as unavoidable fixed costs. Avoidable fixed costs, like traceable fixed costs, are directly related to an individual department. Unavoidable fixed costs, like common fixed costs, are indirectly related to any of the departments. We use the avoidable and unavoidable terminology based on the relationship between the fixed cost and a specific department. Fixed costs that are directly related to an individual department will be incurred if the department is operating, and those fixed costs will not be incurred if the department is closed. The traceable terminology fits better in multiple-location scenarios.

A challenge presented by fixed costs in a single location is in those fixed costs that are directly related to an individual department only in part. These avoidable fixed costs are only partially avoided/escaped when a department is closed because the fixed cost relates to two or more departments, or because the fixed cost relates to the whole location, but can be partially reduced when one department is closed. Examples of partially avoidable fixed costs are a manager's salary, some insurance premiums, and some utilities.

If a store has a single insurance policy to cover the value of the store's inventory and one of the store's three departments is closed, then the premium for the insurance policy may be adjusted downward to reflect the smaller amount of inventory in the two remaining departments. In this case the insurance premium is partially avoidable in relation to any of the individual departments.

When evaluating a business with a single location and multiple departments, the avoidable fixed costs are examples of relevant costs that must be identified and recognized in any analysis. For decision makers to make well-informed decisions, they need to know and include those costs that are relevant to the decision and exclude those that are irrelevant. If a specific department is not performing well or as expected, management may decide to review and evaluate the department to see whether it should continue to operate or be closed. The costs relevant to the specific department would include all those that are directly related, in whole or in part, to the specific department. The relevant costs are those that would be avoided/escaped if the department were closed.

The single-location environment requires each fixed cost to be identified as avoidable or unavoidable in relation to each department.

Remember, revenue and variable costs are always directly and completely related to their respective departments. The revenue generated can be directly traced to each department, as can the variable costs, such as the cost of products and employees. The work in this section deals specifically with the fixed costs. The avoidable and unavoidable behaviors belong solely to the fixed costs.

Figure 7.6 provides an illustration of a single location with multiple departments.

A small retailer might own or lease a single building with a modest space of 10,000 square feet and carry outdoor equipment, sporting goods, and grilling equipment to cater to the local market. The sporting goods department uses 2,200 square feet of the building space, the outdoor equipment department uses 2,800 square feet, and the grilling equipment department uses 2,000 square feet, while the shipping/receiving docks and offices use the remaining 3,000 square feet.

Constrained Resources

A constrained resource is any individual product resource or input that limits (or constrains) the overall production capacity. The term "constrained resource" refers to a resource or input that comes from outside the firm while the term "bottleneck" (which we have examined above) refers to internal limitations. Within current productive capacity boundaries (short-time horizon in which capacity cannot easily be changed), a constrained resource may not be increased or expanded because of conditions outside our immediate control. Any of the product inputs could be a constrained resource. Direct materials, direct labor, or manufacturing overhead (specifically land, buildings and facilities, and equipment) are susceptible to supply interruptions or overall limits that are beyond our control without significant investment. A machine running at full capacity may be a constrained resource if an additional machine cannot be purchased or the machine's efficiency cannot be increased easily or quickly.

A raw material may be a constrained resource if additional amounts of the raw material cannot be obtained because of poor harvests, transportation issues, or simply lack of supply. Labor can be a constrained resource if the firm's labor force is at full capacity or if people with the appropriate skills cannot be hired or trained quickly.

The constrained resource becomes a critical issue when the firm has greater demand for their product(s) than the capacity of the constrained resource. In such a scenario, owners and managers

Drop/Keep Department Analysis					
Initial Income Statement Item	Total	Store	Repair	Distribution	Distribution
Revenue	$250,000	$125,000	$75,000	$50,000	$50,000
Variable Cost	$105,000	$50,000	$25,000	$30,000	$30,000
Contribution Margin	$145,000	$75,000	$50,000	$20,000	$20,000
Fixed Costs:					
Salaries	$50,000	$29,500	$12,500	$8,000	$8,000
Advertising	$15,000	$1,000	$7,500	$6,500	$6,500
Utilities	$2,000	$500	$500	$1,000	$0
Depreciation—Fixtures	$5,000	$1,000	$2,000	$2,000	$0
Rent	$20,000	$10,000	$6,000	$4,000	$0
Insurance	$3,000	$2,000	$500	$500	$500
General Administrative	$30,000	$15,000	$9,000	$6,000	$0
Total Fixed Costs	$125,000	$59,000	$38,000	$28,000	$15,000
Net Operating Income	$20,000	$16,000	$12,000	($8,000)	$5,000

Fixed Cost Analysis:	Total Assigned to Distribution	Unavoidable	Avoidable
Fixed Costs:			
Salaries	$8,000		$8,000
Advertising	$6,500		$6,500
Utilities	$1,000	$1,000	
Depreciation—Fixtures	$2,000	$2,000	
Rent	$4,000	$4,000	
Insurance	$500		$500
General Administrative	$6,000	$6,000	
Total	$28,000	$13,000	$15,000
		Common	Traceable
		Committed	Discretionary

Incremental Analysis:	
CM Lost	($20,000)
Avoidable FC	$15,000
NOI Impact	($5,000)

Fig. 7.6 Drop/Keep Department Analysis

must understand how to maximize the constrained resource. To maximize a constrained resource, the contribution margin per unit of each affected product must be converted to the contribution margin generated by the constrained resource when producing the product.

To convert a product's contribution margin per unit to the contribution margin based on the constrained resource for that product, we will follow a four-step process:

1. The unit contribution margin much be calculated for each product.
2. The demand for each product must be converted from units of product to the amount of the constrained resource required to meet the unit demand.
3. The unit contribution margin for each product must be converted to the contribution margin generated by the constrained resource when processing each product unit.

Constrained Resource Analysis

Basic Product Information

	Annual Unit Demand	Selling Price	Variable Costs: Direct Material	Direct Labor	Variable Overhead	Total VC
Baseballs—Game	144,000	$12.00	$1.75	$0.90	$0.25	$2.90
Baseballs—Practice	90,000	$7.00	$1.25	$0.45	$0.13	$1.83
Softballs—Game	132,000	$16.00	$2.80	$1.80	$0.50	$5.10
Softballs—Practice	96,000	$11.00	$2.20	$0.90	$0.25	$3.35

1) Find the Contribution Margin per Unit of Product

Rank based on CM/unit:	2		4		1		3	
Per Unit:	Baseballs—Game		Baseballs—Practice		Softballs—Game		Softballs—Practice	
Selling Price	$12.00		$7.00		$16.00		$11.00	
VC	$2.90	24.17%	$1.83	26.07%	$5.10	31.88%	$3.35	30.45%
CM	$9.10	75.83%	$5.18	73.93%	$10.90	68.13%	$7.65	69.55%

2) Convert product demand to constrained resources required

	Baseballs—Game			Baseballs—Practice			Softballs—Game			Softballs—Practice			Total Demand
Montly Demand	12,000			7,500			11,000			8,000			
Stitching Time per ball	3	minutes		1.5	minutes		6	minutes		3	minutes		
Total Stitching time required	36,000	minutes	+	11,250	minutes	+	66,000	minutes	+	24,000	minutes	=	137,250

3) Convert the CM/unit to CM/constrained resource

Rank based on CM/hour:	2		1		4		3	
	Baseballs—Game		Baseballs—Practice		Softballs—Game		Softballs—Practice	
CM per minute	$3.03	per minute	$3.45	per minute	$1.82	per minute	$2.55	per minute
CM per hour	$182.00	per hour	$207.00	per hour	$109.00	per hour	$153.00	per hour
Total Stitching time available	125,000	minutes	(The Constraint)					

4) Prioritize production based on CM/constrained resource

What is our producation priority? (Highest CM/constrained resource)

	CM/Min	Individual Minutes	Cummulative Minutes
Baseballs—Practice	$3.45	11,250	11.250
Baseballs—Game	$3.03	36.000	47.250
Softballs—Practice	$2.55	24.000	71,000
Softballs—Game	$1.82	53,750	125,000

(The lowest CM/constraint is produced LAST)

Fig. 7.7 Constrained Resource Analysis

4. The production must be prioritized based on the amount of contribution margin the constrained resource can generate for each product, prioritizing production from the product with the highest contribution margin with respect to the constrained resource, down to the product with the lowest contribution margin.

Figure 7.7 shows the four-step process to analyze a constrained resource for a firm producing two different baseballs and two different softballs. The constraint is the stitching machine, and the firm cannot purchase an additional stitching machine.

The process to convert a product's contribution margin per unit into a contribution margin based on the constrained resources depends on how much of the constrained resource a single unit of the product uses. The following table lists possible constrained resources and possible measurements of a constrained resource a unit of product may use.

Constrained Resource	Measurement
Direct material	Ounce, liter, meter, kilogram, or other amount of the specific material
Direct labor	Minutes, hours, days, or other amount of time
Equipment/Machinery	Minutes, hours, or other amount of time

The results of analyzing constrained resources should provide decision makers with the information they need to appropriately organize and prioritize production to maximize the amount of contribution margin the constrained resource can effectively produce.

8 INTERMEDIATE-TERM DECISIONS

How do we make temporary changes in our capacity without a significant investment?

LEARNING OBJECTIVES

LO1: Calculate the costs of making a part/product versus buying the part/product (outsourcing).

LO2: Describe and explain the decision criteria used to evaluate the decisions to make or buy a part/product.

LO3: Prepare an overtime analysis.

LO4: Describe and explain the decision criteria used to evaluate the decision to pay overtime.

LO5: Identify and describe the concepts of the time value of money.

LO6: Calculate the present value of a lump-sum cash flow and an annuity cash flow.

LO7: Calculate the net present value for replacing equipment.

THE QUESTIONS WE TRY TO ANSWER

- Should we continue to make a part for our product or should we purchase the part from a contract manufacturer?
- Can we afford to pay overtime?

In this chapter, we discuss decisions that cause a minor or temporary change to a firm's physical productive output capacity. We call these types of decisions intermediate-term decisions because these decisions could affect the firm's physical productive capacity, to some degree, and cannot be implemented in a short period of time. These changes are minor or temporary changes, or they could be permanent changes to the firm's productive capacity without requiring significant investment. Although the effects of these decisions can impact the firm for multiple years into the future, the driving cause to make these decisions is still the physical productive capacity of the firm.

From the time horizon perspective, the intermediate term will impact the firm in the future. As we consider the information needed for making internal decisions, we must also consider the effects on an intermediate-term horizon because these types of decisions may impact the firm for multiple years, but the time horizon is not the predominant factor that causes the need for these decisions—it is the capacity of the firm that is the driver.

The effect a decision has on the *current productive capacity* of the firm will be the predominant factor to distinguish intermediate-term decisions from those we consider short term or long term. An intermediate-term decision may impact, to some degree, the current productive capacity of the firm, but the impact is either minor or temporary in nature and can be reversed or changed relatively easily or quickly, or the decision could permanently impact the firm's physical productive capacity without significant investment. In either case, the decisions we address in this chapter can be made relatively quickly even though the impact of a decision can affect multiple future years.

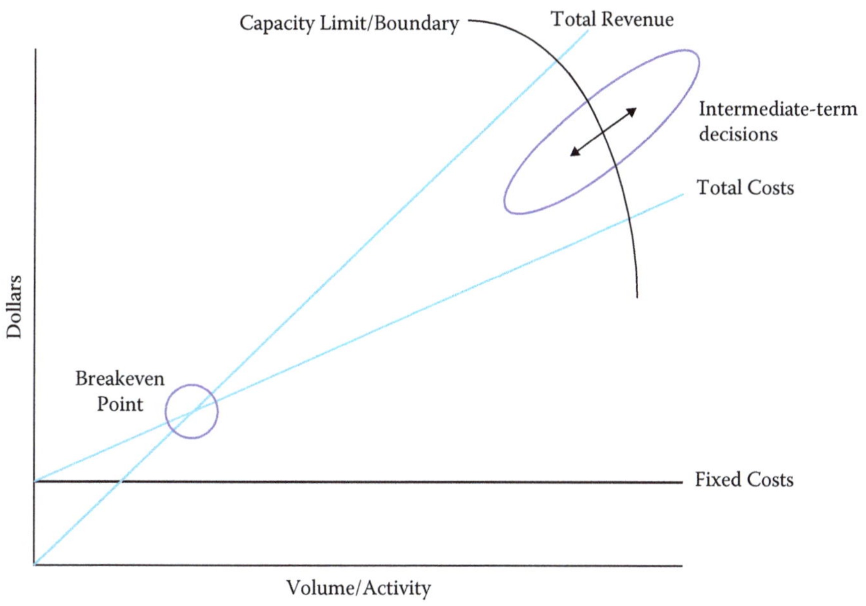

Fig. 8.1 Intermediate Term Decisions

To help us visualize the minor or temporary productive capacity decisions, Figure 8.1 presents a rendition of the CVP graph we discussed in Chapter 3, illustrating where intermediate-term decisions affect the firm in terms of the CVP concepts.

Generally, the minor or temporary capacity decisions in this chapter will cause the productive capacity (or boundary) of the firm to straddle its capacity boundary by temporarily increasing its productive capacity. Temporary capacity changes may be modified, reversed, or expanded in the future, but our analysis will focus on both the effect of a temporary change in capacity, as well as a permanent change in capacity without significant additional investment.

The types of decisions presented in this chapter will all use an incremental analysis approach. The costs that are different between the decision options are the costs that are relevant to the decision. If a cost will be paid no matter the decision, then that cost is not an incremental cost and hence becomes irrelevant to the decision.

Relevant incremental costs can sometimes be difficult to identify because a specific cost may be only partly related to the decision. Some costs may represent activities or resources that are shared between two or more parts, assemblies, or products, such as supervisors' salaries and some types of equipment. Such costs are usually fixed costs, which are partially avoidable and partially unavoidable; the avoidable portion of any fixed cost should be included as a relevant cost to make the item.

MAKE OR BUY DECISIONS

The decision for a firm to make a part (or product) itself or to buy it from a contract manufacturer affects the overall productive capacity of the firm; contracting with an outside manufacturer to make the part increases the productive capacity of the firm. A firm would be interested in contracting an outside manufacturer when the third party can produce the part with equal or better quality at a lower price.

By contracting an outside manufacturer, the firm will increase its overall capacity because the space and resources that were dedicated to producing the part will then become available for other uses. If the firm has developed a new product and would like to produce the product, using a contract manufacturer to take over some portion of current production would free up employees, space, and equipment that can be redirected to the new product. In such a case, the decision to contract an outside manufacturer creates a potentially permanent change in the overall capacity of the firm. The firm is leveraging the productive capacity of the contract manufacturer and redirecting current productive capacity to new manufacturing activities, effectively increasing the firm's overall productive capacity without significant additional investment.

In the analysis related to make/buy decisions, we compare the costs of manufacturing the part to the costs of purchasing the same item from an outside manufacturer. To produce a product internally, the firm pays for direct materials, direct labor, and manufacturing overhead to produce the item. Externally, the firm would pay a single purchase price for the item. If the firm has a new product they would like to produce, we include an estimate of the potential contribution margin the new product would generate in place of the item that could be produced by an outside manufacturer as an opportunity cost of making the product.

In the make/buy decision, direct materials, direct labor, and variable overhead are the variable costs of the item, and the per-unit product costs are multiplied by the total number of units that would be produced by the contract manufacturer. If the firm makes the items, then the firm will have to pay for the direct materials, direct labor, and the variable manufacturing overhead.

FIXED MANUFACTURING OVERHEAD

The challenge of ascertaining the cost to make an item relates to the fixed manufacturing overhead costs (FOH) incurred to make the item. We must separate the unavoidable fixed costs from the avoidable fixed costs. The avoidable fixed costs are those fixed costs that will not be paid; they will go away or the firm will escape them, if the contract manufacturer produces the product.

An example of an avoidable fixed cost might be the production manager's salary. The production manager's salary would be paid if the firm makes the item, but the production manager would not be paid if the item is produced by an outside manufacturer. The production manager's salary would be added to the cost of making the item because the salary will be paid if the item is made but will not be paid if the item is produced by an outside manufacturer; the production manager's salary is an avoidable fixed cost.

OPPORTUNITY COST

In general terms, an opportunity cost is a benefit that will be forfeited because of the decision made. A full-time college student has an opportunity cost of full-time wages because he or she has made the decision to attend school full time instead of working full time. The opportunity cost of going to a football game might be the wages and tips a person could earn if they worked at a restaurant and didn't attend the game. The opportunity cost of going to the beach instead of attending your managerial accounting class might be getting a lower grade on the final exam.

In the make/buy decision, the opportunity cost is the potential contribution margin from a new product or service. The contribution margin of the new product is treated as an opportunity cost. Such an opportunity cost can be considered as 1) an additional cost of making the item or 2) a reduction in the cost of purchasing the item from an outside manufacturer.

If the opportunity cost is treated as an additional cost of making the current item, then the opportunity cost should be added to the total cost of making the item. If the opportunity cost is treated as a reduction in the purchase price of the item from an outside manufacturer, then the opportunity cost should be subtracted from the total cost to purchase the item. Either approach will generate the same result.

Figure 8.2 shows the analysis to support the decision of either making or buying a specific wire bundle used in dental chairs. The chairs dentists use in their exam rooms are complex and specialized pieces of equipment. The back of the dental chair can be tilted back and then up, the whole chair can be raised or lowered, and the footrest can be raised or lowered separately. Each of the movement functions requires separate electrical connections for which the manufacturer may wrap or bundle multiple wires into a single strand to more easily assemble the chair in the factory and then install the chair in a dental office. The product design manager for the dental chairs would like to know whether making the wire bundles is more or less cost efficient than contracting an outside manufacturer to make the wire bundles.

The opportunity cost shown in the example is the $45,000 contribution margin that could be generated if the wire bundles were made by an outside manufacturer and the current space used to make wire bundles was instead used to expand the dental chair assembly area. The total cost of making the wire bundles includes the direct materials and direct labor, the variable manufacturing overhead, the avoidable supervisor's salary (fixed manufacturing overhead), and the forfeited contribution margin of not expanding the chair assembly area. The example shows, in the Make column, the opportunity cost as an additional cost to make the wire bundles. The other approach is to show the opportunity cost as a reduction to the outside purchase price in the Buy column.

Make/Buy Decision Analysis

Estimated Units	20,000 dental chairs			Make	Buy
Per Unit VC Info:			DM	$320,000	
DM	$16.00		DL	$420,000	
DL	$21.00		VOH	$170,000	
VOH	$8.50		Avoidable Fixed Costs:		
			Supervisor Salary	$45,000	
FC Info:					
Supervisor Salary	$45,000	(100% avoidable/escapable)	Outside purchase cost		$1,040,000
Depreciation – Equipment	$20,000	(unavoidable & irrelevant)			
Allocated general overhead	$80,000	(unavoidable & irrelevant)	Opportunity cost (forgone SM/CM)	$45,000	
Rent	$60,000	(unavoidable & irrelevant)			
			Total Cost	$1,000,000	$1,040,000
Outside purchase Price per Unit	$52		Different	($40,000)	

Fig. 8.2 Make/Buy Example

OUTSOURCING DECISIONS

Outsourcing decisions, for our purposes, will relate to the various business service operations of payroll, human resources, invoicing and collections, employee benefits, and other types of internal functions or services that support the overall business operations. We will look at the payroll function and how to analyze it to determine whether the function should continue as an internal function or whether it should be outsourced to a third-party provider.

The payroll function is one that firms commonly choose to outsource for both financial and nonfinancial reasons. Payroll is a distinct function with common but specific interrelationships with other functions. Because payroll is a self-contained function with commonly understood relationships with other parts of the firm, the function can be outsourced effectively to a third party. Although the function can be outsourced, the firm must evaluate both the financial and nonfinancial aspects of the payroll function to make an outsourcing determination.

The nonfinancial aspects of payroll are important considerations and can significantly influence the outsourcing decision. In the United States, payroll has a tremendous amount of regulatory reporting and oversight at the local, state, and federal levels of government. Regulatory issues include, but are not limited to, such areas as overtime, minimum wages, worker's compensation insurance, and unemployment insurance. Employers of various sizes have very different reporting requirements as well as remitting requirements, which can range from less than a week to a calendar quarter, for taxes and other withholdings.

Substantial effort is required to comply with such regulatory oversight, and specialized employee skill resources must be dedicated to achieve and maintain compliance. Maintaining an internal payroll function can be constrained by a lack of qualified people with payroll skills and experience. The inability to find qualified candidates to hire as employees can be a deciding factor to outsource, even though a firm may have sufficient economic resources to have an in-house payroll function.

The financial aspects of the payroll function include the costs associated with information technology and employing properly trained and skilled employees. The following chart shows some of the costs related to the payroll function:

Cost	Cost Measurements
Salaries and wages	Hourly and salary
Employee benefits	Insurance premiums, benefit costs
Professional education	Cost of seminars and workshops
Information technology	Computers, networks, software
Facilities	Rent, utilities, maintenance
Worker's compensation insurance	Premiums
Unemployment insurance	Premiums
Outside CPAs	Professional fees
Outside employment attorneys	Professional fees

The financial analysis of outsourcing an internal function is identical to the analysis used in the make/buy decision. The total cost of providing the internal function is compared to the total cost of outsourcing the function to a third party.

PAYING OVERTIME

One significant source of temporarily increasing the overall capacity of a firm occurs when employees are willing to work overtime, which is the amount of time an employee works in excess of the typical 40-hour work week. In production facilities, a single shift is an eight-hour period of time when production is in process. Firms can run one, two, or even three shifts in a 24-hour period, depending on the demand for the product. If a firm has either one or two shifts working, then the firm has the time capacity for employees to temporarily work more than their standard 40-hour week without opening an additional full 8-hour shift. Employees working overtime are usually paid more per hour than during their regular shift, often as high as 1.5 to 2 times the regular wage rate. Many different overtime arrangements can be structured, but we will use the standard time-and-a-half to compute overtime wages.

When evaluating the decision to have employees work overtime, managers must be aware of the increased costs of paying overtime, and they must know whether they can afford to pay the increased overtime wages without damaging the firm financially. The decision to offer overtime is based on the amount of contribution margin the firm generates from the product(s) that cannot be made during a regular shift and which requires some additional time to finish producing.

To make the decision to offer overtime, the contribution margin of the product that cannot be produced in sufficient quantities to meet demand within a regular shift must be enough to at least cover the overtime wages. We can also say that the product's contribution margin must be greater than the increase in the wages paid to employees to work overtime.

When evaluating the overtime decision, the contribution margin of each product must be converted to the contribution margin generated for each hour the employees work to produce that product. The products are prioritized for production based on the amount of contribution margin each product generates per direct-labor hour.

Our analysis is almost identical to our work in Chapter 7 regarding constrained resources. While the objective of the constrained resource analysis in Chapter 7 was to prioritize production, our objective here in Chapter 8 is to understand whether the firm can afford to temporarily increase the amount of direct labor hours for the purpose of increasing production. Although direct labor hours can be a constrained resource when the demand for a product is greater than can be produced in one or two full shifts, the constraint of a full shift can be alleviated by working overtime, which gives direct labor a unique ability to effectively eliminate a constraint on a temporary basis.

Figure 8.3 illustrates the analysis to determine whether or not overtime can be paid. The process is similar to the constrained resources analysis with an additional step:

1. The unit contribution margin much be calculated for each product.
2. The demand for each product must be converted from units of product to the amount of the constrained resource required to meet the unit demand—direct labor hours.
3. The unit contribution margin for each product must be converted to the contribution margin generated by the constrained resource (direct labor hours) when processing each product unit.

4. The production must be prioritized based on the amount of contribution margin the constrained resource (direct labor hours) can generate for each product: prioritizing production from the product with the highest contribution margin with respect to the constrained resource, down to the product with the lowest contribution margin.

5. The contribution margin per hour of the last product should be added to the regular hourly wage rate to find the total amount a firm could pay for additional production.

The conversion of the contribution margin from a per-unit basis to a direct-labor-hour basis is accomplished in steps 2 and 3. In step 4, the production is prioritized based on the amount of contribution margin generated per direct labor hour. (Notice that the priorities are different on a direct-labor-hour basis than we saw in Chapter 7 when the constraint was machine hours on the stitching machine.)

The total number of direct labor hours available is 10,000 hours, while in step 2 we identify 10,917 total hours needed to make enough product to meet expected demand. The 917-hour difference affects the last product produced, practice baseballs. Without the employees working 917 hours more than the single shift, we will not be able to meet demand for the practice baseballs.

Step 5 demonstrates the total amount of $29.50 per direct labor hour, which the firm could pay for additional production. The total amount the firm is willing to pay is the regular wage per direct labor hour ($18.00 per direct labor hour), plus the contribution per direct labor hour ($11.50 per direct labor hour) of the product, which needs additional time to produce enough units to meet demand. Practice baseballs have enough demand to require 1,250 direct labor hours, but only 333 direct labor hours are available during the shift. To meet demand, the firm will need an additional 917 direct labor hours to produce enough practice baseballs to meet demand.

Time Value of Money

The principles, concepts, and ideas related to the time value of money (TVM) provide a myriad of tools for accountants, bankers, managers, investors, money managers, portfolio managers, and many other financial professionals to evaluate different scenarios where money is received or paid over a multiple-year time horizon. The TVM principles can be used to evaluate the effect time has on the value of the actual money received at different points in time because money is subject to the opportunities to earn a rate of interest or return.

A common, ongoing example of the TVM principles at work is inflation. Inflation is the erosion of a currency's purchasing power because of general increase in prices. Inflation causes a currency to lose value, or to devalue, from one year to the next. Inflation is typically quoted and discussed on an annual basis and is a common topic in both the popular and professional press. Time-value-of-money concepts and tools can be used to quantify the impact inflation has on an amount of money. We commonly see TVM concepts and tools being used to show the effects of inflation in a range of areas, including retirement planning and with social programs such as Social Security in the United States.

Constrained Resource—Overtime Analysis

Basic Product Information	Annual Unit Demand	Selling Price	Variable Costs: Direct Material	Direct Labor	Variable Overhead	Total VC
Baseballs–Game	144,000	$12.00	$1.75	$5.40	$1.50	$8.65
Baseballs–Practice	90,000	$7.00	$1.25	$3.00	$0.83	$5.08
Softballs–Game	132,000	$16.00	$2.80	$6.00	$1.67	$10.47
Softballs–Practice	96,000	$11.00	$2.20	$5.40	$1.50	$9.10

1) Find the Contribution Margin per Unit

Rank based on CM/unit	2		4		1		3	
Per Unit:	Baseballs–Game		Baseballs–Practice		Softballs–Game		Softballs–Practice	
Selling Price	$12.00		$7.00		$16.00		$11.00	
VC	$8.65	72.08%	$5.08	72.62%	$10.47	65.42%	$9.10	82.73%
CM	$3.35	27.92%	$1.92	27.38%	$5.53	34.58%	$1.90	17.27%

2) Convert product demand to constrained resources required

	Baseballs–Game			Baseballs–Practice			Softballs–Game			Softballs–Practice			Total DL Hours Need to Meet Demand
Montly Demand	12,000			7,500			11,000			8,000			
Direct labor time per unit	18	minutes		10	minutes		20	minutes		18	minutes		
Total direct labor minutes required	216,000	minutes	+	75,000	minutes	+	220,000	minutes	+	144,000	minutes	=	
Total direct labor hours required	3,600	hours		1,250	hours		3,667	hours		2,400	hours		10.917

3) Convert the CM/unit to CM/constrained resource

Rank based on CM/hour	2		1		4		3	
	Baseballs–Game		Baseballs–Practice		Softballs–Game		Softballs–Practice	
CM per direct labor minute	$0.19	per minute	$0.19	per minute	$0.28	per minute	$0.11	per minute
CM per direct labor hour	$11.17	per hour	$11.50	per hour	$16.60	per hour	$6.33	per hour
Total direct labor time available	10,000	hours	(The Constraint)					

4) Prioritize production based on CM/constrained resource

What is our producation priority?
(Highest CM/constrained resource)

	CM/HR	Individual Hours	Cummulative Hours	
Baseballs–Game	$11.17	3,600	3,600	
Softballs–Game	$16.60	3,667	7,267	
Softballs–Practice	$6.33	2,400	9,667	
Baseballs–Practice	$11.50	333	10,000	(The lowest CM/constraint is produced LAST)

5) Potential additional amounts that could be paid to employees

Current regular wage rate per hour	$18.00
Contribution margin per hour of constratined resource of lowest priority product	$11.50
Total amount the firm could pay employees to produce game softballs	$29.50
Total amount the firm could pay emplohyees to produce game softballs	$29.50
Overtime wage rate per hour–1.5 × regular rate	$27.00
Contribution margin per available after overtime	$2.50

Fig. 8.3 Paying Overtime

Compound and Simple Interest

As an example of inflation, in 1986 a ticket to a new movie on opening weekend cost about $2. Today, a ticket to a new movie on opening weekend might cost $15. We could say that $2 in 1986 is worth about $15 today because they both have the same purchasing power of one movie ticket on an opening weekend. Two dollars in 1986 has inflated to $15 today.

For our purposes in this textbook, we can effectively use TVM concepts and tools to evaluate various options related to decisions such as replacing old equipment, adding new equipment, expanding a production facility, adding a new brand or product line, opening a new location, creating a new service line, buying a business, and other decisions that require large amounts of capital to be invested, and generate financial benefits over multiple years into the future.

In Figure 8.4, an initial deposit of $100 into a savings account at a bank that earns 10 percent compound interest each year grows, or compounds, to an ending balance of $133.10 at the end of three years.

Each year the bank deposits the interest they promised into the savings account. The amount of interest earned at the end of each year is 10 percent of the balance in the savings account at the beginning of the year. Each year the balance of the savings account increases, which causes the following year's interest to also increase. As the savings account balance increases, the amount of interest earned during each year in the account grows from $10 at the end of year one to $11 at the end of year two, and to $12.10 at the end of year three. This is an example of compound interest because the interest earned in a given year is based on the account's beginning balance, which includes both the original deposit and the interest previously earned.

In Figure 8.5 we deal with the same savings account, except this account earns a simple rate of interest (not a compounded rate of interest).

Simple interest is earned each year on only the original deposit, or balance, in the account. In this example, only $10 of interest is earned in a year and the interest accumulating in the account is not included in the annual interest calculation.

At the end of the third year, the savings account earning compound interest has a balance of $133.10, while the savings account earning simple interest has a balance of $130.00. Although these

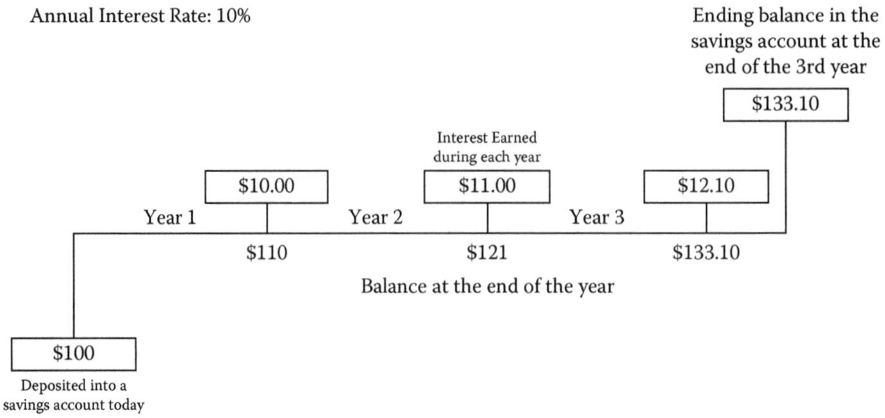

Fig. 8.4 Cash Flow Diagram Compound Interest Example

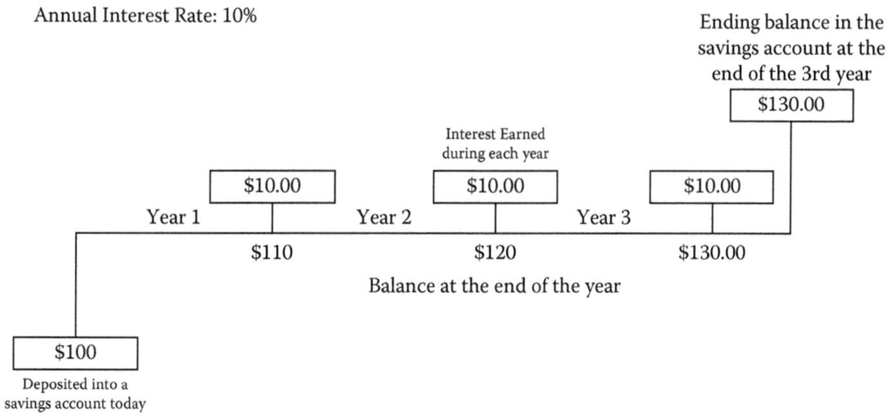

Fig. 8.5 Cash Flow Diagram Compound Interest Example

two examples show a small difference of $3.10, the difference between compound interest and simple interest balances increases exponentially over time. This exponential increase led Albert Einstein to call compound interest "the eighth wonder of the world."

Cash Flow Streams

The time-value-of-money concepts and tools all use some form of cash flow in their calculations. As we will discuss further in the chapter, present value and future value calculations use one of two basic types of cash flows: a lump-sum cash flow or an annuity cash flow. The two types of cash flows have unique properties and are used in TVM calculations based on those properties.

Lump-Sum Cash Flows

A lump-sum cash flow is characterized by a specific amount of cash at a specific point in time. See, for example, a business that generates the following amounts of cash each year after all the expenses have been paid:

2013	$80,000
2014	$65,000
2015	$72,000
2016	$88,000
2017	$91,000
2018	$76,000

We can classify series of cash flows as a series of individual lump-sum amounts. Each amount is a unique amount and each amount happens at a different point or period in time. Lump-sum cash flows are also known as irregular cash flows because either the amounts are different, the intervals are different, or both. Each individual lump-sum amount in a lump-sum, or irregular, cash flow must be discounted or compounded separately.

Annuity Cash Flows

An annuity is characterized by a stream of cash flows that are equivalent in amount, occurring at equivalent intervals of time. A business pays the following amounts as a dividend to its preferred stock shareholders at the end of each of the following years:

2013	$35,000
2014	$35,000
2015	$35,000
2016	$35,000
2017	$35,000
2018	$35,000

We can classify this series, or stream, of cash flows as an annuity. Each cash flow is the same amount (an equivalent amount of $35,000) and is paid at the end of each year (equivalent time interval). We can further classify this annuity stream as an ordinary annuity because the cash flow occurs at the end of each period. If the cash flows were paid at the beginning of each year, we would classify the annuity as an annuity due.

TVM calculations for annuities will generate different results depending on whether the annuity is an ordinary annuity (cash flows at the end of each period) or an annuity due (cash flows at the beginning of each period), because the timing of the first cash flow (whether at the beginning or end of a period) will impact both the present value and the future value.

Figure 8.6 illustrates the timing difference of the first cash flow between an ordinary annuity and an annuity due.

An example of common annuity cash flow stream is an automobile loan. The bank loans a person $20,000 to purchase a vehicle and the person pays back the loan with equal monthly payments to the bank. The monthly payments on the car loan are usually the same each month for the term of

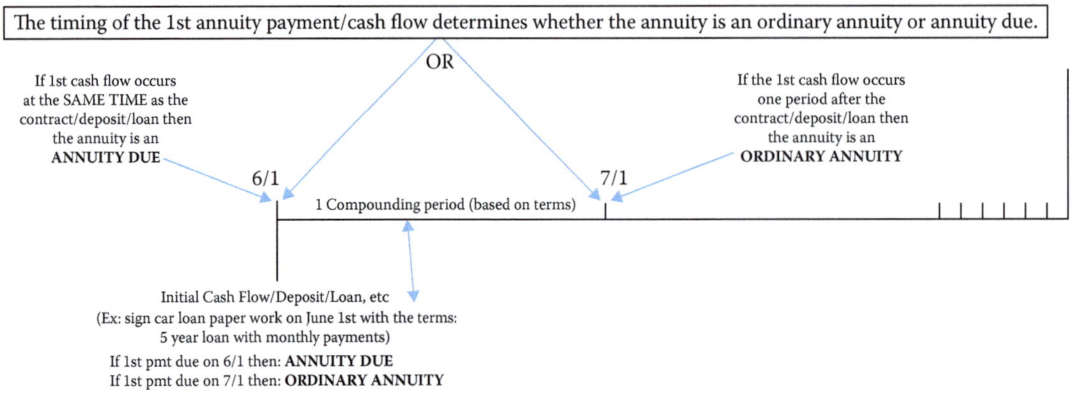

Fig. 8.6 Cash Flow Diagram Annuity Comparison

the loan. Because the payments made are equivalent amounts each time a payment is made and the payments are made at equivalent monthly intervals, we can classify the payment stream on this loan as an annuity cash flow. To determine whether the annuity is an ordinary annuity or an annuity due, we need to know when the first payment is due after the bank has made the loan. Most automobile loans are structured to have the first payment made at least one month after the loan is made, making the annuity stream of the payment an ordinary annuity.

In this textbook, we will assume all annuity cash flow stream are ordinary annuities and that the cash flows happen at the end of each given period. We will also refer to annuity cash flow streams simply as an annuity. The distinctions between an ordinary annuity and an annuity due are important factors not only in other academic courses but also in practice. Our goal in this textbook is to introduce these topics and begin to use them in very specific situations, all of which will be structured as ordinary annuities.

Present Value

Present value is the value of a future amount of money in terms of today's dollars. If you take a $5 bill out of your wallet right now, its present value is $5 because you have the money right now. If you take a $5 bill out of your wallet one year from now, it will most likely not buy quite as much as the same $5 could buy today. As we discussed earlier, prices generally go up in most economies, which makes $5 today worth more (because it can buy more) than $5 one year into the future.

The process of quantifying a future amount of money into its value in today's dollars is called discounting, or present valuing. An amount of money in the future is discounted (or shrunk) to today's dollars. The process of discounting uses both the amount of time between today and when the money will be received or paid and the interest rate (or discount rate) related to the cash flow.

Earlier we talked about inflation and the effect of general price increases. For our work in this course, we will use an interest rate (often called a discount rate) that a firm must earn in their business to discount the future cash flows back to today's value (we can also say we will present-value the future cash flows). The discount rate that firms select is referred to as the required rate of return or the minimum required rate of return. The present value of a future cash flow will be smaller than the future value because the present value can earn the interest rate or discount rate each year, which increases its value over the time period. Because money can earn interest or a rate of return over time, we can visualize the future value of an amount shrinking to its present value. Also, compounding a present value into the future can be visualized as growing the amount.

Figure 8.7 provides the formula that can be used to discount a lump-sum cash flow:

When a single dollar is used in the formula, the product is generally referred to as a factor, and a table of factors is provided at the end of this chapter for various periods and various interest or discount rates.

$$\text{Present Value} = \frac{\$1}{(1 + i)^n}$$

Fig. 8.7 Present Value Lump-Sum Formula

Present Value Tables

To facilitate our work discounting future cash flows back to today's value, we can use present value tables to find the discounting factor. As we just discussed, when the present value formula is used with a single dollar, the result is called a factor. A present value table is a table of factors for a given number of cash flows and a given set of interest or discount rates.

We have provided a set of present value and future value tables in Appendix A, and two sample present value tables are included in this chapter to illustrate how to use present value tables. Note that the decisions we address in this textbook all require future cash flows to be discounted back to today's values, so we will be working with only the present value tables.

Future value tables provide factors for compounding amounts into the future. We won't use future value tables in this textbook since the decisions we address all deal with current decisions that require future cash flows discounted back to today's value.

Figure 8.8 presents the present value factors for a lump sum of a single dollar. To discount $100 five years from now at a discount rate of 10 percent, we need the present value factor. The present value factor is found by going down the left column of the table to the row denoted 5, and then across the row to the 10 percent column to find the table factor of 0.620921. The table factor 0.620921 is multiplied by $100 to calculate the present value of $62.0921. We can say that $62.0921 could be deposited in an account, earning 10 percent compounded annually, and at the end of five years will be worth $100. We can also say that $100 discounted at 10 percent for five years has a present value of $62.091.

Each lump sum, or irregular, cash flow must be discounted separately or individually. The present value factor for lump sums will always be less than one.

Figure 8.9 presents the present value factors for an annuity cash flows. To discount a five-year $100 annuity at 10 percent, we need the present value factor of an annuity. The present value factor is found by going down the left column of the table to the row denoted 5, and then across the row to the 10 percent column to find the table factor of 3.790787. The $100 annual annuity is multiplied by the present value of an annuity table factor of 3.790787 to calculate the present value of $379.08 (rounded), the five annual cash flows. The present value of an annuity factor is a single factor multiplied by a single cash flow that discounts all of the cash flows in the annuity cash flow stream at the same time.

Formula: $1/(1+i)^n$

Present Value of a: $1.00 lump sum

	Interest Rate or Discount Rate Per Compounding Period (or per cash flow)							
n	5.00%	6.00%	7.00%	8.00%	9.00%	10.00%	11.00%	12.00%
1	0.952381	0.943396	0.934579	0.925926	0.917431	0.909091	0.900901	0.892857
2	0.907029	0.889996	0.873439	0.857339	0.841680	0.826446	0.811622	0.797194
3	0.863838	0.839619	0.816298	0.793832	0.772183	0.751315	0.731191	0.711780
4	0.822702	0.792094	0.762895	0.735030	0.708425	0.683013	0.658731	0.635518
5	0.783526	0.747258	0.712986	0.680583	0.649931	0.620921	0.593451	0.567427

Fig. 8.8 Present Value Factor Table Lump Sum

Formula: $(1/i)[1-(1/(1+i)^n)]$

Present Value of a: $1.00 ordinary annuity (or annuity in arrears)

	Interest Rate or Discount Rate Per Compounding Period (or per cash flow)							
n	5.00%	6.00%	7.00%	8.00%	9.00%	10.00%	11.00%	12.00%
1	0.952381	0.943396	0.934579	0.925926	0.917431	0.909091	0.900901	0.892857
2	1.859410	1.833393	1.808018	1.783265	1.759111	1.735537	1.712523	1.668102
3	2.723248	2.673012	2.624316	2.577097	2.531295	2.486852	2.443715	2.361153
4	3.545951	3.465106	3.387211	3.312127	3.239720	3.169865	3.102446	2.974471
5	4.329477	4.212364	4.100197	3.992710	3.889651	3.790787	3.695897	3.517231

Fig. 8.9 Present Value Factor Table - Ordinary Annuity Cash Flows

The annuity cash flow stream can be discounted in one calculation, using one table factor, because of the nature of annuity: equivalent amounts at equivalent intervals. The present value factor for an annuity cash flow will always be more than one, except with a single cash flow (the first row of the present value of an annuity table).

The left column is labeled as "n," which denotes the number of total cash flows on the annuity table and the nth cash flow on the lump sum table. In this textbook, we work with annual cash flows, cash flows that occur at the end of a year. For purposes of calculating the time value of money, "n" is the number of cash flows, and if the cash flows occur more frequently than once a year, the cash flows per year must be multiplied by the number of years to calculate "n." For example, if a firm pays a quarterly dividend for three years, then three years multiplied by quarterly dividend payments would generate an "n" of 12.

Typically, interest or discount rates are quoted on an annual basis such as a 12 percent required rate of return, or 13 percent minimum rate of return, or 10 percent discount rate, all of which refer to the rate for a 12-month period of time.

In this textbook, the cash flows are identified as annual cash flows, or cash flows that happen at the end of year. If the cash flows occur more frequently than once a year, the interest or discount rate must be adjusted to match the frequency of cash flows in a year. To adjust the interest or discount rate, the rate should be divided by the number of cash flows in a given year.

For cash flows occurring more frequently than once a year, the interest or discount rate must be divided by the number of cash flows per year, and the number of years must be multiplied by the number of cash flows per year. This clarification is important for structuring TVM problems, although we limit our application of TVM principles to annual cash flows, which match annual interest or discount rates, to maintain simplicity while introducing and using the concepts of the time value of money.

Future Value

Future value is the value of an amount of money in terms of future dollars. Over time, money can earn interest, or a rate of return, which is added to the original balance each period, and the total amount of money increases, or grows. In our interest example earlier in the chapter, the $100 deposit grew to $133.10 by the end of the third year. The $133.10 is the future value of the $100 deposit made today when earning 10 percent annual interest, or a 10 percent rate of return.

The future value of both single lump-sum amounts and annuity cash flows can be calculated. The different cash flows require different formulas. Future values are useful in areas such as retirement planning, investment planning, and business valuations.

Revenue/Cash Flow Increases and Cost Decreases

As we apply the TVM principles in this textbook to scenarios with multi-year time horizons, our work will entail only present value calculations because all the scenarios we will address require decisions that must be made today, based on future cash flows. Each scenario will have present values and future values of both lump-sums and annuity cash flow streams, and any future cash flows must be discounted, or shrunk, back to their values in today's dollars.

An important aspect of some of the scenarios we will address is the need to find the financial benefit in the scenario. For our purposes, both an increase in cash flow and a decrease in expense will be treated as cash inflows. If a scenario includes reduction in future expenses below the current expenses related to the scenario, then the amount of the expense decrease is equivalent to an increase in cash inflow. Both increased cash inflows and decreased cash outflows generate the same effect, and we will treat them both as positive cash inflows. This is particularly important when evaluating decisions, such as replacing equipment, where only cost savings are relevant.

NET PRESENT VALUE AND THE CASH FLOW DIAGRAM TOOL (© 2014 BY J. BROOKS PEACOCK)

Net present value (NPV) is a useful tool for comparing projects and options that impact annual cash flows over the span of multiple years. These projects and options usually have some type of initial investment to purchase needed equipment or other assets, and then produce either annual cash inflows or a reduction in annual cash outflows, for a number of years in the future. As with any TVM computation, an interest rate, discount rate, or rate of return must be used to calculate a present value. All of the TVM scenarios in this textbook relate to internal investment decisions, commonly expansion decisions, that owners and managers must make on a regular basis.

When using NPV, three (3) common cash flows must be identified in the scenario:

1. Initial investment (cash outflow)
2. Ongoing cash flows (cash inflows)
3. Salvage or terminal values (cash inflows)

Functionally, the present value of all the cash inflows are added together and then compared to the total present value of all the cash outflows. The total present value of the cash outflows is subtracted from the total present value of the cash inflows. The difference between the total present value of the cash inflows and the total present value of the cash outflows is the net present value of the project or investment option. To discount all the cash flows of a project or option, we use the firm's required rate of return, or discount rate.

Figure 8.10 presents the Cash Flow Diagram Tool (CFDT © 2014 by J. Brooks Peacock), designed to assist in structuring the information in a net present value scenario. The top half of the diagram includes the cash outflows, while the bottom half of the diagram includes the cash outflows. The left side of the diagram denotes today, and moving to the right represents moving into the future.

A firm establishes a minimum required rate of return that must be applied to any internal project or investment option. The required rate of return is the interest, or discount, rate used to discount the value of the future cash flows of a project. Management will use some type of estimate of the cost of capital plus an additional return, which factors in such things as estimated risk or desired profitability. The required rate of return can be thought of as a hurdle rate, or a rate of return a project must generate to be worth further consideration.

Figure 8.11 presents both the traditional spreadsheet layout and the cash flow diagram tool (© 2014 by J. Brooks Peacock) layout depicting the analysis of the same project. The firm has a potential project that requires a $25,000 piece of equipment and $1,500 to install the equipment (a total of $26,500 of initial investment) that will generate $9,250 of cash flow at the end of each year for five (5) years. At the end of the project, the equipment will be sold for an estimated $5,000 (salvage value). The firm requires a 12 percent compounded annual rate of return.

The future stream of $9,250 per year and the $5,000 salvage value are discounted back to today's value (their present value) and added together for a total present value of cash inflows of $36,181.37.

The initial investment of $26,500 is required now to start the project, is already in today's dollars, and is the total present value of cash outflows.

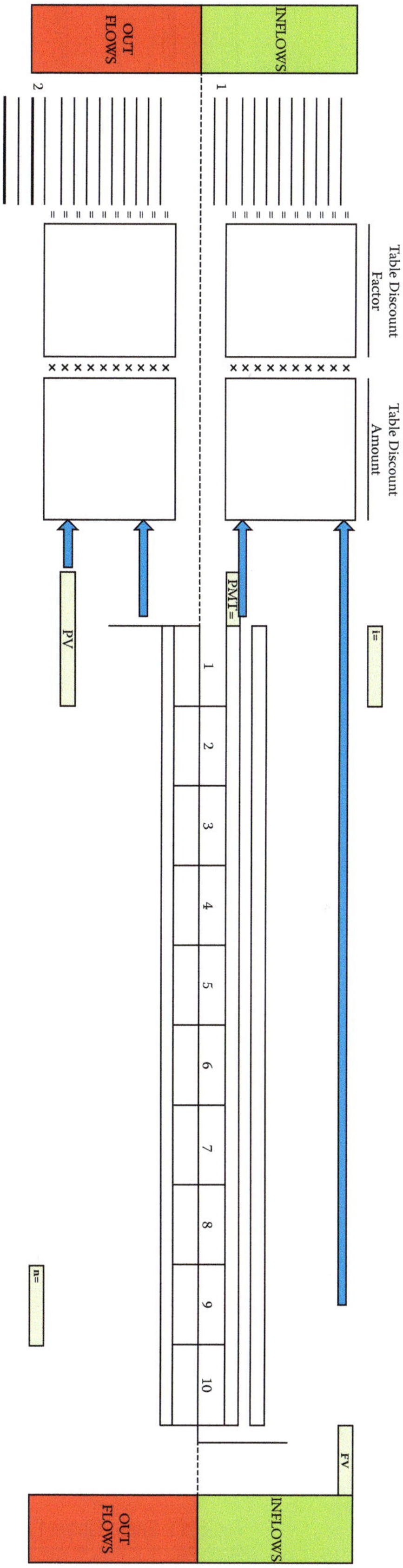

Fig. 8.10 Cash Flow Diagram Tool (© 2014 by J. Brooks Peacock)

Layout Differences
Spreadsheet Format & Cash Flow Diagram Tool

	Machine A
Purchase Price	$25,000
Cost to Install	$1,500
Annual Cost Savings	$9,250
Estimated Salvage Value	$5,000
Estimated Useful Life	5
Required Rate of Return	12%

Machine A	Today	Year 1	Year 2	Year 3	Year 4	Year 5	Year 5 Salvage Value	Total	
Purchase Price	($25,000.00)								
Cost to Install	($1,500.00)								
Annual Cost Savings		$9,250	$9,250	$9,250	$9,250	$9,250	$5,000		
Annual Cash Flow	($26,500.00)	$9,250	$9,250	$9,250	$9,250	$9,250	$5,000		
Present Value Factor	1	0.89286	0.79719	0.71178	0.63552	0.56743	0.56743		
Present Value	($26,500.00)	$8,258.96	$7,374.01	$6,583.97	$5,878.56	$5,248.73	$2,837.15	$9,681.37	Net Present Value

Machine A

PV		PV Table Factor		Cash Flow
$2,837.15	=	0.56743	×	$5,000
$5,248.73	=	0.56743	×	$9,250
$5,878.56	=	0.63552	×	$9,250
$6,583.97	=	0.71178	×	$9,250
$7,374.01	=	0.79719	×	$9,250
$8,258.96	=	0.89286	×	$9,250
$36,181.37	Total PV of Cash Inflows			
$25,000.00	=	1	×	$25,000
$1,500.00	=	1	×	$1,500
$26,500.00	Total PV of Cash Outflows			
$9,681.37	Net Present Value			

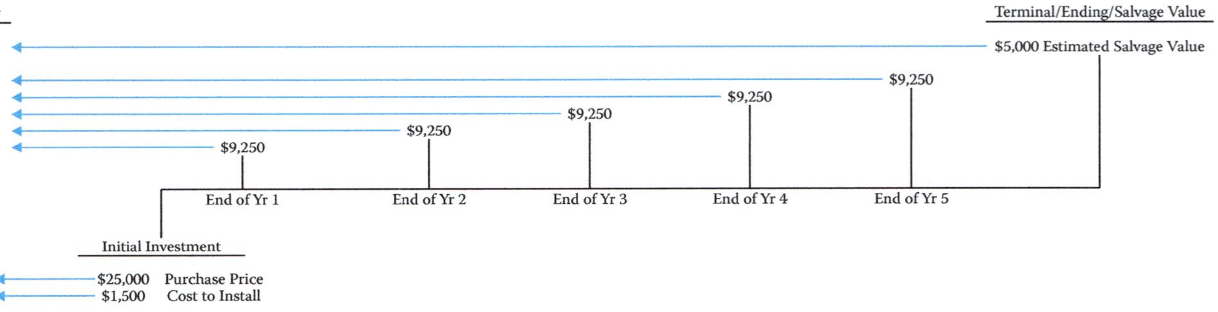

Fig. 8.11 Spreadsheet Format and Tool

The total present value of the cash outflows is subtracted from the total present value of cash inflows to calculate the $9,681.37 net present value of the project.

To facilitate our application of TVM and NPV concepts, we will use the traditional spreadsheet format as well as the cash flow diagram tool (© 2014 by J. Brooks Peacock). Both work well and accomplish the same results while providing different graphical views of a project.

REPLACING EQUIPMENT

Equipment wears out and becomes less efficient with use over time. At some point, the old equipment will need to be replaced. When replacing old equipment, managers must evaluate the various new equipment options. Replacing old equipment is an important decision because the new equipment could make the manufacturing process more efficient and increase the overall productive capacity of the firm. Although new equipment can be purchased and installed quickly, the new equipment will benefit the firm for many years in the future. Because the new equipment will impact future cash flows, the decision to replace equipment will be greatly influenced by the current value of those future cash flow changes, and we must apply some of the TVM principles by discounting the future cash flow changes back to their values in terms of today's dollars. As an example, a firm may choose between two different machines to replace a current machine. The following examples compare the cash flows of two machines that could be purchased to replace a current machine, using both the spreadsheet tool and the cash flow diagram tool.

Replacing Old Equipment
Net Present Value–Spreadsheet Format

	Machine A	Machine B
Purchase Price	$50,000	$60,000
Cost to Install	$4,500	$2,000
Annual Cost Savings	$18,000	$22,000
Estimated Useful Life	5	7
Required Rate of Return	12%	12%

Machine A	Today	Year 1	Year 2	Year 3	Year 4	Year 5	Total
Purchase Price	($50,000)						
Cost to Install	($4,500)						
Annual Cost Savings		$18,000	$18,000	$18,000	$18,000	$18,000	
Annual Cash Flow	($54,500)	$18,000	$18,000	$18,000	$18,000	$18,000	
Present Value Factor	1	0.89286	0.79719	0.71178	0.63552	0.56743	
Present Value	($54,500.00)	$16,071.48	$14,349.42	$12,812.04	$11,439.36	$10,213.74	$10,386.04

Machine B	Today	Year 1	Year 2	Year 3	Year 4	Year 5	Year 6	Year 7	Total
Purchase Price	($60,000)								
Cost to Install	($2,000)								
Annual Cost Savings		$22,000	$22,000	$22,000	$22,000	$22,000	$22,000	$22,000	
Annual Cash Flow	($62,000)	$22,000	$22,000	$22,000	$22,000	$22,000	$22,000	$22,000	
Present Value Factor	1	0.89286	0.79719	0.71178	0.63552	0.56743	0.50663	0.45235	
Present Value	($62,000.00)	$19,642.92	$17,538.18	$15,659.16	$13,981.44	$12,483.46	$11,145.86	$9,951.70	$38,402.72

Fig. 8.12 Equipment Schedule Spreadsheet

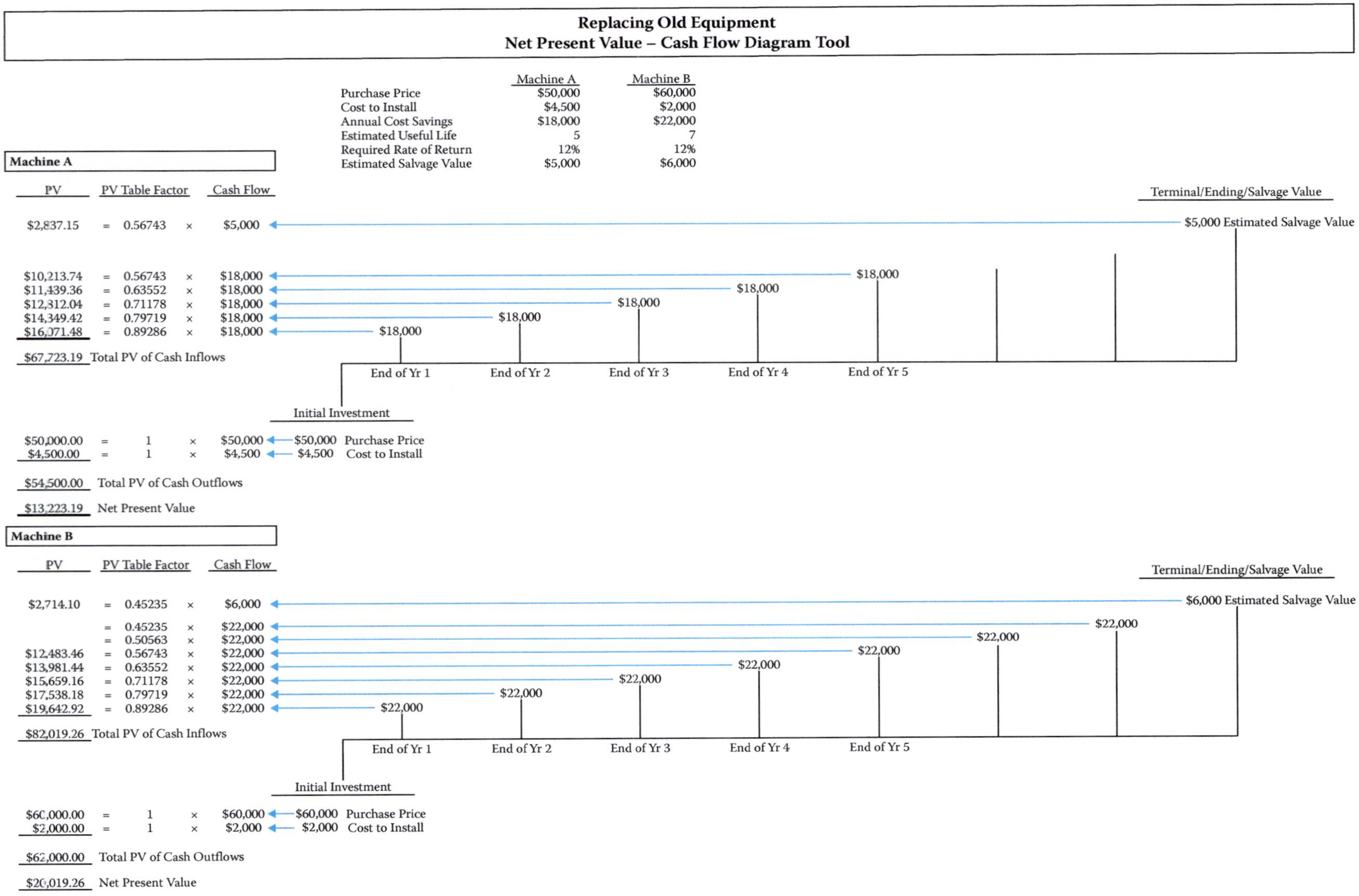

Fig. 8.13 Equipment CFDT

9

LONG-TERM CAPITAL INVESTMENT DECISIONS

How do we make the best decisions to permanently expand physical capacity?

THE QUESTIONS WE TRY TO ANSWER

- How long does it take for a project to generate and repay the initial investment?
- Does a project meet the firm's acceptable minimum standards of performance?
- Which of the acceptable projects should be completed first?

A firm's investment capital is limited. For owners and managers to make informed decisions about how to allocate and employ the firm's capital, they need tools to analyze the available investment options. These types of capital allocation decisions generally relate to proposed projects that would permanently increase the firm's physical productive capacity. Time also plays an important role in evaluating the decisions because of their multi-year effect. Because these decisions affect the firm many years in the future, they are commonly referred to as long-term decisions or long-term capital investment decisions. Although these types of decisions affect the firm over many years, the reason firms make these decisions is because the demand for their products or services is greater than their current physical productive capacity and they must increase their capacity to meet the demand. The demand in the market and the capacity of the firm are the issues that drive the need to invest capital and permanently increase capacity.

In this chapter, we explore four (4) tools used to evaluate proposed projects that permanently increase the firm's physical productive capacity. These tools provide valuable information to decision makers:

1. Payback period
2. Simple rate of return
3. Net present value
4. Internal rate of return

LEARNING OBJECTIVES

LO1: Describe, explain, and calculate the payback period of a project.

LO2: Describe, explain, and calculate the simple rate of return of a project.

LO3: Calculate the net present value of a project.

LO4: Describe, explain, and calculate the profitability index of a project.

LO5: Rank/prioritize multiple projects using the profitability index.

LO6: Describe, explain, and calculate the internal rate of return for a project.

LO7: Rank/prioritize multiple projects using the internal rate of return.

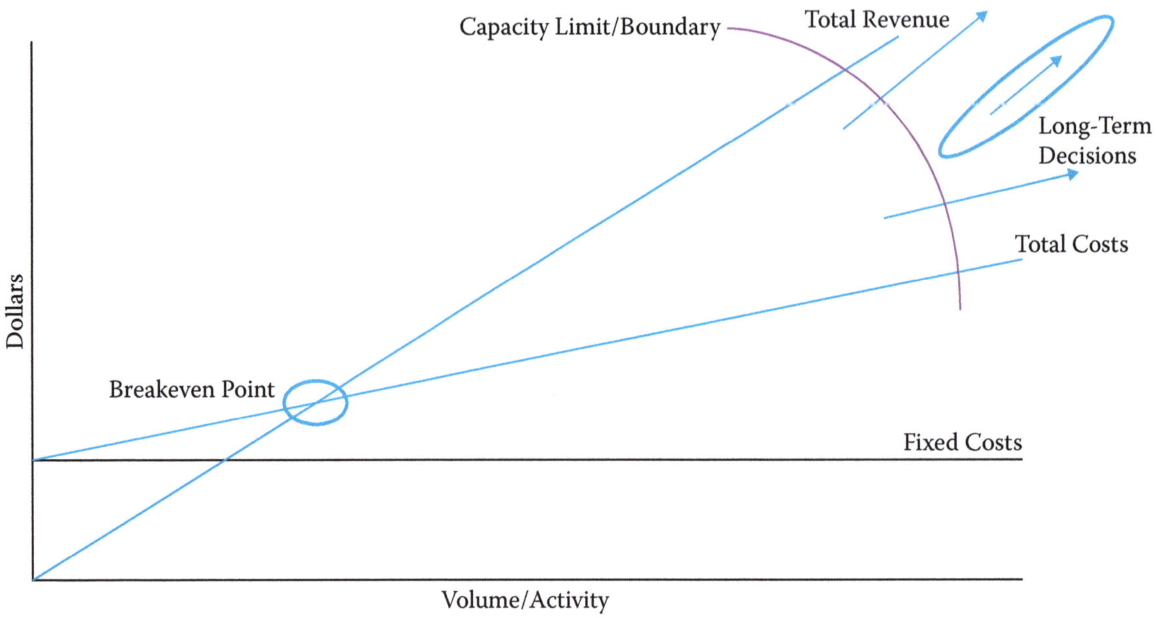

Fig. 9.1 Long-Term Capital Decisions

Figure 9.1 shows the relationship of long-term capital investment decisions to the productive capacity of a firm on the traditional CVP diagram.

TOOLS FOR LONG-TERM CAPITAL INVESTMENT DECISIONS

Permanent capacity decisions require tools to evaluate potential options by first screening the available options and then prioritizing the options. The concepts and tools covered in this chapter can be grouped into two very general categories: one group that does not use TVM concepts and one group that uses TVM concepts.

The tools we cover are used to evaluate a project's liquidity, profitability, screening, and prioritizing of potential projects or investments. The following chart summarizes the tools and concepts in this chapter along with their major attributes:

Tool / Concept	TVM	Screening	Prioritizing	NOI / Cash Flow
Payback period (liquidity)	No	Yes	No	Cash Flow
Simple rate of return (profitability)	No	Yes	No	NOI
Net present value	Yes	Yes	No	Cash Flow
Profitability index	Yes	Yes	Yes	Cash Flow
Internal rate of return	Yes	Yes	Yes	Cash Flow

PAYBACK PERIOD

Payback period is a relatively quick and straightforward method of analyzing permanent capacity investment projects and of evaluating a project's effect on firm liquidity. The payback period can also be viewed as a measure of the project's breakeven point: the point in time when the fixed and variable costs of the project have been covered, or paid, by the project's cash flows, and the project begins to be profitable.

The payback period uses the actual cash flows of a project to determine how long before the project repays the initial investment. As a measure of liquidity, the payback period quantifies how fast the project returns the initial investment made to carry out the project.

We can look at the liquidity of a project in terms of how quickly the project creates enough cash to cover, or pay back, the initial investment. On a balance sheet, the assets and liabilities are listed in order of liquidity. The assets are listed in the order of how quickly the assets can be converted into cash. The liabilities are listed in order or due date. Both represent liquidity, the time in which the firm expects to receive or pay cash.

Using cash flows that have not been discounted provides a measure of liquidity or is the breakeven point of a project. Because the cash flows are not discounted, the payback period doesn't use any factors for the time value of money or for any minimum required performance standards. Although the undiscounted cash flows provide valuable understanding of a project's liquidity or breakeven point, that understanding is limited because the time value of money is not considered. Another limitation is that the cash flows after the payback period are not considered.

The payback period formula divides the annual cash flow of the project into the initial investment of the project.

$$\text{Payback Period} = \frac{\text{Initial Investment}}{\text{Annual Cash Flow}}$$

Figure 9.2 presents the payback period of a project with three (3) potential cash flow scenarios for the project. The project has an initial investment of $76,500 and the scenarios represent possible cash flow streams the project could generate. The various cash flows streams are determined by those responsible for the project.

Scenarios 1 and 3 are irregular lump-sum cash flow streams because the cash flow is different, or unique, each year. Scenario 2 is an annuity cash flow stream. The Annual column is the estimated annual cash flow generated by the project as provided by the project's management. The Cumulative column is the running total of the cash flows generated by the project since its inception. The Investment Remaining column shows the amount of initial investment that has not yet been recovered at the end of the year. The payback period is the time it takes to generate cash flow equal to the initial investment.

Scenario 1 has a payback period of 4.15 years. At the end of year 4, the project has $4,000 of initial investment that has not yet been recovered. During year 5, the project is expected to generate $27,500 of cash flow. To calculate the amount of time during year 5 to generate the remaining investment, the $4,000 is divided by $27,500, which is 0.15 of a year.

Scenario 3 has a payback period of 2 years. The scenario has a stream of irregular, lump-sum cash flows unique to each year. The first two years happen to have an estimated cash flow of exactly the amount of the initial investment.

Backyard Pizzeria Payback Period Example

Initial Investment $76,500

Cash Flow Scenario #1	Annual	Cummulative	Investment Remaining	Payback Period Calculation			
Year 1	$15,000	$15,000	$61,500				
Year 2	$18,000	$33,000	$43,500	Investment Remaining	$4,000	=	0.15
Year 3	$17,500	$50,500	$26,000	Yr 5 Cash Flow	$27,500		
Year 4	$22,000	$72,500	$4,000				
Year 5	$27,500	$100,000	($23,500)	Payback Period is 4.15 years			

Cash Flow Scenario #2—annuity cash flow stream	Annual	Cummulative	Investment Remaining	Payback Period Calculation			
Year 1	$21,200	$21,200	$55,300				
Year 2	$21,200	$42,400	$34,100	Initial Investment	$76,500	=	3.61
Year 3	$21,200	$63,600	$12,900	Annual Cash Flow	$21,200		
Year 4	$21,200	$84,800	($8,300)				
Year 5	$21,200	$106,000	($29,500)	Payback Period is 3.61 years			

Cash Flow Scenario #3	Annual	Cummulative	Investment Remaining	Payback Period Calculation	
Year 1	$42,000	$42,000	$34,500		
Year 2	$34,500	$76,500	$0	Investment Remaining	$0
Year 3	$7,500	$84,000	($7,500)		
Year 4	$2,500	$86,500	($10,000)	Payback Period is 2 years	
Year 5	$5,000	$91,500	($15,000)		

Fig. 9.2 Payback Period Example

Scenario 2 has a payback period of 3.61 years. The scenario has an annuity cash flow stream of $21,200 each year. Because an annuity is a cash flow stream of equivalent amounts at equivalent intervals, the initial investment of $76,500 can be divided by the $21,200 annual annuity to calculate the payback period.

The payback period calculation is straightforward and provides a measure of how quickly the project will recover the initial investment. Without any other considerations, the shortest payback period is the preferred choice.

The payback period has two significant drawbacks. As mentioned, the method does not account for the time value of money. Second, the payback period does not account for any cash flows that occur after the payback period. The following table shows the payback period for each scenario along with the amount of cash flow generated after the payback period, the unaccounted cash flows.

	Payback Period	Unaccounted Cash Flows
Scenario 1	4.15 years	$23,500
Scenario 2	3.61 years	$29,500
Scenario 3	2.00 years	$15,000

Scenario 3 would be the preferred choice using the payback period, because Scenario 3 has the shortest payback period, or the greatest liquidity of the three (3) projects. The unaccounted cash flows provide some insight into the limitation of the payback period because after the payback period, additional cash flows are not included in the payback period.

SIMPLE RATE OF RETURN

The simple rate of return is the annual rate of return for the project based on net operating income. Net operating income is used in this calculation to capture the effect of depreciation—the wear, tear, and use of the assets in the production of revenue and cash—even though depreciation is a non-cash expense. The other methods all use annual cash flows. Because the initial investment is paid at the beginning of the project, the cash flows of the project are skewed compared to the performance of the project. This is the only method in this chapter that uses net operating income.

In this chapter, the difference between annual cash flow and net operating income is depreciation. Annual cash flow minus depreciation equals net operating income, and net operating income plus depreciation equals annual cash flow. For our work in this textbook, we assume and use the straight-line method of depreciation whenever depreciation is presented or required to be calculated.

Often the information for a project will not include all the information we would like to have, so we need to be able to derive cash flows from net operating income and to derive net operating income from cash flows. To maintain relative simplicity in the project information, we will limit the difference between cash flows and net operating income to depreciation only, even though a project could have other non-cash differences besides depreciation. Our goal is to understand how the simple rate of return is calculated and what the method communicates, while avoiding unnecessary detail.

Annual Cash Flow	Net Operating Income
Less: Depreciation	Plus: Depreciation
Net Operating	Income Annual Cash Flow

Figure 9.3 is a continuation from the payback period example. The initial investment is $76,500, and we will use the $21,200 annual annuity cash flow from Scenario 2. To calculate the simple rate of return, we also need to know either the annual depreciation or the net operating income. This example provides information about the useful life, salvage value, and depreciation method used to calculate the annual depreciation expense.

The formula for the simple rate of return is annual net operating income divided by initial investment (or by average project assets).

$$\text{Simple Rate of Return} = \frac{\text{Annual Net Operating Income}}{\text{Initial Investment (or average project assets)}}$$

Or

$$\text{Simple Rate of Return} = \frac{\text{Average Annual Net Cash Flows} - \text{Annual Depreciation Expense}}{\text{Initial Investment (or average project assets)}}$$

Backyard Pizzeria Simple Rate of Return		
Initial Investment	$76,500	
Estimated Useful Life	10 years	
Estimated Salvage Value	$7,500	
Depreciation Method	Straight-Line	
Annual Revenue	$65,700	
Annual Cash Expenses	$44,500	
Annual Cash Flow	$21,200	
Annual Depreciation	$6,900	
Net Operating Income	$14,300	
Simple Rate of Return:		
Annual Net Operating Income	$14,300	= 20.72%
Depreciable Cost of Investment	$69,000	

Depreciable cost = initial investment – salvage value

Fig. 9.3 Simple Rate of Return Example

TIME VALUE OF MONEY TOOLS

In Chapter 8 we introduced the time-value-of-money concepts including discounting, compounding, present value, future value, cash flows, interest/discount/required rate, cash flow streams, cash flow frequency, and the cash flow diagram tool (© 2014 by J. Brooks Peacock). In this chapter, we will use the TVM concepts again when using net present value (NPV), profitability index, and the internal rate of return to evaluate long-term capital investment decisions.

We analyze long-term capital investment options for permanent capacity changes in two steps: 1) screening the projects to determine whether a project meets the minimum requirements, then 2) prioritizing the projects that meet the minimum criteria.

Projects are screened using net present value to find acceptable projects. The acceptable projects are then prioritized using the profitability index. Both steps are needed because a firm may have many different potential projects, and those projects that require higher levels of investment will have a higher potential NPV solely based on their size.

CASH FLOW DIAGRAM TOOL (© 2014 BY J. BROOKS PEACOCK)

The cash flow diagram tool (CFDT © 2014 by J. Brooks Peacock) is a graphical display that can be used with many different TVM scenarios. In this chapter, we will apply the CFDT (© 2014 by J. Brooks Peacock) with the scenarios using TVM concepts including net present value, profitability index, and internal rate of return. To assist with applying the CFDT (© 2014 by J. Brooks Peacock), we will discuss the tool's layout.

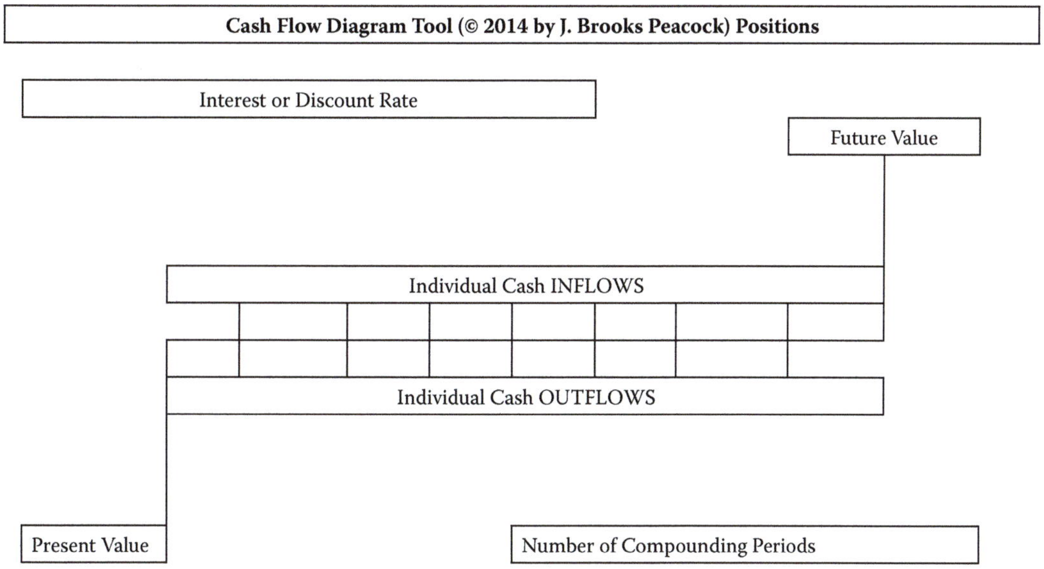

Fig. 9.4 CFDT Positions

Figure 9.4 presents the cash flow diagram tool (© 2014 by J. Brooks Peacock) without any numerical information. The figure identifies the positions of the CFDT (© 2014 by J. Brooks Peacock) used for the general application of TVM concepts.

CFDT	Position Application
Present value	Initial investment
Future value	Salvage or terminal value(s)
Individual cash inflows	Cash inflows from the project operation
Individual cash outflows	Cash outflows for additional project investment
Interest or discount rate	The rate of return used for compounding or discounting
Number of compounding periods	The number of cash flow occurrences

Figure 9.5 presents the time element in the CFDT (© 2014 by J. Brooks Peacock). The left side of the diagram is today, and moving right across the diagram represents future time periods. The CFDT (© 2014 by J. Brooks Peacock) provides a visual display of the timing of the various cash flows.

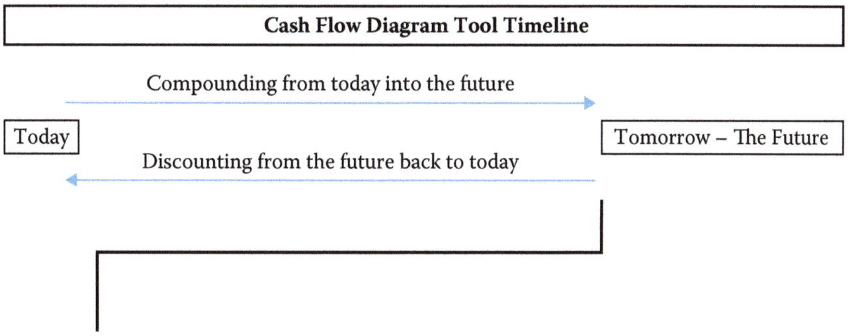

Fig. 9.5 CFDT Timeline

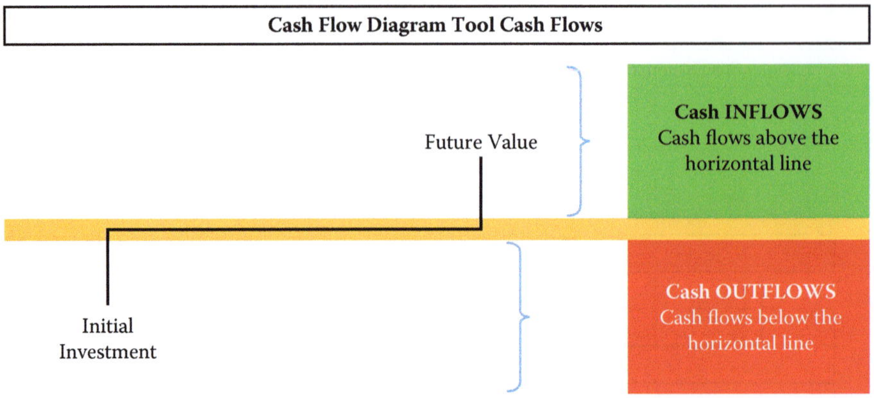

Fig. 9.6 CFDT Cash Flows

Figure 9.6 illustrates the direction of the cash flows in the CFDT (© 2014 by J. Brooks Peacock). All of the cash inflows of a project are used above the horizontal line, while all of the cash outflows of a project are used below the horizontal line.

The net present value concept will be presented in two formats:

1. Spreadsheet or Schedule Format
2. Cash flow diagram tool (© 2014 by J. Brooks Peacock) format

The spreadsheet or schedule format is a traditional format used for structuring net present value scenarios. The CFDT (© 2014 by J. Brooks Peacock) format is a more graphical display for structuring net present value scenarios. Both formats are manual tools to demonstrate the mechanics of discounting applied to the net present value analysis for screening projects that require significant capital investment into a firm's productive capacity.

NET PRESENT VALUE

Net present value analysis compares the total present value of the cash inflows (PV-CI) to the total present value of cash outflows (PV-CO) of a project. If the PV-CI is greater than the PV-CO, then the project is acceptable because the project is expected to meet the minimum requirement. The minimum requirement for our purposes is the minimum required rate of return determined by the firm. This minimum required rate of return is also known as the required rate of return or the discount rate.

The discount rate is an arbitrary rate set by the firm as a way of measuring an adequate return on its capital. The discount rate theoretically implies the rate of return needed to pay for the investment and operation of the project as well as provide an additional return required by stakeholders. The firm's management might use historical returns, industry returns, and other types of returns to establish the discount rate. Management may also include some rate of return to represent the level of risk taken as projects are executed. We should also recognize that the discount rate is an arbitrary rate of return used to screen projects for a minimum level of performance.

The following two figures, Figures 9.7 and 9.8, illustrate the use of the net present value concept for each of the three cash flow scenarios from the payback period discussion for Backyard Pizzeria earlier in the chapter. The three cash flow scenarios are possible cash flows from a project to permanently expand the productive capacity at Backyard Pizzeria.

Figure 9.7 presents the net present value analysis in a spreadsheet or schedule format, and Figure 9.8 presents the net present value analysis using the cash flow diagram tool (© 2014 by J. Brooks Peacock).

PROFITABILITY INDEX

While NPV can be used to screen projects and investment options using a minimum required rate of return, the NPV analysis does not provide information to help prioritize projects and options once the minimum standards have been met. When a firm determines the projects and investment options that meet its minimum criteria (specifically the required rate of return), we can then use the profitability index to help prioritize the acceptable options.

The profitability index is calculated by dividing a project's net present value by its initial investment. The objective is to evaluate a project's use of capital to generate cash flow in excess of the minimum required rate of return. We can think of the profitability index as a tool to measure the capital efficiency of a project because the net present value is compared to the investment required to generate that net present value.

$$\text{Profitability Index} = \frac{\text{Net Present Value}}{\text{Initial Investment}}$$

In Figure 9.9, the three project scenarios used to calculate net present value are presented in the cash flow diagram tool (© 2014 by J. Brooks Peacock) format. Each scenario is an acceptable project because it generates a positive net present value. Because each scenario is acceptable, the scenarios must be prioritized to effectively allocate the limited amount of capital available for investment.

INTERNAL RATE OF RETURN

The internal rate of return (IRR) is the interest rate, or discount rate, within a project at which the present value of the cash inflows, PV-CI, equals the present value of the cash outflows, PV-CO. The internal rate of return is the discount rate that generates a zero (0) net present value in a project.

The IRR is unique to each project and can be useful both as a screening tool and a prioritization tool to evaluate capital investment in capacity projects. The drawbacks of using IRR include the possibility that either two rates of return are calculated or the possibility that no rate of return can be calculated. Depending on the amount and timing of the cash flows, the IRR calculation may possibly produce two rates of return or no rate of return.

Backyard Pizzeria
Net Present Value—Spreadsheet Format

Initial Investment	$76,500
Estimated Salvage Value	$7,500
Discount Rate	18.50%

Cash Flow Scenario #1

	Annual
Year 1	$15,000
Year 2	$18,000
Year 3	$17,500
Year 4	$22,000
Year 5	$27,500

Cash Flow Scenario #2—annuity cash flow stream

	Annual
Year 1	$21,200
Year 2	$21,200
Year 3	$21,200
Year 4	$21,200
Year 5	$21,200

Cash Flow Scenario #3

	Annual
Year 1	$42,000
Year 2	$34,500
Year 3	$7,500
Year 4	$2,500
Year 5	$5,000

	Scenarios								
	1			2 - As Lump Sums			3		
	Cash Flow	Table Factor	Present Value	Cash Flow	Table Factor	Present Value	Cash Flow	Table Factor	Present Value
Initial Investment - Today	($76,500)	1.00	($76,500.00)	($76,500)	1	–$76,500.00	($76,500)	1	–$76,500.00
Cash Inflows:									
Year 1	$15,000	0.8438819	$12,658.23	$21,200	0.8438819	$17,890.30	$42,000	0.84388186	$35,443.04
Year 2	$18,000	0.7121366	$12,818.46	$21,200	0.7121366	$15,097.30	$34,500	0.71213659	$24,568.71
Year 3	$17,500	0.6009591	$10,516.79	$21,200	0.6009591	$11,740.33	$7,500	0.60095915	$4,507.19
Year 4	$22,000	0.5071385	$11,157.05	$21,200	0.5071385	$10,751.34	$2,500	0.50713852	$1,267.85
Year 5	$27,500	0.427965	$11,769.04	$21,200	0.427965	$9,072.86	$5,000	0.427965	$2,139.82
Salvage Value - Year 5	$7,500	0.427965	$3,209.74	$7,500.00	0.427965	$3,209.74	$7,500	0.427965	$3,209.74
Net Present Value			($14370.71)			–$7,738.14			($5,363.65)

2 - As An Annuity			
	Cash Flow	Table Factor	Present Value
Initial Investment—Today	($76,500)	1.00	($76,500)
Cash Inflows:			
Year 1	$21,200	3.0920811	$65,552.12
Year 2			
Year 3			
Year 4			
Year 5			
Salvage Value—Year 5	$7,500	0.427965	$3,209.74
Net Present Value			($7,738.14)

Fig. 9.7 NPV Scenario Tables

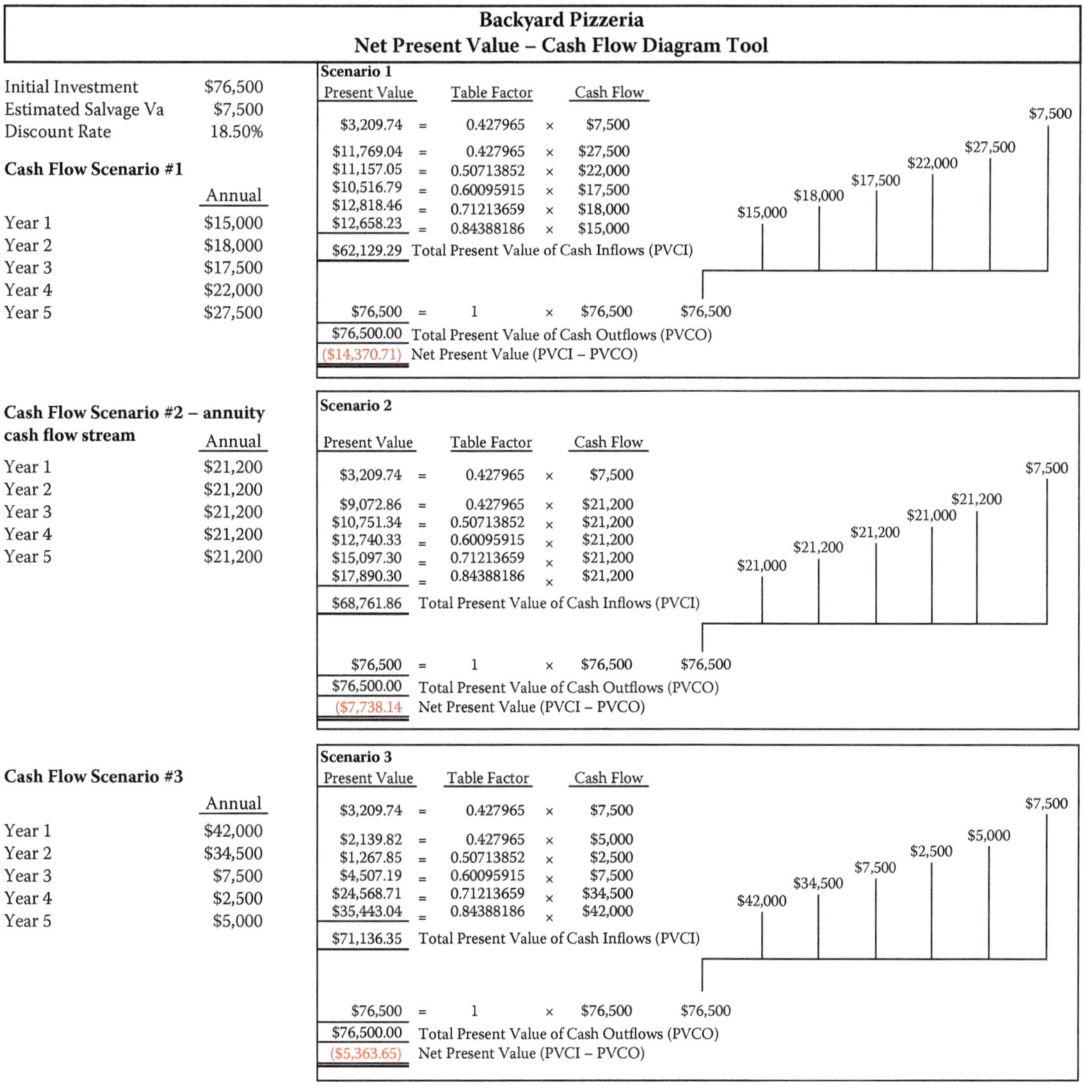

Fig. 9.8 NVP Scenario CFDT

The benefits of using IRR include finding the unique rate of return in a project. The calculation for IRR can be done in a spreadsheet program with IRR functions, on a business calculator that accommodates uneven cash flows, or by calculating the present value table factor for the project and referring to a present value table. While spreadsheets and calculators can provide a point value for IRR, we will illustrate finding IRR by calculating a table factor and using a present value table.

By calculating a table factor and using a present value table, our work will identify a range of discounts rates wherein the IRR for a project resides. The illustration uses an annuity cash flow stream to simplify the process and uses the following equation to calculate the project's table factor:

Project Table Factor = Annual Cash Inflow / Initial Investment

Once the project table factor has been calculated, it is used with the present value of an annuity table to find the IRR range. The table is used by moving down the left column to the row that corresponds with the number of annuity cash flows, then moving to the right across the row. As we

Backyard Pizzeria
Net Present Value with profitability Index

Initial Investment	$67,500
Estimated Salvage Value	$12,500
Discount Rate	18.50%
Cash Flow Scenario #1	Annual
Year 1	$21,000
Year 2	$22,500
Year 3	$27,000
Year 4	$27,500
Year 5	$30,000

Scenario 1

Present Value		Table Factor		Cash Flow
$5,349.56	=	0.427965	×	$12,500
$12,838.95	=	0.427965	×	$30,000
$13,946.31	=	0.50713852	×	$27,500
$16,225.90	=	0.60095915	×	$27,000
$16,023.07	=	0.71213659	×	$22,500
$17,721.52	=	0.84388186	×	$21,000
$82,105.31	Total Present Value of Cash Inflows (PVCI)			
$67,500	=	1	×	$67,500
$67,500.00	Total Present Value of Cash Outflows (PVCO)			
$14,605.31	Net Present Value (PVCI – PVCO)			

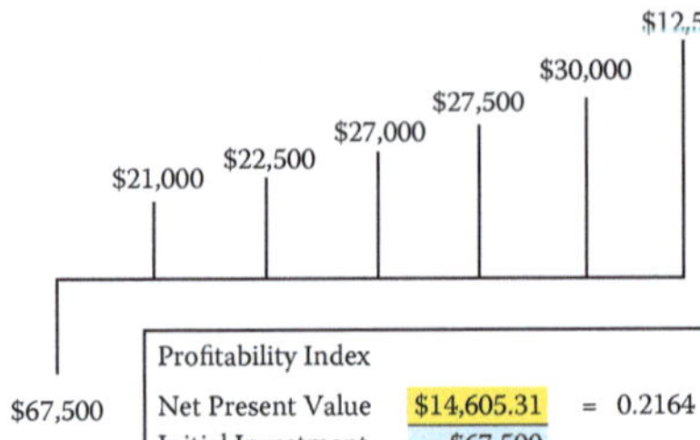

Profitability Index		
Net Present Value	$14,605.31	= 0.2164
Initial Investment	$67,500	

Initial Investment	$60,000
Estimated Salvage Value	$10,000
Discount Rate	18.50%
Cash Flow Scenario #2 – annuity cash flow stream	Annual
Year 1	$21,500
Year 2	$21,500
Year 3	$21,000
Year 4	$21,500
Year 5	$21,500

Scenario 2

Present Value		Table Factor		Cash Flow
$4,279.65	=	0.427965	×	$10,000
$9,201.25	=	0.427965	×	$21,500
$10,903.48	=	0.50713852	×	$21,500
$12,920.62	=	0.60095915	×	$21,500
$15,310.94	=	0.71213659	×	$21,500
$18,143.46	=	0.84388186	×	$21,500
$70,759.39	Total Present Value of Cash Inflows (PVCI)			
$60,000	=	1	×	$60,000
$60,000.00	Total Present Value of Cash Outflows (PVCO)			
$10,759.39	Net Present Value (PVCI – PVCO)			

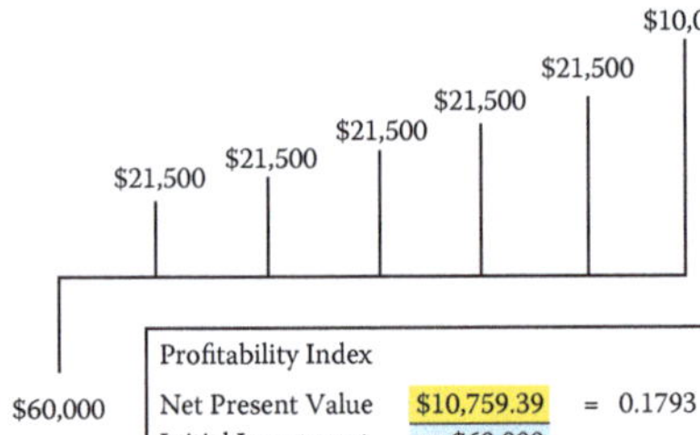

Profitability Index		
Net Present Value	$10,759.39	= 0.1793
Initial Investment	$60,000	

Initial Investment	$1,250,000
Estimated Salvage Value	$150,000
Discount Rate	18.50%
Cash Flow Scenario #3	Annual
Year 1	$225,000
Year 2	$350,000
Year 3	$450,000
Year 4	$490,000
Year 5	$575,000

Scenario 3

Present Value		Table Factor		Cash Flow
$64,194.75	=	0.427965	×	$150,000
$246,079.87	=	0.427965	×	$575,000
$248,497.87	=	0.50713852	×	$490,000
$270,431.62	=	0.60095915	×	$450,000
$249,247.81	=	0.71213659	×	$350,000
$189,873.42	=	0.84388186	×	$225,000
$1,268,325.34	Total Present Value of Cash Inflows (PVCI)			
$1,250,000	=	1	×	$1,250,000
$1,250,000.00	Total Present Value of Cash Outflows (PVCO)			
$18,325.34	Net Present Value (PVCI – PVCO)			

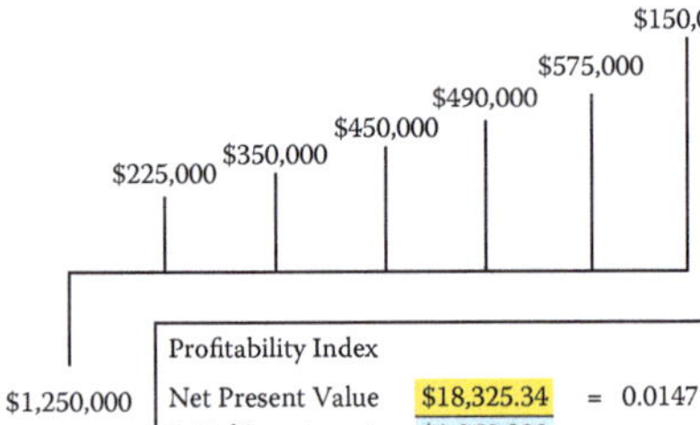

Profitability Index		
Net Present Value	$18,325.34	= 0.0147
Initial Investment	$1,250,000	

Fig. 9.9 NPV with PI Example

move across the row, the project's table factor will most likely fit between two interest rate columns on the present value of an annuity table. The IRR for the project will be expressed as being between the interest rates of the two columns.

Figure 9.10 illustrates the comparison of three potential projects that would increase the capacity for Backyard Pizzeria The options include

1. opening eight small locations (A-Small),
2. opening three large locations (B-Large), and
3. purchasing six cargo vans and six pizza trailers (C-Mobile).

The illustration includes the summary analysis for payback period, simple rate of return, net present value, profitability index, and internal rate of return to not only demonstrate the internal rate of return, but also to provide some context in which all the methods discussed in this chapter fit together.

Beaver Pizza Expansion Options		A- Small	B- Large	C- Trailers
Internal Rate of Return				
Annuity Factor		5.6	7.6	3.5
Table Rate		1296-13%	5%-6%	21%-22%
Required Rate of Return		10%	10%	10%
Calculated IRR		12.22%	6.61%	22.94%
Calculator Key Values	n	10	10	7
	i	Solve	Solve	Solve
	PV	($8,400,000)	($8,250,000)	($798,000)
	PMT	$1,500,000	$1,080,000	$228,000
	FV	$0	$1,000,000	$162,000

Fig. 9.10 IRR Example

The internal rate of return has a number of drawbacks, including the potential to generate two IRRs for a single project as well as the potential of having no solution. As with any type of financial analysis, any single rate, period, value, percentage, or other metric produced by analysis or calculation is not sufficient evidence upon which a decision may confidently be made. The art and science of investment analysis revolves around finding, calculating, analyzing, and collecting many data points and using multiple metrics to create a comprehensive picture and provide decision makers with an understanding of the available options.

NEW FACILITIES

Expanding an existing facility or building a new facility is a common long-term capital investment decision. New facilities can take a long time to build, they impact the firm for many years in the future, and they permanently change the productive capacity of the firm. As we discussed earlier, a capital investment project shifts the productive capacity boundary out to the right on the traditional cost-volume-profit (CVP) diagram.

For most facility construction projects, the project includes many costs for such things as architecture, permits, structural reviews, local building code compliance, site preparation, construction, landscaping and land improvement. If the project is new facility construction, the costs will also include land acquisition, title and recording fees, sales commissions, and other transactions, as well as more extensive site preparation costs such as excavation or the demolition of old structures.

From the time a location is purchased, through construction and use, the nature and impact of facility projects span many years. These types of projects also require large amounts of capital, which causes the results of the analysis of such projects to be very different from the analyses we saw in Chapters 7 and 8. For example, the payback period for a facility's project will potentially be much longer than for replacing a piece of equipment.

Facilities projects also have some different cash flow streams than previous projects we've analyzed. These projects can lower operating costs, reduce waste, or generate additional contribution margin by increasing productive capacity. Although the cash flows may appear in different forms, the analysis tools are still the same basic tools as with any project: payback period, simple rate of return, net present value, profitability index, and internal rate of return.

KEEP OR DISPOSE OF A SEGMENT

Keeping a segment open or selling the segment is a decision that can have a significant impact on a firm's productive capacity, profitability, and strategic direction. In our analysis in this area, we will assume that if a segment will be disposed of, it will be done by selling the segment. A segment may also be disposed of by closing the segment, which may well be a viable option, but our analysis for closing a segment would be similar to that of closing a department, as discussed in Chapter 8.

Profitable Segment

Keeping a segment open requires that it generate a positive segment margin, which can also be viewed as segment profit. If a segment is generating a positive segment margin, it is generating its own profit, which then contributes to the overall common fixed costs of the business. With a positive segment margin (a profitable segment), the natural decision is to keep the segment operating unless there is significant evidence that the firm could engage in another activity that would generate greater segment margin and be a better strategic fit for the firm overall. The analysis of a profitable segment places significant importance on the opportunity cost of possible alternative operations.

Unprofitable Segment

A segment that does not generate a positive segment margin (that is an unprofitable segment) appears, at first glance, to be a likely candidate to closed or sold. One of the issues an unprofitable segment presents is in ascertaining the value of any intercompany products or services the segment provides to other areas of the business that either cannot be obtained from an outside provider or are significantly more expensive to acquire from an outside provider.

PURCHASE A BUSINESS

Purchasing a business is a seemingly straightforward analysis: If the target business has a positive net present value, then the target business should be purchased. One of the difficulties of a business purchase is the viability of business at the given purchase price. A business offered for sale may be functional and even profitable, but the potential buyer must consider the potential investments the business will require to meet their strategic plan. A new owner may feel the target business will need significant capital improvements in the future to remain competitive or to achieve the owner's desired strategic outcome.

10

CREATING VALUE

How can we create value in the firm?

LEARNING OBJECTIVES

LO1: Describe, explain, and calculate the DuPont method of return on investment.

LO2: Describe, explain, and calculate Economic Value Added®

LO3: Describe and explain the value chain.

LO4: Describe and explain the production process timeline.

LO5: Calculate the delivery cycle efficiency and the manufacturing cycle efficiency.

LO6: Describe, explain, and calculate customer lifetime value.

THE QUESTIONS WE TRY TO ANSWER

- What drives value in a firm?
- How can we generate value?
- How can we know if we have generated value?

Creating value is not limited to increasing the price of a firm's stock or paying more dividends to the owners or shareholders. Creating value encompasses all the value related to all of a firm's stakeholders: customers, clients, employees, industries, communities, regions, and other stakeholders, in addition to the firm's owners. Although a firm must address the issue of value to all its stakeholders, our work in this chapter will be limited to the financial and operational value a firm creates. We will assume the predominant driver of financial value is net income, or profit. Without a profit, a firm will not be able to expand, let alone be able to stay in business. We recognize that profit is the driver of financial value and we recognize that other types of value are driven by other measures and results. In this chapter, we will limit our work to addressing financial value using the following tools:

1. DuPont analysis
2. Economic Value Added®
3. Value chain
4. Manufacturing cycle efficiency
5. Customer lifetime value

DUPONT ANALYSIS

In the 1802, the E.I. du Pont de Nemours and Company, generally known as the DuPont Company, was founded by Éleuthère Irénée du Pont to manufacture gunpowder. The firm expanded into dynamite production and smokeless powders. In 1912, Donaldson Brown, who was working for the DuPont

Company as a salesman, expanded (or decomposed) the return on equity (ROE) calculation, into three constituent formulas:

$$\text{ROE} = \text{Net Income} / \text{Equity}$$
$$\text{ROE} = \text{Return on Assets} \times \text{Financial Leverage}$$
$$\text{ROE} = \text{Profit Margin} \times \text{Asset Turnover} \times \text{Financial Leverage}$$

In Chapter 6, we used the return on investment (ROI) to evaluate the current performance of a business or its operating segments. The DuPont analysis is an advanced continuation of the ROI calculation.

Basic DuPont Analysis Formula

$$\underbrace{\frac{\text{Net Income}}{\text{Total Revenue}} \times \frac{\text{Total Revenue}}{\text{Total Assets}}}_{\text{Return on Assets}} \times \underbrace{\frac{\text{Total Assets}}{\text{Total Equity}}}_{\text{Financial Leverage}}$$

Fig. 10.1 DuPont Formula

The formula for ROE is a combination of the formulas for return on assets and financial leverage. The return on assets formula is a combination of profit margin and asset turnover. While return on equity is an outstanding ratio, the ratio provides a single metric that tells us essentially the results of what happened, without providing any insights on how the return on equity was generated. Understanding ROE and what happened is an important starting point. Crucial explanations come from expanding the ROE formula into its constituent parts to identify and understand how the results were achieved.

Figure 10.2 presents the operating results of a firm for two consecutive years. In both years, management achieved the same result: ROE of 6.25%. Using the DuPont analysis to separate the ROE calculation into its constituent parts, we see that management achieved the 6.25% ROE results by increasing asset turnover and by financial leverage to offset a decrease in profitability.

In DuPont analysis, as in any ratio analysis, any given ration cannot continue in the same direction, up or down, indefinitely. For a firm to increase asset turnover, decrease profit margin, and generate a consistent 6.25% return on equity is unsustainable. Sustainable business activity must respond to changing economic and market conditions, which will inevitably cause fluctuation in financial results, and hence fluctuations in financial ratios.

ECONOMIC VALUE ADDED®

Economic Value Added® (EVA®) is a tool developed by and a service mark of Stern Value Management. The idea of EVA® is to ascertain the creation of wealth and value generated by a firm above the actual rate of return required by current creditors and owners of the firm; this is known as the weighted-average cost of capital (WACC).

In Chapter 6, we used residual income as a method of evaluating a business's or segment's operating performance. The idea of residual income is to try and measure any excess profit generated by a firm in addition to a required rate of return. We will essentially extend the residual income analysis by using EVA®, which is a more stringent analysis.

Both the residual income method and EVA® seek to quantify the creation of growth and value. In this chapter, we use the calculation for EVA® uses the following formula:

DuPont Analysis

	2016	2017
Revenue	$1,250,000	$2,950,000
Expenses	$1,125,000	S2,762,500
Net Income	$125,000	$187,500
Total Assets	S3,175,000	$5,200,000
Total Liabilities	$1,175,000	S2,200,000
Total Equity	$2,000,000	$3,000,000

Return on Equity

$$\frac{\text{Net Income}}{\text{Equity}} = \text{Return on Equity}$$

DuPont Analysis

$$\underbrace{\frac{\text{Net Income}}{\text{Total Revenue}} \times \frac{\text{Total Revenue}}{\text{Total Assets}}}_{\text{Return on Assets}} \times \underbrace{\frac{\text{Total Assets}}{\text{Total Equity}}}_{\text{Financial Leverage}}$$

2016 Results

ROE: $\frac{\$125,000}{\$2,000,000} = \boxed{6.25\%}$

DuPont: $\frac{\text{Profit Margin}}{10.00\%} \times \frac{\text{Asset Turnover}}{0.39} \times \frac{\text{Finacial Leverage}}{1.59} = \boxed{6.25\%}$

$\frac{\$125,000}{\$1,250,000} \times \frac{\$1,250,000}{\$3,175,000} \times \frac{\$3,175,000}{\$2,000,000}$

2017 Results

ROE: $\frac{\$187,500}{\$3,000,000} = \boxed{6.25\%}$

DuPont: $\frac{\text{Profit Margin}}{6.36\%} \times \frac{\text{Asset Turnover}}{0.57} \times \frac{\text{Finacial Leverage}}{1.73} = \boxed{6.25\%}$

$\frac{\$187,500}{\$2,950,000} \times \frac{\$2,950,000}{\$5,200,000} \times \frac{\$5,200,000}{\$3,000,000}$

Fig. 10.2 DuPont Analysis Example

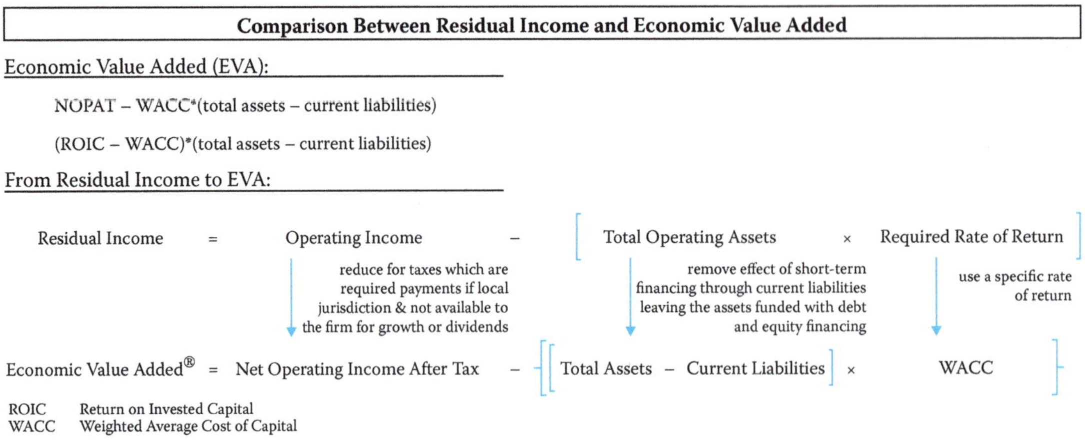

Fig. 10.3 RI and EVA

$$\text{EVA}^{®} = \text{net operating income after taxes} - [(\text{total assets} - \text{current liabilities}) * \text{WACC}]$$

The EVA® model developed by Stern Value Management uses two terms not presented in this textbook:

NOPAT—net operating profit after tax
ROIC—return on invested capital

To maintain congruency and reduce potential confusion, we have modified the original EVA® formula. We use net operating income after taxes to replace NOPAT and we substitute (total assets – current liabilities) for ROIC, both of which provide a measure of invested capital.

We can use residual income and EVA® to compare and contrast the two approaches.

Figure 10.3 illustrates the similar structures of both residual income and EVA® and identifies their differences. One contrast between the approaches is that while both estimate the amount of value created in a firm, with residual income being a basic approach, EVA® represents the more stringent or difficult threshold to achieve.

VALUE CHAIN

The system of processes executed by a firm to create and deliver their products or services is known as a value chain. The concept of the value chain was described and popularized by Michael Porter in his 1985 book *Competitive Advantage: Creating and Sustaining Superior Performance*. The idea is to identify all the business processes within a firm that must be executed to make and deliver a product or to create and deliver a service. The value of a business is created by repeatable processes that create consistent, high-quality outputs in the form of products or services. Those processes can then be monitored, evaluated, enhanced, refined, eliminated, or otherwise changed to meet the needs of the firm.

The value chain concept identifies the activities, or processes, in a firm as either primary or support activities. The following list gives a breakdown of the activities:

Primary	Activities	Support Activities
Inbound	Logistics	Firm Infrastructure
Operations	Human	Resource Management
Outbound	Logistics	Technology
Marketing and Sales	Procurement	
Service		

Value chain activities are those that generate value in the production of a product or delivery of a service and are not necessarily correlated to cost or the incurrence of costs. A highly value-added process may not incur much cost, while a non-highly value-added process may incur significant cost. The key is to first identify and expand the activities that add value and then examine the costs.

PRODUCTION PROCESS EFFICIENCY—DELIVERY AND MANUFACTURING CYCLE EFFICIENCIES

In a manufacturing firm, the manufacturing process can be examined to increase efficiency and hence increase the value created by the firm. Identifying and understanding the processes that add value to the product or service—and hence to the firm's customers as well as its shareholders—are critical to the a firm's intentional efforts to create value. The time expended in various production processes in a firm has a significant impact on the customer's experience and satisfaction with the firm, along with a significant impact on the financial value generated.

The objective of evaluating the efficiency of the production process is to eliminate as much time as possible from the non-value-added processes and to increase the overall proportion of value-added processes: to maximize the time spent on value-added activities and minimize the time spent on non-value-added activities.

For our purposes, the efficiency of the production process is the relationship of value-added time to the total production time in a firm. The production process begins with the customer order and ends when the customer receives the product or service. The production process timeline includes both the delivery cycle and the manufacturing cycle.

Figure 10.4 illustrates the production process timeline.

As we evaluate the efficiency of the production process, we will examine the production process in units of time such as minutes, hours, days, and months.

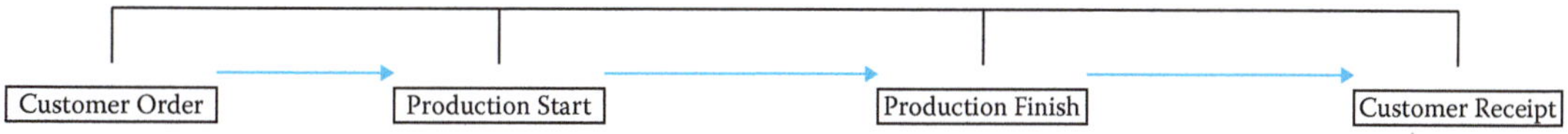

Fig. 10.4 Production Process Timeline

Delivery Cycle Efficiency

The delivery cycle begins at the time a customer places an order and ends when the customer receives the product or service they ordered. The delivery cycle is the same time period as the production process timeline. Delivery cycle efficiency is the relationship of value-added time to non-value-added time in the full delivery cycle, or production process timeline. The following formula is used to calculate delivery cycle efficiency:

Delivery Cycle Efficiency = Processing Time / Total Delivery Cycle Time

Manufacturing Cycle Efficiency

The manufacturing cycle begins at the time production starts and ends when the production is complete. The manufacturing cycle contains all the processes to convert materials into a product or to generate and provide the service. Manufacturing cycle efficiency compares the value-added time to the total manufacturing cycle time of the firm.

Manufacturing Cycle Efficiency = Processing Time / Total Manufacturing Cycle Time

Manufacturing operations vary widely depending on the product, manufacturing methods, physical space, vendor capabilities (e.g., providing just-in-time inventory deliveries), and other issues. The manufacturing cycle contains the crucial value-added element in the firm: processing materials into products. Whether a firm manufactures a product or delivers a service, the concept of the manufacturing cycle is equally applicable.

For both delivery cycle efficiency and manufacturing cycle efficiency, the goal is to first identify the value-added processing time as it relates to the delivery and manufacturing cycles and then to work on reducing or eliminating as much non-value-added time as possible while increasing the efficiency of the value-added processing time. The results of these efforts should be an increase in the value-added processing time as a proportion to the total delivery and manufacturing cycles.

Figure 10.5 illustrates the delivery and manufacturing cycles as part of the production process timeline.

CUSTOMER LIFETIME VALUE

Customer lifetime value (CLV) is a measurement of the financial value of a customer relationship and is a forward-looking measurement. The CLV model essentially discounts the future cash flows from a customer relationship while including an effect of customer retention.

Figure 10.6 presents the formula used to calculate the value of a customer relationship.

As with many analyses, the relationship between the formula constituents is assumed to be constant. In practice, the contribution margin a customer relationship generates may differ from year to year, as might the retention rate. This formula also assumes an ongoing—and, importantly, unending—relationship. Although a customer relationship in perpetuity may not be realistic, the calculation

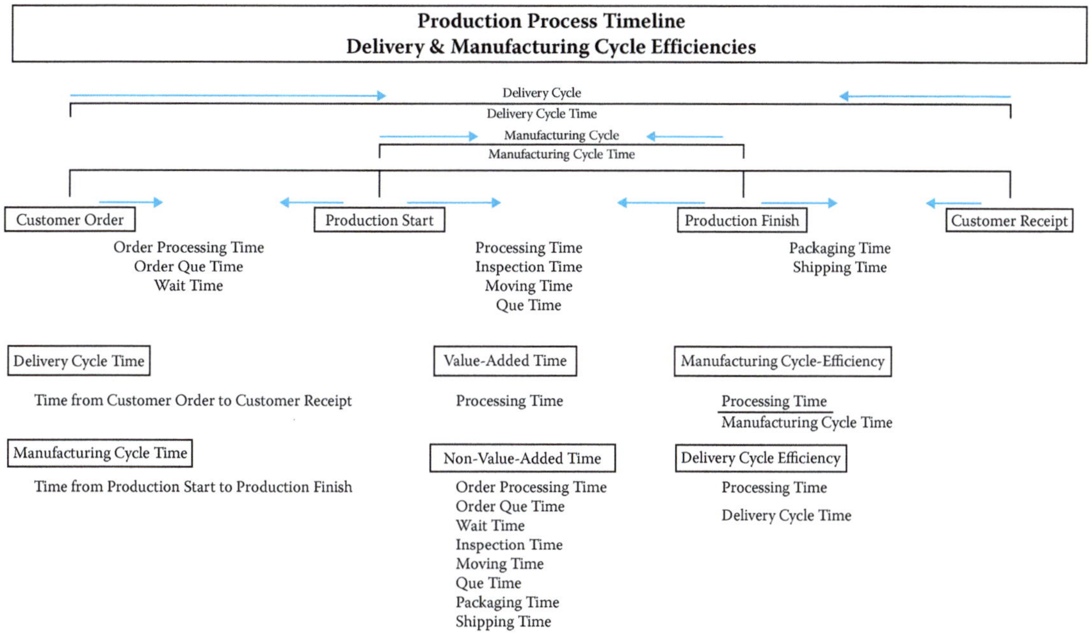

Fig. 10.5 Manufacturing and Delivery Cycle Efficiency

does provide a view of the potential value of the customer relationship and may provide context for decisions regarding the efforts to maintain current customer relationships.

The effort to quantify the value of a long-term customer relationship can lay a solid foundation for a firm to make better decisions regarding customer service levels, relationship building efforts, and other activities. The CLV analysis can also be an effective tool to focus a firm's attention and efforts on its long-term goals and objectives while preventing too much influence from short-term performance results. The CLV model is a useful tool to evaluate customer relationships and stratify those relationships into similar service levels. A firm may use CLV to help determine the levels of service, attention, and effort it can or should provide to its customers based on the value of those customers to the firm. Levels of services can be created and offered to customers, allowing them to choose the level of service they receive, knowing the cost of that increase.

Customer Lifetime Value

$$\textbf{Customer Lifetime Value} = \textbf{Customer CM/year (\$)} \star \left[\frac{\textbf{Retention Rate (\%)}}{\textbf{(1+Discount rate (\%) – Retention rate (\%)}}\right]$$

Customer CM/year ($)	The dollar amount of contribution margin generated in the first year of the customer relationship
Retention Rate (%)	Percentage of customer who continue their relationship in a given year
Discount rate (%)	The discount rate used by the firm to express their cost of capital when discounting future cash flows

Fig. 10.6 CLV Formula

APPENDIX

PRESENT VALUE FACTOR TABLE—LUMP SUM

Formula: $1/(1+i)^n$

Present Value of a: $1.00 lump sum

Interest Rate or Discount Rate Per Compounding Period (or per cash flow)

	0.50%	1.00%	2.00%	3.00%	4.00%	5.00%	6.00%	7.00%	8.00%	9.00%	10.00%	11.00%	12.00%	13.00%	14.00%	15.00%	16.00%	17.00%	18.00%	18.50%
1	0.995025	0.990099	0.980392	0.970874	0.961538	0.952381	0.943396	0.934579	0.925926	0.917431	0.909091	0.900901	0.892857	0.884956	0.877193	0.869565	0.862069	0.854701	0.847458	0.843882
2	0.990075	0.980296	0.961169	0.942596	0.924556	0.907029	0.889996	0.873439	0.857339	0.841680	0.826446	0.811622	0.797194	0.783147	0.769468	0.756144	0.743163	0.730514	0.718184	0.712137
3	0.985149	0.970590	0.942322	0.915142	0.888996	0.863838	0.839619	0.816298	0.793832	0.772183	0.751315	0.731191	0.711780	0.693050	0.674972	0.657516	0.640658	0.624371	0.608631	0.600959
4	0.980248	0.960980	0.923845	0.888487	0.854804	0.822702	0.792094	0.762895	0.735030	0.708425	0.683013	0.658731	0.635518	0.613319	0.592080	0.571753	0.552291	0.533650	0.515789	0.507139
5	0.975371	0.951466	0.905731	0.862609	0.821927	0.783526	0.747258	0.712986	0.680583	0.649931	0.620921	0.593451	0.567427	0.542760	0.519369	0.497177	0.476113	0.456111	0.437109	0.427965
6	0.970518	0.942045	0.887971	0.837484	0.790315	0.746215	0.704961	0.666342	0.630170	0.596267	0.564474	0.534641	0.506631	0.480319	0.455587	0.432328	0.410442	0.389839	0.370432	0.361152
7	0.965690	0.932718	0.870560	0.813092	0.759918	0.710681	0.665057	0.622750	0.583490	0.547034	0.513158	0.481658	0.452349	0.425061	0.399637	0.375937	0.353830	0.333195	0.313925	0.304770
8	0.960885	0.923483	0.853490	0.789409	0.730690	0.676839	0.627412	0.582009	0.540269	0.501866	0.466507	0.433926	0.403883	0.376160	0.350559	0.326902	0.305025	0.284782	0.266038	0.257189
9	0.956105	0.914340	0.836755	0.766417	0.702587	0.644609	0.591898	0.543934	0.500249	0.460428	0.424098	0.390925	0.360610	0.332885	0.307508	0.284262	0.262953	0.243404	0.225456	0.217038
10	0.951348	0.905287	0.820348	0.744094	0.675564	0.613913	0.558395	0.508349	0.463193	0.422411	0.385543	0.352184	0.321973	0.294588	0.269744	0.247185	0.226684	0.208037	0.191064	0.183154
11	0.946615	0.896324	0.804263	0.722421	0.649581	0.584679	0.526788	0.475093	0.428883	0.387533	0.350494	0.317283	0.287476	0.260698	0.236617	0.214943	0.195417	0.177810	0.161919	0.154560
12	0.941905	0.887449	0.788493	0.701380	0.624597	0.556837	0.496969	0.444012	0.397114	0.355535	0.318631	0.285841	0.256675	0.230706	0.207559	0.186907	0.168463	0.151974	0.137220	0.130431
13	0.937219	0.878663	0.773033	0.680951	0.600574	0.530321	0.468839	0.414964	0.367698	0.326179	0.289664	0.257514	0.229174	0.204165	0.182069	0.162528	0.145227	0.129892	0.116288	0.110068
14	0.932556	0.869963	0.757875	0.661118	0.577475	0.505068	0.442301	0.387817	0.340461	0.299246	0.263331	0.231995	0.204620	0.180677	0.159710	0.141329	0.125195	0.111019	0.098549	0.092884
15	0.927917	0.861349	0.743015	0.641862	0.555265	0.481017	0.417265	0.362446	0.315242	0.274538	0.239392	0.209004	0.182696	0.159891	0.140096	0.122894	0.107927	0.094888	0.083516	0.078384

PRESENT VALUE FACTOR TABLE—ORDINARY ANNUITY CASH FLOWS

Formula: $(1/i)[1-(1/(1+i)^n)]$
Present Value of a: $1.00

Interest Rate or Discount Rate Per Compounding Period (or per cash flow)

	0.50%	1.00%	2.00%	3.00%	4.00%	5.00%	6.00%	7.00%	8.00%	9.00%	10.00%	11.00%	12.00%	12.50%	13.00%	14.00%	15.00%	16.00%	17.00%	18.00%	18.50%
1	0.995025	0.990099	0.980392	0.970874	0.961538	0.952381	0.943396	0.934579	0.925926	0.917431	0.909091	0.900901	0.892857	0.888889	0.884956	0.877193	0.869565	0.862069	0.854701	0.847458	0.843882
2	1.985099	1.970395	1.941561	1.913470	1.872668	1.859410	1.833393	1.808018	1.783265	1.759111	1.735537	1.712523	1.690051	1.679012	1.668102	1.646661	1.625709	1.605232	1.585214	1.565642	1.556018
3	2.970248	2.940985	2.883883	2.828611	2.748964	2.723248	2.673012	2.624316	2.577097	2.531295	2.486852	2.443715	2.401831	2.381344	2.361153	2.321632	2.283225	2.245890	2.209585	2.174273	2.156978
4	3.950496	3.901966	3.807729	3.717098	3.587526	3.545951	3.465106	3.387211	3.312127	3.239720	3.169865	3.102446	3.037349	3.005639	2.974471	2.913712	2.854978	2.798181	2.743235	2.690062	2.664116
5	4.925866	4.853431	4.713460	4.579707	4.389977	4.329477	4.212364	4.100197	3.992710	3.889651	3.790787	3.695897	3.604776	3.560568	3.517231	3.433081	3.352155	3.274294	3.199346	3.127171	3.092081
6	5.896384	5.795476	5.601431	5.417191	5.157872	5.075692	4.917324	4.766540	4.622880	4.485919	4.355261	4.230538	4.111407	4.053839	3.997550	3.888668	3.784483	3.684736	3.589185	3.497603	3.453233
7	6.862074	6.728195	6.471991	6.230283	5.892701	5.786373	5.582381	5.389289	5.206370	5.032953	4.868419	4.712196	4.563757	4.492301	4.422610	4.288305	4.160420	4.038565	3.922380	3.811528	3.758003
8	7.822959	7.651678	7.325481	7.019692	6.595886	6.463213	6.209794	5.971299	5.746639	5.534819	5.334926	5.146123	4.967640	4.882045	4.798770	4.638864	4.487322	4.343591	4.207163	4.077566	4.015192
9	8.779064	8.566018	8.162237	7.786109	7.268790	7.107822	6.801692	6.515232	6.246888	5.995247	5.759024	5.537048	5.328250	5.228485	5.131655	4.946372	4.771584	4.606544	4.450566	4.303022	4.232230
10	9.730412	9.471305	8.982585	8.530203	7.912718	7.721735	7.360087	7.023582	6.710081	6.417658	6.144567	5.889232	5.650223	5.536431	5.426243	5.216116	5.018769	4.833227	4.658604	4.494086	4.415384
11	10.677027	10.367628	9.786848	9.252624	8.528917	8.306414	7.886875	7.498674	7.138964	6.805191	6.495061	6.206515	5.937699	5.810161	5.686941	5.452733	5.233712	5.028644	4.836413	4.656005	4.569944
12	11.618932	11.255077	10.575341	9.954004	9.118581	8.863252	8.383844	7.942686	7.536078	7.160725	6.813692	6.492356	6.194374	6.053476	5.917647	5.660292	5.420619	5.197107	4.988387	4.793225	4.700375
13	12.556151	12.133740	11.348374	10.634955	9.682852	9.393573	8.852683	8.357651	7.903776	7.486904	7.103356	6.749870	6.423548	6.269757	6.121812	5.842362	5.583147	5.342334	5.118280	4.909513	4.810443
14	13.488708	13.003703	12.106249	11.296073	10.222825	9.898641	9.294984	8.745468	8.244237	7.786150	7.366687	6.981865	6.628168	6.462006	6.302488	6.002072	5.724476	5.467529	5.229299	5.008062	4.903327
15	14.416625	13.865053	12.849264	11.937935	10.739546	10.379658	9.712249	9.107914	8.559479	8.060688	7.606080	7.190870	6.810864	6.632894	6.462379	6.142168	5.847370	5.575456	5.324187	5.091578	4.981711

Printed by Libri Plureos GmbH in Hamburg,
Germany

9 781631 893476